Experiments in psychology
a workbook for students

Experiments in psychology

a workbook for students

Jonathan Beer

Weidenfeld and Nicolson
London

First published in Great Britain by
George Weidenfeld and Nicolson Ltd
91 Clapham High St, London SW4

ISBN 0 297 78080 8

Printed in Great Britain by
Butler & Tanner Ltd, Frome and London

Contents

Using this book

Most people starting a course in psychology, whether an A-level or degree course, are starting from scratch. Many of these students have no scientific background, they may wither at the sight of a mathematical formula, and yet they find that all practical work in psychology involves mathematics in a particularly virulent form – statistical analysis. Psychology is not an exact science. In chemistry, stuff A reacts with stuff B to give you stuff C – every time. The stuff of psychology is the behaviour of people and animals. This behaviour is so adaptable and varied that it is hard to distinguish what is reacting with what. An experiment in psychology must be carefully designed to tease out the bits of behaviour you are interested in. The statistical analysis is part of this design.

Do not be daunted by the formulae. Like all mathematics they are simply a succinct way of describing a straightforward series of steps. I have explained these steps non-mathematically (I am no mathematician). If you care to follow what the tests are doing and how they do it, I hope you will see that they do make sense. If you don't care to follow them you can use them just the same by substituting your results in the worked examples of each test.

Like any other science, psychology is a collection of systematic observations of the world. I have referred to these observations, the practical work of psychology, as 'experiments'. This will upset some readers; strictly speaking, an experiment is a particular sort of observation designed to establish a causal relationship between events (see page 138 for a full explanation). However, the term 'experiment' is used much more generally in everyday language and I have followed this usage. Many perfectly legitimate and valuable studies are not experiments in the strict sense and I have included some of these designs in the suggestions for experiments in Part II.

The aim of this book is to enable and encourage the reader to plan and carry out his own experiments in psychology. It is a practical book. A fuller discussion of some of the theoretical points and the background information for the experiments can be found in a general textbook. There are several general textbooks now available, suitable for A-level and degree courses. I recommend using *Understanding Psychology* by Dobson, Hardy, Heyes, Humphreys and Humphreys, published by Weidenfeld and Nicolson. I have referred to this textbook, where possible, throughout this workbook. These references, enclosed in square brackets, are to index headings in *Understanding Psychology*. Of course, these index headings will be similar in other general textbooks, which could be used in the same way.

Part I

The scientific method: an introduction

Everything that happens in the world, the blink of an eye, a river flooding, the formation of a chain of mountains, my putting on my wellingtons, is an event. All events are related in some way to other events in the world. The river flooding, for example, may be caused by one thing – a recent heavy fall of rain – and be the cause of something else – a soggy dining room carpet. The flooding would also be related, in a different way, to many other events merely by their happening at the same time.

Humans have always been interested in these relationships between events in the world and have many different ways for examining them. A photographer is interested in events that share the same time and space; a novelist explores possible relationships between events; an historian is concerned with events in the past; the scientist is ultimately concerned with events in the future.

Scientists try to understand general laws or principles governing events rather than refer to any specific instances. Science says, 'Events of this *sort* are related to events of that *sort*: they have done so in the past, they will do so in the future.' It is this power of science to talk about the future that has led to its dominance of our lives. Science is so useful – and for two reasons. First, being able to predict the future allows us, to some extent, to control it – or at least to get out of the way when we can't. Secondly, prediction allows us to test our scientific knowledge and hence to change and improve it when necessary.

Hypotheses

Science, then, attempts to describe general principles or laws governing how events interact. The problem is that we cannot directly observe general principles and laws, only particular instances of them. From these particular observations the scientist infers (or guesses) an underlying general principle. This inference (or guess) is his hypothesis.

I have observed when driving down small country lanes that whenever I get stuck behind a car crawling along the road there is a woman behind the wheel. Several hypotheses have occurred to me: that women usually drive slower than men; that there is a world conspiracy of women to slow me down; that I only notice the occasion if there is a woman behind the wheel. How did I reach these and which, if any, is really a general law?

Induction

This process of arriving at a hypothesis from particular observations is the process of **induction.** It can be contrasted with the reverse procedure, deduction, the tool of the detective.

Philip Marlowe, Raymond Chandler's private eye, stumbles across a body in *The High Window*: 'The bullet had gone in at the temple. The set-up was for suicide. But people like Louis Vannier do not commit suicide. A blackmailer, even a scared blackmailer, has a sense of power, and loves it.' Here the detective concludes that Vannier was murdered. Marlowe has arrived at a description of a particular event (that Vannier, the blackmailer, did not commit suicide), from a general statement (that blackmailers don't commit suicide). This is deduction. At some time in the past Marlowe must have formed, by induction, the hypothesis that blackmailers don't commit suicide – presumably from observations of blackmailers not going in for suicide and suicides not going in for blackmail.

So far we have ignored a rather daunting problem. Looking at the world we are faced with an infinite number of events. How can we tell which particular ones are related – which of innumerable possible hypotheses will repay investigation? The answer is that, before testing, we can't. There is no logically rigorous method of generating useful hypotheses. In practice, however, this is rarely a problem. Humans are incorrigible hypothesis makers and our observations are highly selective: we unconsciously look for patterns and evidence of relationships between events. This habit is so strong that it can be difficult to stop. When we have too few instances of a particular event to form a reasonable hypothesis, or if the significant relationships are obscure, why then we go ahead and form unreasonable ones and use them just the same. A superstition is born.

The second half of this book is a collection of hypotheses that should prove fruitful. They can be used as recipes for investigations but each one has suggestions for variation. They will also serve as models for forming your own hypotheses – there is no reason why you should not start by breaking new ground.

It may seem a little odd that all scientific research starts off in this way with a series of guesses, inspired or otherwise. Surely, anyone can make a guess. Perhaps so. What distinguishes the scientist – and occupies most of his time – is the testing of his hypotheses.

Testing the hypothesis

The testing of a hypothesis is, in theory, very simple. The scientist uses it to predict the future (i.e. one small part of the future) and then sees if his predictions come to pass. If they do then his hypothesis or theory is supported. Of course, like palm-reading and other ways of predicting the future, the predictions coming to pass is not *proof* that his hypothesis is right; he could have been lucky. If they often come to pass he could be *very* lucky: he can never prove finally that his hypothesis is a true statement of the underlying laws. If his predictions do not come to pass then the hypothesis, in that form, is refuted and must be abandoned or changed.

In the end, the measure of a hypothesis is how useful it is, not how safe from refutation you can make it. As an example take the behaviour of traffic lights and the hypothesis that the red light always follows the single amber. This cannot be *proved*. 'Always' is a long time and one faulty set of lights would be enough to refute it. A safer hypothesis would be that a red light *sometimes* follows an amber light. Any number of faulty traffic lights would not refute this hypothesis as long as red follows amber sometimes. However, this hypothesis would not be terribly useful to a driver approaching an amber light.

The psychologist deals with the behaviour of humans and animals. This is a good deal more variable than that of a traffic signal and he must try to steer a course between the twin perils of saying something interesting, but wrong (all women have better linguistic ability than men) and saying something true, but useless (some women have better linguistic ability than men). To do this the psychologist needs to make quantitative statements (how many women have better linguistic ability than men) and to be able to estimate how sure he can be of this prediction. All this involves the use of statistical analysis. Statistics are simply a tool of the experimenter and, like many tools - a calculator or an electric drill - it is not necessary to know exactly how it works to use it: all you need is the manual.

The first part of this book is a 'workshop manual' for practical psychological investigation.

Variables

Variables are simply types of events that can vary. The weather is a variable. The time of the day, my mood and what I had for lunch are all variables. In an experiment we are interested in two particular variables which we guess are connected in some way. This guess is our *hypothesis*; the two variables in the hypothesis are the **experimental variables.**

Experimental variables

The experimental variables in the hypothesis could be connected in several ways. In some experiments we are looking for a causal relationship between the experimental variables: that is, a change in one variable *causes* a change in the other. In this case one variable supposedly *depends* on the other and is called the **dependent variable.** The other variable is called the **independent variable.** To establish a causal relationship the experimenter manipulates the independent variable (IV) and looks for a consequent change in the dependent variable (DV) (see p. 000).

Example: Demonstration 1
The independent variable to be manipulated is the figure to be shown to the subject:

1.

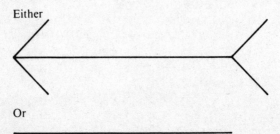

As the subject's stimulus is changed we look for a consequent change in the dependent variable: that is, where he judges the mid-point of the line to be. The hypothesis suggests that by changing the figure, by adding the arrow-heads, we *cause* a change in the perceived mid-point. Often the problem is not quite so clear.

Example: Experiment 18
This experiment follows up one of the hypotheses suggested in the first chapter (p. 4), that is, that women drive slower than men. The experimental variables are driving speed and the sex of the driver. Common sense suggests that the driving speed is the dependent variable. This 'depends' on the sex of the driver – the independent variable – although in this case the iv is not manipulated by the experimenter. In fact, we cannot be sure that these two variables are causally related in such an experiment.

In other experiments no causal relationship between the experimental variables is suggested.

Example: Demonstration 2
The experimental variables here are the subjects' preferred way of folding their arms and clasping their fingers. There is no reason to suppose that either depends on or is caused by the other. Neither is manipulated by the experimenter. In this case it is better to consider them simply as two experimental variables.

The experimental effect
This is any relationship, causal or otherwise, between the two experimental variables. The whole business of experimentation is aimed at discovering and measuring this experimental effect.

Other variables – errors

Of course many other factors (variables) will affect the dependent variable in your experiment other than the independent variable. All of these can obscure any experimental effect that may be there. The effects of these other variables are called **errors.** They can be of two sorts.

Constant errors and random errors
In E 18, sex differences in driving speeds, we measure the speed of every car that travels towards us down a particular stretch of road and note the sex of the driver. All these drivers are different. Some may be tired and slow, others late for an

appointment and racing. All these variables should be random however and not favour one sex or another. These are **random errors.**

Suppose, on the other hand, that we had chosen a street that had a night-club whose principal attractions, to judge by the life-size photographs outside, were several stunningly beautiful young ladies. This sight may have little or no effect on the passing female motorist. The male motorist however might well show a tendency to slow down and gaze. In this case the error is always in the same direction, slowing the males down – **a constant error.**

This constant error will produce in our results an apparent experimental effect, that males drive slower than females. This may be totally false. Random errors can obscure an experimental effect; constant errors can produce a spurious one. The task of the experimenter is to eliminate as many of these errors as possible including *all* constant errors.

Removing errors
One way of removing errors (unwanted variables) is simply to stop them varying by keeping conditions constant throughout the experiment. In D 1, changes in the brightness of the figures could be controlled by using a standard illumination; random distracting noises could be controlled by using a quiet room and so on. Which variables are controlled needs common sense as the vast majority of conditions that could change during the experiment will have little or no effect on the experimental variables and the control of these conditions may be quite impractical. It would be pointless in E 18 trying to keep the street constant throughout the experiment. On the other hand, it might be as well to discard measurements made when a police car was standing in the street. Some significant variables may be impossible to control. It would be impossible to select a group of human subjects all having the same age, motivation, genetics, upbringing, personality, intelligence etcetera. Yet all of these may and probably will affect their behaviour, the dependent variable, to some extent. Several basic designs of experiment can be used to get round these problems.

Experimental designs

Repeated measures
In this design one subject appears under both conditions of the IV. For example, in D 1, each subject marks the apparent mid-point of both the straight line and the arrow figure (p. 6). These positions are compared. The difference between the two responses cannot be the result of variations in intelligence, personality, and so on as the same subject performs both tasks. Several random errors have been eliminated.

But beware. A constant error may have crept in. The presentations of the two figures cannot be identical: one must come first, the other second. This simple difference could produce an **order effect.** If the two figures are always presented in the same order this error would always be in the same direction – a constant error. This problem can be overcome by varying the order of presentation. Every other subject is shown the arrow figure first; the others see the simple line first. Balancing an order effect so that it does not produce a constant error is known as **counterbalancing.**

A similar problem, the position effect, arises if the two figures are presented simultaneously. One must be on the right, one on the left. Again it is necessary to counterbalance these positions. As an alternative to counterbalancing the order or positions of the two figures can be **randomized.** The arrow figure is assigned to the first presentation by the toss of a coin (p. 148).

Counterbalancing and randomization do not remove an order effect, they just prevent the order effect becoming a constant error. As a random error it may still obscure the experimental effect. If an order effect is dangerously large, e.g. if subjects were to perform the same IQ test under different conditions, the experimenter may decide against repeated measures and choose a **matched-subjects** design.

Matched subjects

Pairs of subjects are matched as closely as possible for any variables that might affect the DV: that is, age, intelligence, sex and so on. One member of each pair is then assigned randomly to one of the two conditions of the IV. The other member of each pair takes the other condition. The scores are compared between the two members of each matched pair.

Pairs of identical twins make ideal subjects for such a design but even with such well matched subjects there will still be some random variation within each pair. On the other hand errors from order and position effects are avoided. The experimenter must weigh up these advantages and disadvantages together with the practical difficulties of collecting and matching a sufficient number of subjects.

There are other reasons why a repeated-measures design may be impossible. In E 18, one subject could hardly appear under both conditions of the IV. This experiment needs an **independent-subjects** design.

Independent subjects

Each subject is randomly assigned to one or other of the two conditions of the IV. In many experiments subjects assign themselves to the conditions as in E 18. Here the assignments of the subjects to the two conditions, male or female, were made many years ago and not, we trust, by the experimenter.

The problem with this design is that there is a large number of random errors to contend with and these may well swamp and obscure any experimental effect. If the experimental effect is small it may only emerge from the mass of random variation if large numbers of subjects are used.

Single-subject design
Only one subject is used throughout the experiment. Random errors are thus reduced to a minimum. This may appear an attractive design but it has grave drawbacks. It is difficult to draw general conclusions from the results of one subject. It is difficult to be certain that each observation is independent of all the others. There is a temptation to use yourself as a subject, and it is rather unsettling how many such experiments support the experimenter's hypothesis.

It is safer to reserve this design for your pilot studies to get some idea of the size of the experimental effect and the practicability of the experiment.

Random errors and the experimental effect

As we have just seen, we can never get rid of all errors. At best we can reduce them by controlling the experiment, choosing a suitable design and ensuring that all constant errors are eliminated by counterbalancing or randomization. There will always be random errors in any experiment.

When we look at our results there will be a difference in the scores of the two experimental groups. This difference may be the result of random error or of the experimental effect. What we must decide is 'how likely is it that the difference between the two groups is the result of random error *alone*?' If this is very improbable then we can conclude that there must also be some experimental effect.

Happily even random events have the decency to obey some rules and we can use these to find out the probability of our observed differences being the result of random errors alone. Statistical analysis is simply the use of these rules.

Probability and significance

Probability

The probability of an event describes how likely it is the event will happen. Probability is expressed numerically with values from 0 to 1. If the probability of an event is 1, that event always happens. If its probability is 0, it never happens. Probability is represented by the letter p. The familiar example of tossing a coin will show how probabilities can be calculated.

A coin is flipped. Only two things can happen. The coin can land heads or it can land tails. These two events exhaust the possibilities. Probabilities can be added to give the probability of one event *or* another. So, if p(H) is the probability of the coin landing heads, and p(T) is the probability of the coin landing tails, then:

$$p(H) + p(T) = 1$$

This simply says that when you flip a coin it always lands either heads *or* tails.

We also know that:

$$p(H) = p(T)$$

That is, the coin has an equal chance of landing on either heads or tails. It is clear from this that:

$$p(H) = \tfrac{1}{2}, \quad \text{and} \quad p(T) = \tfrac{1}{2}$$

This is a numerical way of saying that if a coin was tossed many times we would expect it to land, say, heads on approximately *half* the tosses. We can make a general rule: if an event has x possible outcomes and they are all equally likely then the probability of each happening is $\tfrac{1}{x}$.

A die has six faces numbered from 1 to 6. If the die is not loaded each of these faces is equally likely to end up on top. The probability of each face, then, is $\tfrac{1}{6}$. Suppose we throw two dice. Now there are 36 different possible outcomes illustrated over the page (4,2 denotes one die falling 4 and the other die falling 2):

1,1	1,2	1,3	1,4	1,5	1,6
2,1	2,2	2,3	2,4	2,5	2,6
3,1	3,2	3,3	3,4	3,5	3,6
4,1	4,2	4,3	4,4	4,5	4,6
5,1	5,2	5,3	5,4	5,5	5,6
6,1	6,2	6,3	6,4	6,5	6,6

Some of these combinations look the same if the dice are thrown together, e.g. 2,1 and 1,2. It is safer to imagine the two dice being thrown one after the other. Each pair above is equally likely; each has a probability of $\frac{1}{36}$.

By adding probabilities we can calculate the probability of general events. For example, what is the probability of scoring more than 10 using two dice? There are 3 ways of doing this: throwing 5,6 *or* 6,5 *or* 6,6. And so,

the probability of scoring more than $10 = \frac{1}{36} + \frac{1}{36} + \frac{1}{36} = \frac{1}{12}$.

What is the probability of throwing a double? There are 6 ways of throwing a double. So:

$$p(\text{double}) = \frac{6}{36} = \frac{1}{6}$$

Similarly, the probability of scoring exactly 8 is $\frac{5}{36}$.

The probability of a sequence of events (e.g. 5,5) using two dice, is found by multiplying together the probabilities of each event. So:

$$p(5,5) = p(5) \times p(5)$$

The probability of throwing a 5 with one die, $p(5)$, is $\frac{1}{6}$. Therefore, as we have already seen, the probability of throwing a pair of 5s, $p(5,5)$, is

$$\tfrac{1}{6} \times \tfrac{1}{6} = \tfrac{1}{36}$$

In the same way we can calculate the probability of tossing two coins and getting two heads, $p(H,H,)$:

$$p(H,H) = p(H) \times p(H) = \tfrac{1}{2} \cdot \tfrac{1}{2} = \tfrac{1}{4}$$

Similarly, the probability of tossing three heads in a row, $p(H,H,H)$, is:

$$\tfrac{1}{2} \cdot \tfrac{1}{2} \cdot \tfrac{1}{2} = \tfrac{1}{8}$$

So we have two rules. Probabilities are **added** for alternatives:

$$p(A \text{ } or \text{ } B \text{ } or \text{ } C \text{ } or \text{ etc.}) = p(A) + p(B) + p(C) + \text{etc.}$$

Probabilities are **multiplied** for sequences:

$$p(A \text{ } and \text{ } B \text{ } and \text{ } C \text{ } and \text{ etc.}) = p(A) \times p(B) \times p(C) \times \text{etc.}$$

Using probability

All these events, dice throws and coin tosses, are random and yet they follow rules. How does this help the experimenter?

Suppose now a shifty-looking individual sidles up to you, produces a very oddly shaped coin, and proposes that you bet on how the coin will land, heads or tails. He claims the coin is fair, that is, it behaves randomly. You have your doubts. You suspect that the coin is biased. You suggest a trial run, say four throws. The coin lands tails four times in a row. Your suspicions deepen but the shifty individual says that this could easily happen with a fair coin. The probability of this run of four tails, with a fair coin, is:

$$\tfrac{1}{2} \cdot \tfrac{1}{2} \cdot \tfrac{1}{2} \cdot \tfrac{1}{2} = \tfrac{1}{16}$$
one chance in sixteen.

It is small but not *too* unlikely. The trial continues and four more tails come up. Now there have been eight in a row. The probability of this is:

$$\tfrac{1}{2} \cdot \tfrac{1}{2} \cdot \tfrac{1}{2} \cdot \tfrac{1}{2} \cdot \tfrac{1}{2} \cdot \tfrac{1}{2} \cdot \tfrac{1}{2} \cdot \tfrac{1}{2} = \tfrac{1}{256} \text{ or } 0.0039$$
about four chances in a thousand.

The shifty character shrugs. It is *possible* that the coin is fair but with these results it is so unlikely that you conclude the coin is biased and refuse to bet – or you bet on tails.

This is exactly the problem of the experimenter at the end of the previous chapter. Are the differences between the experimental groups due to random errors alone or is there an experimental effect? Your hypothesis is that the coin is biased. After four throws the differences between the experimental groups (four tails, no heads) could have been due to random errors alone, $p = \tfrac{1}{16}$. After eight throws, however, the observed difference between the experimental groups is so large, (eight tails, no heads) that it is extremely unlikely that it is due to random errors alone, $p = \tfrac{1}{256}$. We conclude that there is also an experimental effect: the coin must be biased. Note: We could be wrong. The shifty-looking character could be entirely honest, just rather unlucky. We can never be absolutely sure.

Null hypothesis

The hypothesis that the observed differences are due to random error alone is called the **null hypothesis**. In the example above the null hypothesis is that the coin is fair. We rejected this when the probability of getting the observed results using this hypothesis became too small.

But what is *too small*?

Significance

In the previous section we noted that, although it seemed likely the coin was biased, we could always be wrong. In fact we could be wrong in two different ways:

1 Suppose we reject the null hypothesis (as we did) when *in fact* the coin was fair. The run of eight tails was due to chance alone. This is a **type 1 error**, when we decide incorrectly that there is an experimental effect. We wrongly accuse the shifty character of cheating.

2 Alternatively we might decide the coin was fair when *in fact* it was biased. This is a **type 2 error**, when we decide incorrectly that there is no experimental effect. We bet on the coin and lose a lot of money.

We must decide. How small must the probability of the null hypothesis become before we reject the null hypothesis as being too unlikely? This critical value of probability is called the **significance level**.

In any experiment we will observe differences between two groups. If the probability of the null hypothesis (random errors alone) producing these differences falls below this significance level we conclude that there is a **significant difference** between the experimental groups; that there is an experimental effect. If the probability does not fall below this significance level we cannot draw this conclusion.

Levels of significance

Where we draw our significance level will depend on whether we wish to avoid type 1 or type 2 errors. If the significance level is set when the probability of the null hypothesis is very small we will avoid type 1 errors but make many type 2 errors. In our example we will avoid accusing honest people of cheating – but we will lose a lot of money. Conversely, if the significance level is set when the probability is very large we will avoid type 2 errors but make many type 1 errors. We won't lose our money but we will accuse a lot of honest people of cheating.

In practice, scientists are anxious to avoid type 1 errors, that is, drawing false associations between events, and have settled on a significance level of $p = 0.05$. This is known as the 5% significance level. When $p = 0.05$ there are five chances in one hundred that the observed results are caused by random error alone.

If the probability falls to less than 0.01 (or 1%) the results are referred to as *highly significant*. The lower the probability, the higher the significance of the results.

One- and two-tailed tests

We can use a 5% significance level to assess the shifty character's coin. After how many throws could we have rejected the hypothesis that it was fair? After four tails in a row we calculated (p. 13) the probability that the coin was fair:

$$p = (\tfrac{1}{2})^4 = 0.0625$$

After yet another tail, now five in a row:

$$p = (\tfrac{1}{2})^5 = 0.03125$$

The probability has fallen below the 5% level. Is it now safe to reject the coin? *No.*

Our hypothesis stated that the coin was biased. We did not state in which direction, heads or tails. If the coin had turned up heads five times in a row we would have been just as suspicious. We can only reject the null hypothesis if the probability of 'five heads *or* five tails' falls below the 5% significance level.

$$p \text{ (5 heads or 5 tails)} = p(5 \text{ heads}) + p(5 \text{ tails})$$
$$= (\tfrac{1}{2})^5 + (\tfrac{1}{2})^5 = 0.0625, \textit{ not} \text{ significant at the 5\% level}$$

Significance will only be reached after the sixth tail in a row:

$$p(6 \text{ heads or 6 tails}) = (\tfrac{1}{2})^6 + (\tfrac{1}{2})^6 = 0.03125, \text{ significant}$$

Where the experimenter's hypothesis does not specify the direction of the difference between the two experimental groups then a two-tailed test, allowing for both directions, must be used.

Sometimes an experimental hypothesis predicts a difference only in one particular direction. For example, if our shifty friend produced his coin and suggested that he bet only on tails, we might well have suspected a coin biased to tails. If this is our hypothesis we need use only a **one-tailed** test. In this case we are justified in rejecting the coin after only five tails have appeared:

$$p(5 \text{ tails}) = (\tfrac{1}{2})^5 = 0.03125$$

But, if the coin had turned up any number of heads in a row we could not have supported our hypothesis that his coin was biased to tails. Whether to use a one- or two-tailed test will depend on the hypothesis and must be decided *before* the experiment is carried out.

We have been working out probabilities from first principles. This can become very tedious with more complex experiments and in practice we use the ready-computed tables of probability for each statistical test found at the end of the book.

The last two chapters have been dealing with the problems of variables, experimental and random, largely in theory. The following chapters deal with putting that theory into practice.

Measurements

Operational definitions

You have an idea, a hypothesis, which proposes a relationship between two variables. Before setting about testing this hypothesis you must be quite sure of exactly what it states. The variables must be defined. Here is a jolly hypothesis: Dirty jokes are funnier than clean jokes. This seems plausible but what does it mean? What is a dirty joke? What might seem risqué to me might be totally innocuous to you. How am I to decide whether or not I have a joke in the first place? What is a joke? I am not really sure I could define 'funnier' or 'funny', and yet the hypothesis seems to make sense.

Definitions in psychology are notoriously difficult. Endless arguments surround the precise meanings of such terms as intelligence and personality, and often the most important factors are also the hardest to define satisfactorily. The experimenter avoids these problems by using **operational definitions**.

A variable is defined by the operations or procedures used to measure it. If the variable is 'intelligence' this can be defined as the subject's performance on a particular IQ test. The experimenter is saying, 'What I mean by "intelligence" is whatever this test is measuring.' A good example of an operational definition, of friendship, can be found in I 1a. We define *what* we are measuring by describing precisely *how* we are measuring it.

Measurement of variables – how much information?

Any observation or measurement must be selective. We must decide how much of the information available we are going to use. Let's look, for an example, at the dependent variable in Demonstration 5, mathematical ability. First, note that we could argue for ever on a definition of this. We avoid that by using an operational definition: a subject's mathematical ability is defined as his or her performance on a particular set of mathematical questions – a maths test.

Every subject will perform differently, attempt different questions, get different answers right or wrong and arrive at these answers in different ways. How much of this difference in performance will we use? Hardly any of it. We ignore most of the information and use only the number of questions that each answered correctly.

Our selection does not have to stop here. We could ignore the actual score of each subject and record only the rank order of their scores. That is, who came first, who came second and so on down to who came last. Here we have lost more information. A rank-order measure records that one subject did better than another; it does not record by how much.

Finally, we could lose yet more information. By deciding on a pass mark for the test we can assign the subjects to the two discrete categories, 'pass' and 'fail'. Now we cannot distinguish between those who just missed the pass mark and those who failed dismally. From all the information available we know only that those who passed scored more than those who failed.

These three ways of recording the performance in a maths test illustrate the three ways in which variables are measured. These are **continuous measurements, rank-order measurements,** and **discrete measurements**.

Continuous measurements

Variables measured in this way vary *quantitatively*, that is they vary in amount rather than in type, and could take any value along a continuous scale. Height is measured continuously: everyone has a certain amount of it; tall people have rather more than shorter people. A person's height could take on any value from about two to seven feet. In D 4 the dependent variable is the time taken to complete a task. A subject might take any number of seconds to complete it.

In practice the measures are rarely perfectly continuous. In the maths test, where the measure was the number of correct answers, subjects can score only whole-number values. In the same way, age, a common independent variable, is usually recorded as a whole number of years.

Rank-order measurements

The variable again is quantitative but the actual value along a scale is not recorded, just the order along the scale in which the subjects lie. In a horse-race, for example, although the time taken by each horse to run the distance could be measured (a continuous measure) it is easier to record the order in which they passed the finishing-post. Rank orders can be used in this way to avoid the need for sophisticated measuring equipment. More commonly they are used for simplicity of statistical analysis.

Discrete measurements

Where the variable is *qualitative*, varying in type rather than amount, each measurement will fall into a discrete category. Sex is a qualitative variable and hence is measured discretely, male or female, as in E 18 and D 5. Similarly, which hand a subject writes with is measured discretely, left or right, as in D 3. In this experiment it may be necessary to include a third category for any subjects who are truly ambidextrous.

Quantitative variables can also be measured discretely to suit a particular design. This is often done with the independent variable to give two conditions of the IV. In I 1 age is the IV of a developmental study in a primary school. Where two classes are available of, say, five-year-olds and nine-year-olds we would use these two classes as the two conditions of the IV. A quantitative variable can also be measured discretely for the sake of simplicity of measurement or analysis. Using O-level passes in D 5 is an example of this; E 9 is an even better example.

Which to choose?

Where a variable is qualitative the measurement will be discrete. Where it is quantitative we have a choice, as in the measurement of the maths test. The choice is between power and simplicity. The **power** of an experiment or analysis is its ability to reveal an experimental effect among all the random variation. The more information we have about the variables, the more likely we are to find a relationship between them. As we have seen, there is a loss of information from continuous measurement to rank orders and from rank orders to discrete measurement. This loss may result in an experimental result being obscured.

Collecting detailed information, however, can be a difficult and lengthy business and you may have a severely limited amount of time and equipment at your disposal. It is sometimes better to sacrifice some information for a quick and simple experiment.

In a pole-vault attempt the athlete either clears the bar or he doesn't – a discrete measurement. We have sacrificed some information (e.g. by how much he cleared the bar), but imagine the paraphernalia we would need to measure the height of his vault without the discrete measurement – without a bar. Often continuous measurements are very simple. At other times, where resources are limited, a discrete measurement may be the only practicable method.

An important consideration in deciding the type of measurement is the *use* of the information. If we wish to compare our results with a related experiment it might be as well to use the same operational definition of the variable; that is, the same way of measuring it.

In E 18, we are measuring driving speed, a continuous variable. If we wish to compare our results with police speeding statistics we might use a discrete measure – over or under the speed limit on our particular stretch of road. This information could be extracted from the continuous measure at a later date.

Exactly which type of measurement is used will depend on the variable and your resources. The advice here is to extract as much information as possible. That is, take continuous measurements if they can be taken simply. These can always be converted to rank-order or discrete measurements if necessary.

The type of measurement chosen for each variable will decide the type of statistical test you can use.

Selecting a statistical test

The story so far

Take a look at any of the experiments in the second half of the book or one you have dreamt up yourself. You can now identify several stages in the planning of an experiment. There is the hypothesis connecting two variables. These two variables have been defined (operational definition) by the way in which they will be measured. These measurements can be of three general types (continuous, rank-order or discrete). You will be looking for a regular variation between the two variables: as one varies, the other varies (the experimental effect). You also know when it is safe to say that there is an experimental effect by looking at the probability of the null hypothesis.

Now read on

In one instance you have actually calculated that probability. You need never do so again. Statisticians – who like that sort of thing – have already done this. All you have to do is to put your results into a suitable form and read off the probability of the null hypothesis from a table at the end of this book. The suitable form will depend on the statistical test you choose. This choice of statistical test depends on how the variables have been measured.

Selecting the test

Each of the two experimental variables can be continuous (C), or rank-ordered (R), or discrete (D). This gives us a number of possible combinations for the two variables. That is: DD, RR, CC, RC, RD and CD. Each uses a particular test.

DD
Both variables discrete ───────────────► Chi-squared (χ^2) test
p. 24

RR
Both variables rank-ordered ───────────► Rank-order correlation (r)
p. 111

CC
Both variables continuous ─────────────► Product-moment correlation (r)
p. 116

RD
One variable rank-ordered
One variable discrete (two conditions only. If
there are more they can be
considered in pairs)

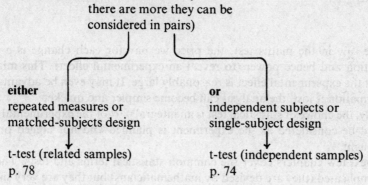

either
repeated measures or
matched-subjects design

Wilcoxon p. 98

or
independent subjects or
single-subject design

Mann-Whitney p. 90

CD
One variable continuous (with reasonably Normal distribution – p. 61)
One variable discrete (two conditions only. If
there are more they can be
considered in pairs)

either
repeated measures or
matched-subjects design

t-test (related samples)
p. 78

or
independent subjects or
single-subject design

t-test (independent samples)
p. 74

(**CD** – other tests. The Sign Test (p. 86) can be used on non-Normal related
samples. It is very simple but rather
weak.

The F-test (p. 82) can be used on Normal samples to
test for difference in variance.)

It is quite possible that your results will not fit into any of these tests for some
reason.

Example:
A common combination of variables in an experiment is: independent variable – discrete, dependent variable – continuous (e.g. E 10 or D 1). This CD combination uses one or other type of t-test and requires that the continuous variable is reasonably normally distributed. It may be that ours is not. (How you can decide is covered on p. 80.)
or:
Your variables may be continuous and ranked (RC). No test is given for this combination.

Do not despair. It is always possible to convert your results to suitable measures. In the maths test described on page 16 the actual scores of the subjects can be expressed as a rank order or as a discrete pass or fail. By changing the type of measurements in this way you can change the variable combinations and hence the statistical test. The possible changes are shown below:

```
CC
 │    ╲RC
 ↓     │  ╲
CD     ↓    RR
 │   ╲ RD
 ↓    ↓
DD    RD
```

As we saw in the maths test, the price we pay for each change is a loss of information and hence power (to reveal an experimental effect). This might not matter if the experimental effect is reasonably large. It may even be advantageous. As information is lost, the analysis can become simpler and quicker.

Finally, the choice of statistical test is an integral part of the experimental design. It should be considered as the experiment is planned and not tagged on as an afterthought.

The next few chapters cover the common statistical terms and tests. They may look complicated (they are devised by mathematicians) but they are very simple to use (they are used by psychologists). You do not need to know what the test is doing to use it in assessing the significance of your results, any more than you need to know what is happening under a car's bonnet to drive the car. However, there are several reasons for going a little deeper and taking a look at the rationale behind the various tests and concepts.

First, some understanding of a test or concept helps greatly in grasping what the test is testing or what the descriptive term is describing. This is particularly important for people like me to whom pithy mathematical formulae do not speak volumes.

Second, all statistical tests are based on assumptions and have limitations, and in practice it is often necessary to take liberties with both. Some familiarity with the works will help in judging how far they can be bent before they break.

Third, there is a mild self-satisfaction for someone as non-mathematical as myself in understanding something with as many xs, square roots and Greek symbols as these things have.

Fourth, and probably most important for the average reader, some other people who matter (examiners and so forth) think that it is important that you understand what is going on (possibly because they too are mildly self-satisfied at having grasped it). It is a good thing to please these people.

I hope one of these reasons appeals to you. I would not recommend that you read these chapters through now. Dip into them as you plan an experiment or when you have some data to play with, or if you need to use a particular concept. Follow the worked example and then substitute your own data.

A calculator is a vast help: there is no virtue in wading through endless figures unnecessarily. A calculator with a memory or two and a square-root function is better. (There *are* calculators with statistical functions preprogrammed.) Some people remember these formulae and carry them around in their heads. I am amazed.

Chi-squared

(DD – both variables discrete)
Examples: D 2, 5; E 7, 9

The most common experiment of this sort has two conditions of each variable. In one variation of E 18 the speed of the driver is measured discretely: over 30 m.p.h. or under 30 m.p.h. Each driver is also either a man or a woman. There are four possible combinations of these conditions:

		Sex	
		Male	Female
Speed	30 +		
	30 −		

This is called a 2 × 2 contingency table. Each subject will fit into one and one only of these four contingencies. The experimenter simply records the number of observations in each contingency:

		Sex		
		Male	Female	Row total
Speed	30 +	47	13	60
	30 −	53	37	90
Column total		100	50	150 Total observations

(these are fictitious and remarkably convenient data)

Our hypothesis states that there is an association between driving-speed and sex. The null hypothesis is that there is no connection between these two. If the null hypothesis is true we would expect that the proportion of males in the faster group (30 + m.p.h.) would be the same as the proportion of males in the slower group, i.e. the same as the proportion of males in the whole sample. We calculate these proportions expected on the basis of the null hypothesis. There are twice as many males as females in the sample: we expect the same proportion among the 60 fast drivers, i.e. 40 males and 20 females. Similarly, of the 90 slower drivers we would expect 60 males and 30 females. These expected (E) values can be quickly calculated for each contingency using the formula:

$$E = \frac{(\text{column total}) \times (\text{row total})}{(\text{total number of observations})}$$

E.g. for males (column total = 100), driving 30 + m.p.h. (row total = 60)

$$E = \frac{100 \times 60}{150} = 40$$

These expected scores are entered on the contingency table. *Observed* scores appear above the diagonal, *expected* scores below:

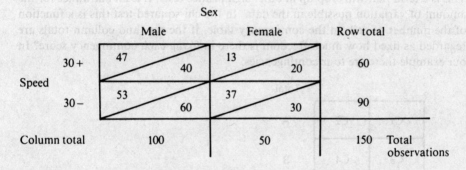

Remember, the *expected* values are on the basis of the null hypothesis. The greater the difference between the observed (O) and the expected (E) scores, the less likely is the null hypothesis. This difference is calculated for each cell:

$$(O - E)$$

This will be positive for some cells and negative for others. We are interested only in the amount of the difference, not the direction. The difference is squared to ensure all differences will appear positive:

$$(O - E)^2$$

If the sample size were very large we would expect fairly large differences from chance alone. To allow for this the squared difference is divided by the expected value of the cell:

$$\frac{(O - E)^2}{E}$$

We can do the same calculation for each cell. The chi-squared statistic (χ^2) is the sum of all these.

$$\chi^2 = \sum \frac{(O-E)^2}{E}$$

Σ (the Greek capital letter 'sigma') means simply 'the sum of all things like this'.

Chi-squared increases as the difference in each cell increases (and the probability of the null hypothesis decreases). This probability, associated with a particular chi-squared value, can be found in Table A under the appropriate **degree of freedom**.

Degrees of freedom

This is a term that will crop up in other significance tests. It is an allowance for the amount of variation possible in the data. In the chi-squared test this is a function of the number of cells in the contingency table. If the row and column totals are regarded as fixed how much freedom is there in fixing each contingency score? In our example there are four contingencies:

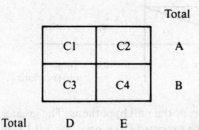

Cell 1 could take any value – but now C2 is decided because:

$$C2 + C1 = A \quad \text{(this total is fixed)}$$

Also C3 is decided:

$$C3 + C1 = D$$

and hence C4 is decided:

$$C3 + C4 = B$$

Only one of the four cells was free to take any value. Once one was fixed all the others were decided. There was one degree of freedom. In larger contingency tables there will be more degrees of freedom.

				Total
C1	C2	C3	C4	A
C5	C6	C7	C8	B
C9	C10	C11	C12	D
Total E	F	G	H	

C1, C2 and C3 can take any value before C4 is decided. Similarly on the second row C5, C6 and C7 can take any value but now *all* the other cells are decided. There are six degrees of freedom.

In general, the degrees of freedom (df) are given by:

$$df = (\text{Number of rows} - 1) \times (\text{Number of columns} - 1)$$

Our 2×2 contingency table has one degree of freedom.

One degree of freedom – Yates's correction

It has been found (by Yates?) that for 2×2 contingency tables the chi-squared statistic gives an underestimate of the probability of the null hypothesis. To allow for this the difference in each cell is reduced slightly. This is **Yates's correction**.

For a 2×2 table (one degree of freedom):

$$\chi^2 = \sum \frac{(|O - E| - \frac{1}{2})^2}{E}$$

(Note: $|O - E|$ means the amount of the difference, ignoring the direction, $+$ or $-$.)

To return to our example:

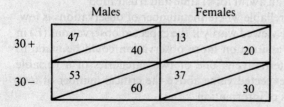

In the top left-hand cell (males driving 30 + m.p.h.):

$$O - E = 47 - 40 + 7$$

Apply Yates's correction:

$$|O - E| - \tfrac{1}{2} = 6\tfrac{1}{2} \quad \text{and} \quad (|O - E| - \tfrac{1}{2})^2 = 42.25$$

Dividing by E:

$$\frac{42.25}{40} = 1.05625$$

We repeat this procedure for all the cells and sum the results:

$$\sum \frac{(|O - E| - \tfrac{1}{2})^2}{E} = 1.05625 + 2.1125 + 0.70417 + 1.4083$$

$$= 5.28 = \text{chi-squared}$$

Turning to Table A, with 1 degree of freedom, our results lie above the 5% significance level ($\chi^2 = 3.84$). We can reject the null hypothesis. These (fictitious) data show a significant relationship between driving speed and the sex of the driver ($p = 0.05$). Follow the worked example.

Limitations of chi-squared

As with all statistical tests the chi-squared is based on certain assumptions about the observations. The chi-squared test assumes that all observations are independent, that the outcome of one observation has no effect on any other. Where more than one observation is made from a single subject there is always the possibility of interaction between observations (for example, an order effect, p. 9). The magnitude of any such interaction will depend on the type of behaviour being observed. You should ask yourself whether a series of observations could be influenced by memory and learning or boredom. Even with independent-subjects designs there may be some interaction. In our example, if two of the drivers were in sight of one another, the second driver might be matching his speed to that of the first to avoid overtaking or coming too close. We must consider scrapping all observations where the driver has another car visible in front of him. These things are best considered at the design stage. This can save an awful lot of time and frustration.

The chi-squared test can be unreliable where the number of observations is low. As a general rule results should be viewed warily if the expected observations (E) in any cell fall below five. In such a situation more observation could be made to increase the expected values. Alternatively, one or two categories of a variable could be combined to bring the expected value above the critical number of five. This will, of course, involve a loss of information.

Chi-squared – test of association: procedure
The test will measure the association between two variables, measured discretely.

Step no.	What to do
1	Draw up a contingency table of A × B cells. A is the number of discrete categories in one variable and B is the number of discrete categories in the other variable. Find the observed frequency (O) of each cell.
2	Find the row totals, column totals and grand total of observations.
3	Find the expected frequency (E) for each cell $$E = \frac{\text{Row total} \times \text{Column total}}{\text{Grand total}}$$

Step no.	Result	What to do
4	$(O-E)$	Take (3) from (1) for each cell, ignoring the sign. NB in a 2×2 contingency table, i.e. one degree of freedom, Yates's correction must be applied $(|O-E| - \frac{1}{2})$.
5	$(O-E)^2$	Square each (4).
6	$\frac{(O-E)^2}{E}$	Divide (5) by (3) for each cell.
7	$\sum \frac{(O-E)^2}{E}$ = chi-squared	Add all (6) to find chi-squared.
8		Look in Table A to find the significant value of chi-squared for $(A-1) \times (B-1)$ degrees of freedom. There is significant association if the observed value exceeds the table value.
9		Interpret this result in terms of the experimental hypothesis.

Chi-squared – test of association: worked example

These results are taken from E 6. Thirty-six subjects were asked to listen to a tape-recording of a passage read from a novel – the model. They were then asked to read aloud, from a different part of the same novel, for the same length of time. Two discrete measures were taken: the speed of reading relative to the model, and their estimation of time relative to the model. The hypothesis suggests that fast reading speeds are associated with over-estimation of reading time.

1   A 2 × 2 contingency table:

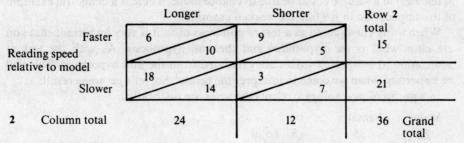

Reading time relative to model

	Longer	Shorter	Row total
Faster	6 10	9 5	15
Slower	18 14	3 7	21

Reading speed relative to model

2   Column total   24   12   36 Grand total

3   Top left cell: $E = \dfrac{15 \times 24}{36} = 10$

Top right cell: $E = \dfrac{15 \times 12}{36} = 5$

Bottom left cell: $E = \dfrac{21 \times 24}{36} = 14$

Bottom right cell: $E = \dfrac{21 \times 12}{36} = 7$

Cell **4**	(O−E)	Yate's Corr. ($\lvert O-E \rvert - \tfrac{1}{2}$)	**5** (O−E)²	**6** $\dfrac{(O-E)^2}{E}$
Top left	4	3.5	12.25	1.225
Top right	4	3.5	12.25	2.45
Bottom left	4	3.5	12.25	0.875
Bottom right	4	3.5	12.25	1.75
				6.300 **7**

Note: Steps **4** and **5** are the same for all cells because, in this case, there is only one degree of freedom. This will not be the case with larger contingency tables.

8   We have $(2-1) \times (2-1) = 1$ degree of freedom. From Table A there is 5% significance if chi-squared exceeds 5.412. There is a significant association between the two variables (p = 0.05).

9   We reject the null hypothesis that the association between reading longer and reading slower is due to random error alone. There is a relationship between reading speed and estimation of time spent reading.

Chi-squared as a test of goodness of fit

So far the chi-squared test has been used as a test of association between the two discrete variables. In the same way it can be used to test the association between a set of observed values and a set of values generated from some theory – to see how well the observations fit the theory and vice versa. Chi-squared here is used as a **test of goodness of fit**. We can use it to test whether a set of figures is normally distributed (p. 61). A common application is to test if the proportions of a variable (e.g. males to females) in a sample could be due to chance alone. There is a delightful example of this application in E 9 (see the worked example).

When using chi-squared as a test of goodness of fit it is very important that you are clear what is the hypothesis and the null hypothesis. As with the test of association, the expected values are generated from the null hypothesis. This will be important when we come to interpret the results. So, let's get some results.

In a group of psychology students the sexes are distributed:

Males	Females	
22	35	= 57 Total

What proportions would I have expected? Well I have no theories that psychology is more attractive to one sex and so I would expect the proportions to be the same. I generate the expected values and proceed:

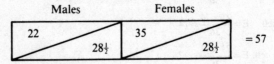

Note: I generated the expected values on the equal proportion hypothesis. This must then be the null hypothesis.

There is one degree of freedom (as soon as the value for one cell is settled the value of the other cell is decided; the total is taken to be fixed). Yates's correction must be applied.

For the first cell:

$$(|O - E| - \tfrac{1}{2}) = (6\tfrac{1}{2} - \tfrac{1}{2}) = 6$$

And so:

$$\frac{(|O - E| - \tfrac{1}{2})^2}{E} = \frac{(6)^2}{28\tfrac{1}{2}} = 1.263$$

The calculation is exactly the same for the second cell as the expected values for the two cells are the same.
So:

$$\sum \frac{(|O - E| - \tfrac{1}{2})^2}{E} = 1.263 + 1.263 = 2.526$$

That is:

$$\chi^2 = 2.526$$

By reference to Table A, I find this is not significant at the 5% level. Can I conclude then that 'psychology *is* equally attractive to males and females'?

No. This is a common error. Imagine that the chi-squared statistic had been significant at the 5% level. I could then reject the null hypothesis (that psychology is equally attractive) – the basis of my expected values. I would have said:

I am 95% certain that psychology is *not* equally attractive to males and females.

With the results I actually obtained all I can say is:

I am *not* 95% certain that psychology is *not* equally attractive to males and females.

This is very different from saying:

I am 95% certain that psychology *is* equally attractive to males and females.

We cannot be reasonably certain in either rejecting or asserting the hypothesis that psychology is equally attractive to both sexes.

In this example the calculation of the expected values was very simple. It can be rather tedious with more complex theories, e.g. that the set of scores is distributed normally.

A worked example of such a test for normality is given on page 36. Before tackling this you will need to have a good look at the Normal distribution (p. 61).

Chi-squared – goodness of fit: procedure

The data will be observations of one discrete variable. These will be compared with expected results generated by a hypothesis. The goodness of fit of the observed results to the hypothesis is measured by a chi-squared test.

Step no.	What to do
1	Draw up a table of results. The table will have one row of N cells. The number of observations in a cell is the observed frequency for that cell (O).
2	Find the total number of observations (Σ O)
3	Generate the expected proportions of observations in each cell on the basis of the hypothesis to be tested. (The sum of these proportions should be 1 – check this.)
4	Find the expected frequency for each cell (E), by multiplying the expected proportion (3) by the total number of observations (2). If E falls below 5 for any cell, either combine two or more cells or take more observations.
	(Note: Σ E = Σ O, check this)

Step no.	Result	What to do
5	$(O-E)$	Take (4) from (1) for each cell, ignoring the sign. If there are only two cells, i.e. one degree of freedom, Yates's correction must be applied ($|O-E|-\frac{1}{2}$).
6	$(O-E)^2$	Square each (5).
7	$\dfrac{(O-E)^2}{E}$	Divide (6) by (4) for each cell.
8	$\sum\dfrac{(O-E)^2}{E}$ $=\chi^2$	Add all (7) to find chi-squared.
9		Look in Table A to find the significant value of chi-squared for (number of cells – 1) degrees of freedom.
10		Interpret this result in terms of the variable and hypothesis.

Chi-squared – goodness of fit: worked example

These results are taken from the first part of E 9. The observed frequencies in cells A, B, C and D are the number of subjects choosing to use one of the four urinals in a men's lavatory. A was nearest the door, B second nearest and so on. The expected frequencies are generated on the hypothesis that there is no preference between A, B, C and D.

		Urinal					
		A	B	C	D	Total	
1	Observed frequencies	12	17	22	29	80	**2**
3	Expected proportions	0.25	0.25	0.25	0.25	1	
4	Expected frequencies	20	20	20	20	80	
5	$(O-E)$	8	3	2	9		
6	$(O-E)^2$	64	9	4	81		
7	$\dfrac{(O-E)^2}{E}$	3.2	0.45	0.2	4.05	$7.9 = \chi^2$	**8**

9   The observed value of chi-squared, 7.9, is greater than the 5% significance value ($\chi^2 = 7.815$) in Table A with 3 degrees of freedom. We can reject the hypothesis of no preference.

10   These results show significant evidence of subjects' preference in their choice of urinal.

Chi-squared – goodness of fit (to a Normal distribution): procedure
A set of scores is claimed to be normally distributed. We can construct a Normal distribution that has the same mean, standard deviation, and sample size as the observed scores. This Normal distribution is then used to generate expected frequencies of scores for comparison with observed frequencies in a chi-squared test. As chi-squared deals with discrete variables we must divide the continuous variable into suitable intervals. The expected frequency in each interval is found from the area under the standard Normal curve (Table B) with the interval expressed as standard (z) scores.

The worked example is illustrated by histograms of the observed and expected scores. This is not necessary but gives a clearer idea of the process. Calculating the expected values is not difficult – but it is tedious. I do not advise this test without a calculator.

Chi-squared – goodness of fit (to a Normal distribution): worked example

These results come from D 1. Each score represents the difference between the perceived mid-point of a line, with and without the arrow-heads, measured from the left of the figure. Each score then is a (d) term in a t-test for related samples (p. 78) where:

$$d = (X_a - X_b)$$

We will check the distribution of these scores, for normality, before proceeding with the t-test. I have not bothered to give details of finding the mean and standard deviation of the scores as this is straightforward and covered elsewhere in the book (mean, page 43, standard deviation, page 46). The sample size is 54. The scores are displayed in the histogram below at intervals of 5 mm.

2. *Distribution of scores observed in D*

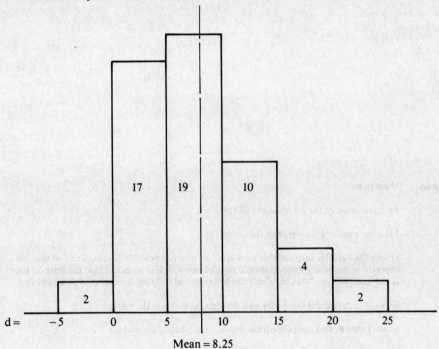

Mean = 8.25

Step no.	What to do
1	Find the mean of the set of scores ($\bar{X}$)
2	Find the standard deviation of the scores (σ).
3	Divide the variable into suitable intervals – as many as possible bearing in mind that the expected score in any interval should not fall below 5. If it turns out that the interval size is too small to avoid this, intervals can be combined to bring the expected value above 5.
4	Express each interval boundary as a standard score from the mean.
5	From Table B, find the proportion between each boundary and the mean.
6	By subtraction, find the proportion of each interval (P).

Step no.	Result	What to do
7	ΣP	Add all (6).
8	$P\dfrac{N}{\Sigma P} = E$	Convert proportions to expected frequencies by multiplying by the number of scores (divided by (7) to ensure that the total expected scores = total observed scores).

2a. A Normal distribution of scores with the same mean and standard deviation as fig. 2

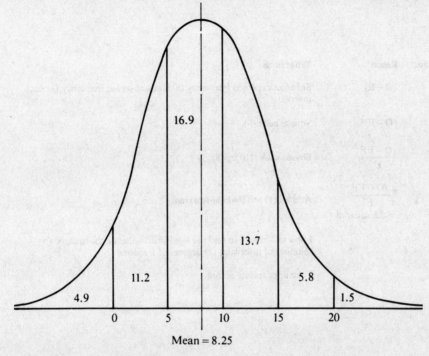

Mean = 8.25

1   Sample mean = 8.25

2   Standard deviation = 6.15

3   Scores are divided into intervals of 5 mm. The histogram (figure 2) shows the observed frequencies.

Calculation of expected normal frequencies

Interval boundary	Difference from mean (8.25)	**4** Expressed as z-score (divided by $\sigma = 6.15$)	**5** Proportion from mean to z	**6** Proportion of interval (P)	**8** Expected frequency (E)
Tail	(less than 0)		0.5	0.0901	4.9
0	8.25	1.34	0.4099		
				0.2080	11.2
5	3.25	0.53	↗ 0.2019		
Mean (8.25)			These must be *added*	0.3122	16.9
10	1.75	0.28	↘ 0.1103		
				0.2540	13.7
15	6.75	1.20	0.3643		
				0.1076	5.8 ↘
20	11.75	1.91	0.4719		= 7.3
				0.0281	1.5 ↗
Tail	(more than 20)		0.5		
			(7) $\Sigma P = 1.0000$		54.0

Step no.	Result	What to do
9	$(O-E)$	Subtract expected frequency (8) from observed frequency for each interval.
10	$(O-E)^2$	Square each (9).
11	$\dfrac{(O-E)^2}{E}$	Divide each (10) by (8).
12	$\sum\dfrac{(O-E)^2}{E}$ = chi-squared	Add all (11) to find chi-squared.
13		Look in Table A to find the significant value of chi-squared for (number of intervals − 1) degrees of freedom.
14		Take appropriate action.

Note: In this case $\Sigma P = 1$ because the total area of the tails were included. So

$$\frac{N}{\Sigma P} = 54$$

Also: the last two intervals have been combined to make E greater than 5 but we will risk the value of the first tail (E = 4.9).

Interval	Observed frequency	**8** Expected frequency	**9** $(O-E)$	**10** $(O-E)^2$	**11** $\dfrac{(O-E)^2}{E}$
Less than 0	2	4.9	−2.9	8.41	1.716
0–5	17	11.2	5.8	33.64	3.004
5–10	19	16.9	2.1	4.41	0.261
10–15	10	13.7	−3.7	13.69	0.999
More than 15	6	7.3	−1.3	1.69	0.232
				12	6.212

Chi-squared = 6.212 (with 4 degrees of freedom).

13 Chi-squared is significant at the 5% level at a value of 9.488. Our results are not significant. We cannot reject the hypothesis that the observed set of scores have a normal distribution.

14 We are safe in carrying on with a t-test.

Descriptive statistics

From chi-squared to t-test

In the chi-squared test both the variables are discrete. We used one variation of E 18 in which one variable was the sex of a driver, the other was the speed of the car (more than 30 m.p.h. or less than 30 m.p.h.). In an effort to get more information from the experiment we could measure the actual speed of the car. This variable is now continuous and will require a different analysis – a t-test.

Before we can statistically compare the performances of male and female drivers we must first be able to describe those performances. As discrete and continuous measurements hold different amounts of information they also differ in how easily they can be described. Measured discretely, the performance of, say, the women is very easy to describe. From the example on p. 24, 13 women drove faster than 30 m.p.h., 37 drove slower. The behaviour of this group of women has been described using all the information.

If a continuous measure of speed were used how could we describe as succinctly the behaviour of the whole group? We might talk about the speed of the average woman, the fastest woman and the slowest but this would use only some of the information collected. Several ways of describing a group of continuous measures have been devised to use as much of the information as possible. We must look at these to understand the t-test.

A set of scores

This example set of scores comes from a real experiment, E 11. The subjects were asked to estimate the height of a friend of mine with whom they had been chatting for half an hour. Some subjects thought he was a professor (the P group); others thought he was an unemployed labourer (the U group). I shall use the estimates (in inches above five feet) of the P group. These 'scores' are set out overleaf:

Subject no.	Estimates of height (X) in inches over 5 ft
1	10
2	9
3	8
4	10
5	8
6	$7\frac{1}{2}$
7	9
8	9
9	$8\frac{1}{2}$

In a succinct description of this set of scores we can give two general measures. First, a measure of **central tendency**; that is, the *typical* score of subjects in this group. Second, a measure of **dispersion**; that is, the amount of *variation* in their scores. You will be using these measures time and again. It might be a good idea to get hold of a set of scores and try them out as you go. Any set of continuous measurements will do: heights, ages or from some of the demonstrations in Part II.

Measures of central tendency

We will be looking at three of these: the **mean**, the **median** and the **mode**.

1. **The mean** (or more properly, the arithmetic mean)
This is by far the most common measure and is the statistical name for what is often loosely called 'the average'. It is calculated by adding up all the individual scores and dividing this total by the number of scores. This can be expressed in symbols:

$$\bar{X} = \frac{\Sigma X}{N}$$

X stands for any individual score. If we wished to identify the score of a particular subject, say subject 4, we label it X_4.

$\bar{X}$ (pronounced 'X bar') is the symbol for the arithmetic mean of X.

Σ is an instruction to 'sum things of this sort' (see p. 26), in this case the instruction is to sum all Xs (the individual scores).

N stands for the number of individual scores.

So, the mean score of the P group is:

$$\bar{X} = \frac{\Sigma X}{N}$$

$$\Sigma X = 10 + 9 + 8 + 10 + 8 + 7\tfrac{1}{2} + 9 + 9 + 8\tfrac{1}{2} = 79$$

and

$$\frac{\Sigma X}{N} = \frac{79}{9} = 8.78 \text{ in}$$

The mean score of the P group, $\bar{X}_p$, is 8.78 inches.

2. The median

The median finds the middle of a set of scores. Half the subjects score above (or equal to) this score, half score below (or equal to) this score. To find this middle score, all the scores are placed in rank order. If there is an odd number of scores the median is the score in the middle of this order. In the P group the rank order of scores is:

$$10, 10, 9, 9, \mathbf{9}, 8\tfrac{1}{2}, 8, 8, 7\tfrac{1}{2}$$

As there are nine scores, the median value is the fifth in this rank order (heavy type). If there is an even number of scores the median value is half way between the middle two scores. Suppose a tenth subject joined the P group and gave an estimate of 7 inches: the median value would be half way between the fifth and sixth scores. That is:

$$\frac{9 + 8\tfrac{1}{2}}{2} = 8.75 \text{ inches}$$

3. The mode

The mode of a group of scores is the most frequently occurring score. If the variable is truly continuous or if the number of scores is small there will be very few if any scores repeated. In this case the mode is meaningless. However, many variables are not truly continuous but measured to the nearest whole number, e.g. height, age, etc., and repetitions can become very common as the number of scores increases.

   In the P group the estimate of nine inches occurs most frequently. This is the modal value.

Which to use?

The mean is the most commonly used measure of central tendency. It is used in several tests of significance and other statistical concepts. It has the attraction of extracting the most information from the set of scores. The value of every score is used in its computation and a change in any score will change the mean. As a purely descriptive term it has some disadvantages. As the mean extracts the same amount of information from each score it is susceptible to extreme, aberrant scores. The value of the mean is rarely an *example* of one of the scores. In many variables the scores are given in whole numbers (age, questions correct on a test, errors in a skilled task and so forth); the arithmetic mean is unlikely to be a whole number and so, in one sense, it is anything but a typical score of the group. In these cases the mean can sound ludicrous and a median or mode is preferable. The average family size is commonly given the modal value of 2 children, rather than the gruesome mean of 2.23 children.

The advice here is to use the mean for all data but give the mode or median value as well if it is more suitable for purely descriptive use.

Measures of dispersion

There are several of these but, again, only three will be covered here: the **range**, the **mean deviation** and the **standard deviation.**

1. The range
The range is simply the difference between the highest and lowest scores in the group. In our example of the P group the highest score is 10 inches, the lowest is $7\frac{1}{2}$ inches; the range of group P scores is $2\frac{1}{2}$ inches.

The advantage of using the range is its simplicity to find and interpret. Its disadvantage is that it extracts very little information from only two scores. Those two scores are the extreme scores of the group and so the range is extremely sensitive to aberrant scores – much more so than the mean which uses information from all the scores.

2. The mean deviation
This title is a shortened version of 'the mean deviation from the mean'. It is computed by finding the mean of individual deviations from the mean of the group.

As we are trying to measure dispersion – the spread of scores – we need a fixed point to measure this spread from. We use the centre of the scores, the mean. First then, we find the mean of the scores ($\bar{X}$). If we now take any individual score (X), there will be a difference between these two. This is the individual's deviation from the mean: symbolically x.

$$x = (X - \bar{X})$$

The score of subject 1 in the P group was 10, the mean of the P group is 8.78. This subject's deviation from the mean is:

$$x = (10 - 8.78) = 1.22 \text{ inches}$$

In this case the deviation is positive. We can do the same for all the scores but because the mean is the arithmetic centre of the scores there will be as much negative deviation as positive deviation; the sum of the deviations will be zero. We are not interested in the direction of the deviation, just its amount, and so we simply ignore the direction (+ or −) and make each deviation positive. This is symbolized:

$$|X - \bar{X}|$$

The mean deviation ($\bar{x}$) is the mean of all these values and is found in the usual way:

$$\bar{x} = \frac{\Sigma|X - \bar{X}|}{N}$$

In our example, the P group:

Subject no.	Score (X)	Deviation $|X - \bar{X}|$
1	10	1.22
2	9	0.22
3	8	0.78
4	10	1.22
5	8	0.78
6	7½	1.28
7	9	0.22
8	9	0.22
9	8½	0.28
Total no. 9 = N	79 = Σ X	6.22 = Σ$|X - \bar{X}|$

$$\bar{X} = \frac{\Sigma X}{N} = \frac{79}{9} = 8.78$$

$$\bar{x} = \frac{\Sigma|X - \bar{X}|}{N} = \frac{6.22}{9} = 0.69 \text{ inches.}$$

The mean deviation of the P group is 0.69 inches.

3. The standard deviation

The standard deviation is very similar to the mean deviation. The rationale behind the two is the same and the computation differs only slightly. But the standard deviation is much more widely used. This is because it forms one of the terms of a very common and useful distribution, the Normal distribution (p. 61). It is slightly more satisfactory mathematically as it does not rely on the user changing certain information (the direction of a negative deviation from the mean). In the mean deviation we used only the amount of the deviation and considered all deviations as positive. Another way of extracting only information of the amount of deviation is to square each deviation. All these squared deviations will be positive:

$$(X - \bar{X})^2$$

We can now calculate the mean of these values:

$$\frac{\Sigma(X-\bar{X})^2}{N}$$

This is called the **variance** of a set of scores.

As we have squared the deviations, the variance will be measured in squared units – in this case, inches squared. To get a measure of dispersion in the original units of the scores we must take a square root:

$$\sqrt{\frac{\Sigma(X-\bar{X})^2}{N}}$$

This is the *standard deviation* of a set of scores, symbolized σ (the Greek lower-case letter sigma). Variance, the square of standard deviation, is thus symbolized σ^2.

The standard deviation is by far the most commonly used measure of dispersion as it crops up time and again in statistical analyses. We are using it here simply as a description of the variability within our group of scores. In most cases, however, we are using such an experimental group as a sample (p. 60) of a larger population and using the standard deviation of the sample as an estimate of the variability within the whole population. When used in this way it is found to give a slight underestimate of the variability and so, in practice, standard deviation is usually calculated as:

$$\sigma = \sqrt{\frac{\Sigma(X-\bar{X})^2}{(N-1)}}$$

The difference between the two is slight and gets slighter as the sample size (N) increases. However, as our sample sizes are often small, we will use this improved version.

Now that you have worked through the reasoning behind this formula perhaps I ought to tell you that there is another, equivalent, formula which may be marginally less tedious as it does away with calculating the individual differences from the mean:

$$\sigma = \sqrt{\frac{\Sigma X^2 - [(\Sigma X)^2/N]}{(N-1)}}$$

Because this formula deals with raw scores rather than differences from a mean, some of the calculation can get up to astronomical figures if each score is large and there are many subjects. This can be a bit frightening without a calculator. Both methods produce the same result and both will be used on the same set of scores, the P group, in the worked examples.

Standard deviation – method 1: procedure

Step no.	Result of step	What to do
1	ΣX	Add together all the individual scores.
2	$\dfrac{\Sigma X}{N} = \bar{X}$	Divide (1) by the number of scores to find the mean.
3	$(X - \bar{X})$	Subtract (2) from each score.
4	$(X - \bar{X})^2$	Square each (3).
5	$\Sigma (X - \bar{X})^2$	Add all (4).
6	$\dfrac{\Sigma (X - \bar{X})^2}{(N-1)} = \sigma^2$	Divide (5) by (number of scores − 1) to find the variance.
7	$\sqrt{\dfrac{\Sigma (X - \bar{X})^2}{(N-1)}} = \sigma$	Take the square root of (6) to find the standard deviation.

Standard deviation – method 1: worked example

Subject no.	Score (X)	**3** Deviation $(X - \bar{X})$	**4** $(X - \bar{X})^2$
1	10	1.22	1.4884
2	9	0.22	0.0484
3	8	0.78	0.6084
4	10	1.22	1.4884
5	8	0.78	0.6084
6	$7\frac{1}{2}$	1.28	1.6384
7	9	0.22	0.0484
8	9	0.22	0.0484
9	$8\frac{1}{2}$	0.28	0.0784
$\overline{9} = (N)$	**1** 79		**5** 6.0556

2 $\quad \dfrac{79}{9} = 8.78$

6 $\quad \dfrac{6.0556}{(9-1)} = 0.75695 \qquad$ **7** $\quad \sqrt{0.75695} = 0.87$

The standard deviation of the scores in group P is 0.87 inches.

It is entirely unnecessary to write all this out as I have done here. Using a calculator the actual sequence of work is slightly different. The mean is calculated. Then, for each score in turn, the deviation and then the squared deviation is calculated and stored in the memory. The memory adds all the squared deviations as they are stored; on recall, step 5 is produced.

Standard deviation – method 2: procedure

Step no.	Result of step	What to do
1	ΣX	Add together all the individual scores.
2	$(\Sigma X)^2$	Square (1).
3	$\dfrac{(\Sigma X)^2}{N}$	Divide (2) by the number of scores.
4	X^2	Square each score.
5	ΣX^2	Add all (4).
6	$\Sigma X^2 - \dfrac{(\Sigma X)^2}{N}$	Subtract (3) from (5).
7	$\dfrac{\Sigma X^2 - [(\Sigma X)^2/N]}{(N-1)} = \sigma^2$	Divide (6) by (number of scores -1) to find the variance.
8	$\sqrt{\dfrac{\Sigma X^2 - [(\Sigma X)^2/N]}{(N-1)}} = \sigma$	Take the square root of (7) to find the standard deviation.

Standard deviation – method 2: worked example

Subject no.	Score (X)	**4** Squared score (X²)
1	10	100
2	9	81
3	8	64
4	10	100
5	8	64
6	$7\frac{1}{2}$	56.25
7	9	81
8	9	81
9	$8\frac{1}{2}$	72.25
9 = N	**1** 79	**5** 699.5

2 $79^2 = 6241$

3 $\dfrac{6241}{9} = 693.4444$

6 $699.5 - 693.4444 = 6.0556$

7 $\dfrac{6.0556}{(9-1)} = 0.75695$

8 $\sqrt{0.75695} = 0.87$

The standard deviation of the scores in group P is 0.87 inches.

If you compare the calculation of the two methods, they are identical from step (5), method 1 and step (6) method 2.

    If the scores are whole-number integers and no calculator is available the second method may be considerably easier as the two squaring steps use whole numbers.

We have considered several statistical methods for describing how the scores in a group are distributed. We can compare these with another way of describing a group of scores - pictorially.

The histogram

The histogram describes the distribution of scores in the form of a diagram. A histogram uses discrete variables and so we must divide a continuous measure into discrete intervals. For an example let's return to our fictitious women drivers in

3. *Histogram of the driving speeds of 400 women*

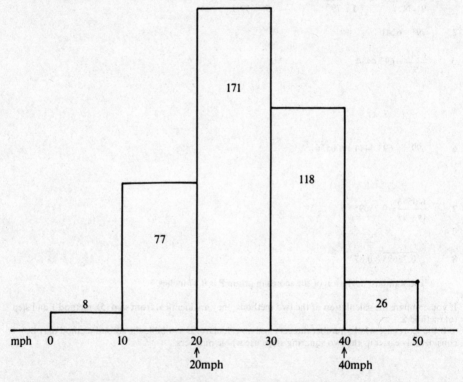

E 18. This time we have got 400 of them. We measured their actual speed of driving down the high street (a continuous measure) but to construct a histogram of the results the speeds can be considered in intervals of 10 m.p.h. The results were as follows:

Speed (m.p.h.)	Frequency (the number of observations)
0–10	8
10–20	77
20–30	171
30–40	118

40–50	26
50+	0
Total	400

These results are displayed in the histogram opposite.

The number of observations in each speed interval is represented by the *area* of each bar. This area can be measured by the height of the bar because the speed is divided into equal intervals and hence the bars have the same width. The whole group is represented by the total area of the figure and so the proportion of women drivers at between, say, 20 m.p.h. and 40 m.p.h. is the proportion of the area of the whole figure between the two verticals, 20 m.p.h. and 40 m.p.h. In this case that proportion is:

$$\frac{(171+118)}{400} = 0.7225 \quad (72.25\%)$$

This histogram displays relatively little of the information we gathered as the speed intervals are quite large. We can display more information if the interval size were reduced to 5 m.p.h.:

4. *Histogram of the driving speeds of the same 400 women;*
   speeds measured in 5mph intervals

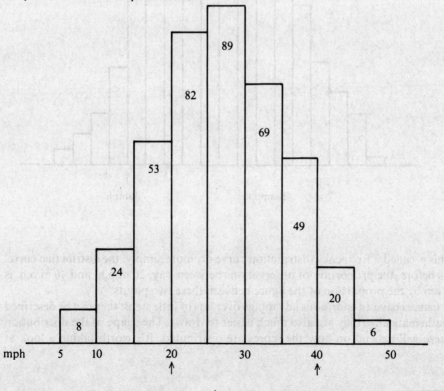

This new figure (*4*) contains more information than the first and hence is more difficult to describe (that is, it takes longer to draw).

If we had a sufficiently large group and the variable was truly continuous, we could continue dividing the interval in this way. As the interval size becomes smaller the outline of the figure becomes smoother and eventually approximates to a continuous curve (*see figures 5 and 6*).

5.

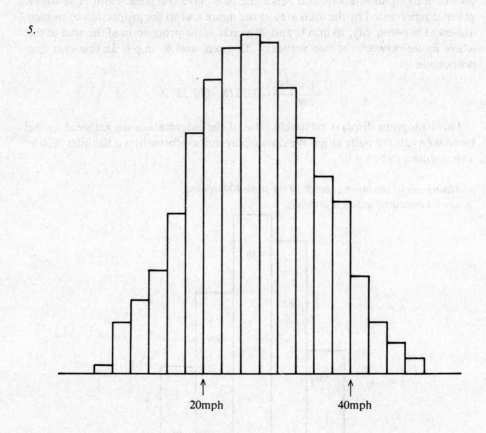

20mph   40mph

This is called a frequency distribution curve or, more simply, **the distribution curve**. As before, the proportion of observations between, say, 20 m.p.h. and 40 m.p.h. is given by the proportion of the figure between these two points.

Curves have an enormous advantage over lots of little steps: they can be described mathematically (they are also much easier to draw). The shape of the distribution curve will depend on how the scores are distributed. It's worth taking a look at

6.

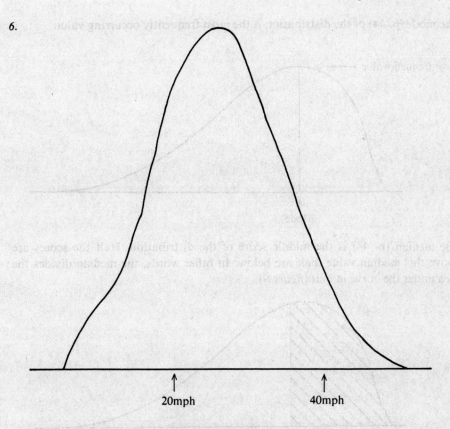

20mph   40mph

how this way of describing a distribution – by shape – compares with the statistical methods we looked at earlier on. Take a distribution curve:

7.

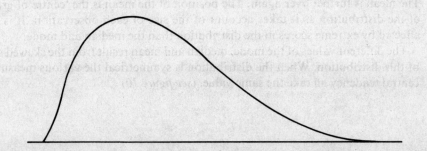

This one is a trifle lop-sided or **skewed**.

The mode (p. 44) of the distribution is the most frequently occurring value.

8.

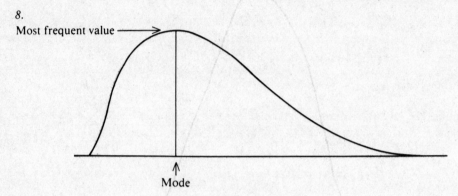

The median (p. 44) is the middle score of the distribution. Half the scores are above this median value, half are below. In other words, the median divides the *area* under the curve in half (*figure 9*).

9.

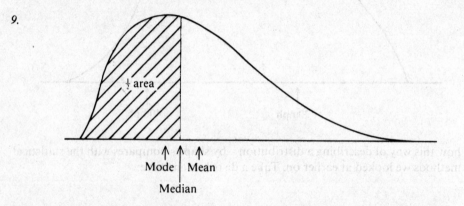

The mean is further over again. The position of the mean is the 'centre of gravity' of the distribution as it takes account of the size of each observation. It is more affected by extreme scores in the distribution than the median and mode.

The different values of the mode, median and mean result from the skewed shape of this distribution. When the distribution is symmetrical the various measures of central tendency all take the same value. (*see figure 10*)

10.

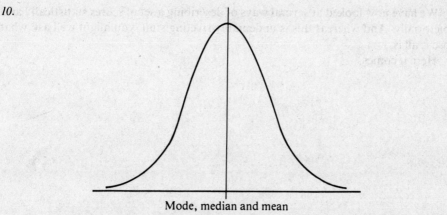

Mode, median and mean

The standard deviation measures the spread of scores around the mean. These two distributions have the same mean but different standard deviations:

11.

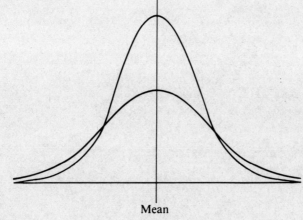

Mean

These two have the same standard deviation, but different means:

12.

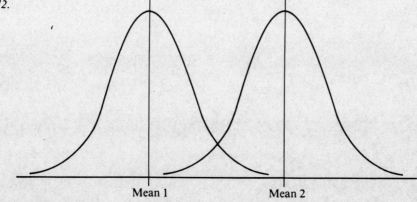

Mean 1   Mean 2

We have now looked at several ways of describing a set of scores statistically and pictorially. And whereas this is undeniably riveting stuff, you might well ask what use it all is.

Here it comes.

The Normal distribution

Here are two histograms (*figures 13 and 14*). The first shows the result of 360 rolls of a pair of dice. The actual frequency of each score (the sum of the two dice) is given inside the bars:

13. Distribution of 360 rolls of a pair of dice

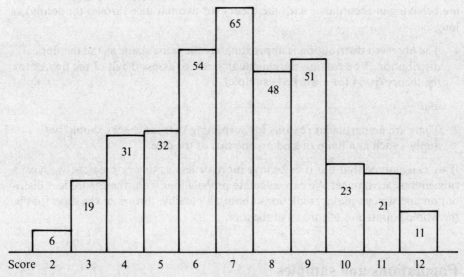

The second histogram (overleaf) shows the theoretical distribution of rolls of a pair of fair dice. The frequency of a particular outcome is expressed as a proportion of all possible outcomes. This is the same as the *probability* of that outcome.

14. Theoretical distribution of a pair of honest dice

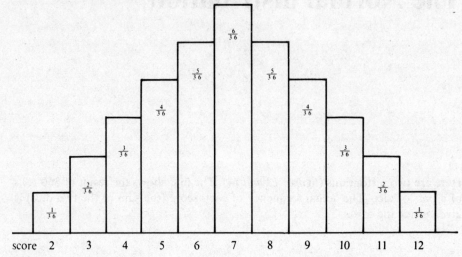

score 2 3 4 5 6 7 8 9 10 11 12

These two distributions have a similar shape. We are safe assuming that the dice are behaving in accordance with the theory (of two fair dice thrown randomly) as long as:

1 The observed distribution is approximately the same shape as the theoretical distribution. You can use the chi-squared test to assess the fit of the figures to the theory (p. 34 for a worked example).

and

2 There are no particular reasons for suspecting that the theory should *not* apply – such as a lump of lead on one side of the dice.

If we can assume that our dice behave more or less as theory predicts, we have a tremendous advantage. We can calculate *probabilities* from the theoretical distribution and we can make predictions about all possible throws of the dice: that is, the whole population of throws of the dice.

Populations and samples

Populations in statistics do not refer only to people but to events that share a common description. We could talk of the population of 'scores of males on a particular maths test'. This means the scores of all the males in the world on this test. It is hardly practical to gather all these. We use a sample of this population.

In the dice example, the population is an infinite number of throws of a pair of dice; the 360 throws in the first distribution (figure 13) are a sample of this population.

The behaviour of dice is rather simple. It would be very useful if the behaviour of our subjects followed such mathematical patterns. Curiously enough, they often do.

The Normal distribution

It so happens that if you go around getting groups of observations and constructing distribution curves, the shapes you end up with are often remarkably similar.

Furthermore, it is possible to derive this typical curve *theoretically* on the assumption of a large number of small independent variations distributed randomly around a particular value (the mean). This is exactly what we believe is happening in our experimental variables; they are affected by countless random errors (p. 10). (You might consider the effect of *constant errors* on a distribution. If there is an error in each observation, always in the same direction, this will shift the position of the mean, giving a bogus experimental effect or removing and obscuring a real one. Random errors will only affect the standard deviation of the distribution.) The name of this useful theoretical curve is the **Normal distribution curve**.

15. *The shape of the Normal distribution*

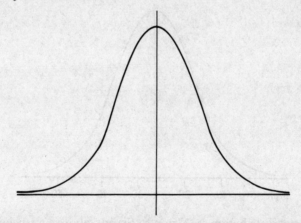

The Normal distribution is a theoretically derived distribution which matches, very closely, the actual distribution of many variables found in the world.

Take another look at the distribution of speeds in the sample of 400 women drivers in the high street, figures 3, 4, 5 and 6 (pp. 52–55). The shape is very similar to the Normal distribution. We will assume that the population of 'women's speeds in the high street' has a Normal distribution.

Because the Normal distribution is theoretically derived it is defined mathematically with a formula. The formula for the Normal distribution is relatively simple and has only two constants: that is, the value of two things in the formula will define it. These two things are the mean and the standard deviation of the distribution.

Unfortunately, we don't know the mean and standard deviation of the *population* of 'women's speeds in the high street', so we will use the mean and standard deviation of our *sample* as a 'best guess'. The mean speed of the sample is 27 m.p.h. The standard deviation is 9 m.p.h.

As we have assumed that the distribution of women's speeds is Normal, and we have decided its mean and standard deviation, we now know all there is to know about it – and it has some very useful properties.

Properties of the Normal distribution

The Normal distribution is symmetrical about its mean. As you can see from figure 16, the frequency of observations falls away on either side of the mean until it approaches – but never reaches – zero. What does this shape mean in real terms?

16.   The Normal distribution of 'women's speeds in the high street'

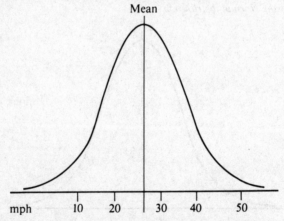

The mean of our distribution is 27 m.p.h. Speeds above and below this value become less frequent the further we move away from the mean. Although in the sample no ladies were observed travelling faster than 50 m.p.h. or slower than 5 m.p.h., we cannot rule out the possibility of women hurtling down the high street at 100 m.p.h. Any value is possible. As the Normal curve never reaches zero but approaches it asymptotically (finally getting there at infinity) extreme scores are always possible but with a very small frequency (i.e. probability). Another property of the Normal curve allows us to calculate the probability of such bizarre occurrences.

The standard deviation measures off constant proportions of the Normal distribution from the mean. The proportion of scores that occur between the mean and one standard deviation above the mean is 0.34 (i.e. 34% of the whole population). This will always be so no matter what the mean or standard deviation of the distribution:

17. *Areas under the normal curve*

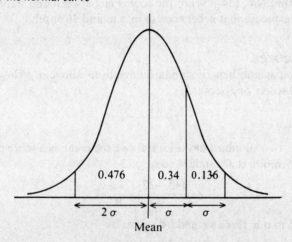

The standard deviation of our distribution is 9 m.p.h. So, we know that 34% of 'women's speeds in the high street' will be between 27 m.p.h. (the mean) and 36 m.p.h. (one standard deviation above the mean).

18. *'Women's speeds in the high street'*

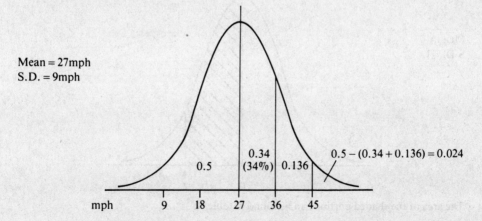

A further 0.136 (13.6%) of observation lies between one standard deviation and two standard deviations above the mean. For our ladies this means that 13.6% will be found driving at speeds between 36 m.p.h. and 45 m.p.h. A total of 47.6% will drive at between 27 m.p.h. and 45 m.p.h. As the Normal distribution is symetrical about the mean, we know that 0.5 of the area under the curve (50% of the whole population) lies above the mean. From this we can deduce that 2.4% (50-47.6) of the women drive at over 45 m.p.h.

Exactly the same deductions can be made about scores below the mean. In this way we know that 68% (34+34) of the scores lie between one standard deviation either side of the mean; that is between 18 m.p.h. and 36 m.p.h.

Standard scores

Scores expressed as numbers of standard deviations above or below the mean are called **standard scores** or z-scores.

$$z = \frac{(X - \bar{X})}{\sigma}$$

In our example, two standard deviations above the mean is a score of 45 m.p.h. In other words, 45 m.p.h. is a standard score of 2.

$$z = \frac{(45 - 27)}{9} = \frac{18}{9} = 2$$

A speed of 24.5 m.p.h. gives a standard scores of

$$\frac{(24.5 - 27)}{9} = \frac{-2.5}{9} = -0.28$$

19. The standard normal distribution

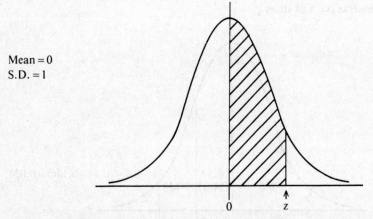

Mean = 0
S.D. = 1

0   z

The area of the shaded portion can be found in table B.

Any Normal distribution expressed in standard scores will have a mean of zero and a standard deviation of 1. This is known as a standard Normal distribution. In figure 19 the area under the curve between the mean and various z-scores is given in Table B.

Using Table B we can find the frequency (that is, the probability) of a particular range of scores. This is exactly equivalent to calculating the probability of the score 'eight tails in a row' in coin tossing (p. 13) and we use our findings in the same way.

Example:
Suppose something is observed hurtling towards us at 60 m.p.h. down the high street. What is it? Could it be a woman driver? Having recently studied a sample of 400 women drivers I am in a position to test this hypothesis. If the thing were a woman driving at 60 m.p.h. she would have a standard score of:

$$z = \frac{60 - 27}{9} = 3.7$$

Before the impact of the thing, I hurriedly refer to Table B and find that 0.4999 of the area under the curve lies between the mean and a standard score of 3.7. That is (0.5–0.4999) of the area lies *above* this standard score.

20.

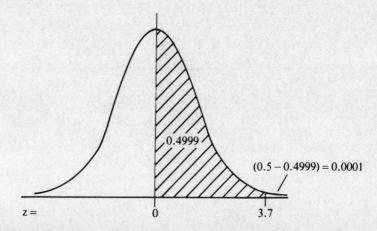

The probability of a woman driving down the high street at 60 m.p.h. or more is 0.0001 (the probability of a standard score of 3.7 or more). I can reject the hypothesis. Whatever is running me over is not a woman (p=0.0001).

This rather flippant example uses the same basic procedure as all significance tests. Compare it with the coin-tossing and chi-squared tests.

There is an observation (a particular score, or a sequence of events or so on). We have a hypothesis, concerning observations of this sort, that we wish to *reject*. (In an experiment this is usually the *null hypothesis*.)

The probability of the observation is calculated on the basis of this hypothesis (usually the null hypothesis). If the probability is very small (less than 0.05) we reject the hypothesis.

The procedure is very straightforward. The difference between the various significance tests is merely in the calculation of the probability. This is simple in the case of coin tossing; it is more complex with a continuous variable as in the last example. We had to find the distribution (women's driving speeds) to which, according to the hypothesis, the particular observation (a woman driving at 60 m.p.h.) belongs. This is exactly the procedure of the t-test.

The t-test

(CD – one variable discrete, with two conditions: one variable continuous, with a reasonably Normal distribution)
Examples: D 1, 4, 5; E 1, 6, 10, 11

This is a very common form of experiment. Typically the discrete variable is the two conditions of the independent variable. The dependent variable, some aspect of the subject's behaviour, is measured continuously. We are looking for a difference in the scores of the subjects under the two conditions of the IV.

If the subjects' scores are more or less normally distributed, the distributions of the two groups of scores can only differ in two ways – the mean and the standard deviation. The t-test measures the significance of differences in the means.

We will use the example of E 11. Two groups of subjects together interview a man. These two groups are the two conditions of the independent variable. One group thinks the man is a professor (the P group); the other thinks he is an unemployed labourer (the U group). They are asked to estimate his height. Their estimates (scores) are the dependent variable. We are looking for a difference in the mean scores of the two groups.

Our experimental hypothesis is that knowledge of a man's occupation affects the subjects' estimate of his height. To put it another way, there is a real difference between these two groups of subjects; they are samples from two different populations.

The null hypothesis is that, when estimating height, knowledge of a man's occupation doesn't matter a hoot; that there is no real difference between the two groups; they are samples of the same population and any difference in their means is due to random error.

We now proceed as usual. We will find the probability of getting our observed results (the difference between the two group means) on the basis of the null hypothesis. The distribution we need to find, then, is the distribution of 'the difference between the means of two samples drawn from the same population'.

We could, if we had the time and patience, collect dozens of sample groups of subjects, show them my friend, get them to estimate his height and work out the mean of each sample. If we used enough samples we could draw up a distribution of these 'sample means'. Having collected all these sample means we could put them all in a hat, draw them out in pairs and find the difference between the two sample means. Each of these values would be a 'difference between the means of two samples drawn from the same population'. If we did this enough times we could build up a distribution of these values and find the mean and standard deviation of this distribution. This is the distribution we have been looking for and we could find it in just the way I described. This is a little daunting – and unnecessary. Because the population is normally distributed we know an awful lot about it and it is possible to arrive at this distribution of 'the difference between the means of two samples drawn from the same population' theoretically from our two original samples, the P group and the U group.

The mean of this distribution is zero; as the sample means will all be more or less the same the difference between any two sample means will be more or less zero.

The standard deviation can be estimated from the two samples. If the samples are of size N_a and N_b and have standard deviations of σ_a and σ_b, then

$$\text{the standard deviation of the difference of sample means} = \sqrt{\frac{\sigma_a}{N_b} + \frac{\sigma_a}{N_b}}$$

When the sample size is large (over 30) this distribution is approximately normal and we can continue as before. Our observation (the difference between our two sample means) is expressed as a standard score by dividing the observed score by the standard deviation of the distribution (p. 46). The mean of the distribution is zero. If the means of the two samples are $\bar{X}_a$ and $\bar{X}_b$, then the difference is:

$$(\bar{X}_a - \bar{X}_b)$$

Expressed as a standard score this becomes:

$$\frac{(\bar{X}_a - \bar{X}_b)}{\sqrt{\frac{\sigma_a}{N_a} + \frac{\sigma_b}{N_b}}} = z$$

It is now simple enough to look up the probability of this standard score or greater by referring to Table B.

One- and two-tailed tests

Before we can decide whether the probability culled from Table B is significant we must consider whether we are using a one- or two-tailed test (p. 14). Does the experimental hypothesis predict the *direction* of the difference in sample means, that is, which sample mean will be bigger, or does it just predict some difference? If the hypothesis does not predict the direction of the difference we must use a two-tailed test.

Example:
We find that the difference between two means has a standard score of 1.75.

From Table B we see that 0.4599 of the total area lies between this z-score and the mean (the shaded part of figure 21). The probability, then, of this score (or greater) is the area of the 'tail'. That is:

21.

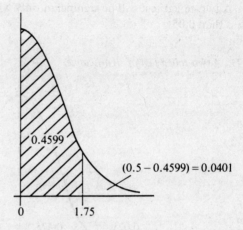

$$(0.5 - 0.4599) = 0.0401$$

The probability is less than 0.05, the 5% significance level.

But we are looking for a significant difference between the mean in **either direction**. We would have been just as satisfied with a standard-score difference of -1.75.

22.

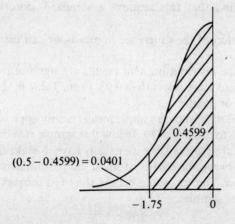

$$(0.5 - 0.4599) = 0.0401$$

The probability of this score is also 0.0401.

In our two-tailed test we must consider the probability of getting differences equal to (or greater than) *either* 1.76 *or* −1.76. This probability is the area of both tails – the sum of the two probabilities:

$$p = (0.0401 + 0.0401) = 0.0802$$

This is not significant at the 5% level.

A two-tailed test will be significant only when the combined area of both tails is less than 0.05.

23. A two-tailed test of significance

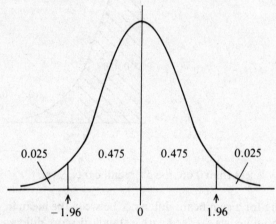

Total area of the two tails = 0.05

By looking at Table B you will find that this requires a standard score of (+ or −) 1.96 or greater.

If the hypothesis predicts the direction of the difference in means we can use a one-tailed test.

We need consider only one tail of the distribution. Our results are significant if the area of the tail cut off by the standard score is less than 0.05. From Table B, this requires a standard score of only 1.65 or greater.

Unfortunately, the distribution of the difference in sample means is only approximately Normal for large sample sizes, that is, over 30. Below this sample size this method can be unreliable. In the limited time available we usually have to make do with small samples. The difference between the means of small samples follows a similar distribution – the t-distribution. The reasoning behind the t-test is exactly the same as we have just seen for larger samples.

24. A one-tailed test of significance

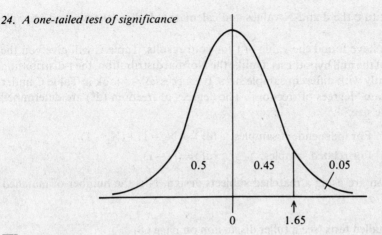

| 0.5 | 0.45 | 0.05 |

0   1.65

The t-test

T, the statistic we compute in the t-test, is equivalent to the z-score of the Normal distribution. It is computed similarly using the same terms; the difference in sample means $(\bar{X}_a - \bar{X}_b)$, and the standard deviation (σ) and sample size (N) of the two samples.

$$t = (\bar{X}_a - \bar{X}_b) \div \sqrt{\frac{[(N_a - 1)\sigma_a^2 + (N_b - 1)\sigma_a^2]}{(N_a - 1) + (N_b - 1)}\left(\frac{1}{N_a} + \frac{1}{N_b}\right)}$$

We can simplify this a little by expressing the standard deviations in terms of the actual scores. (Method 2 for finding the standard deviation, p. 50)

$$t = (\bar{X}_a - \bar{X}_b) \div \sqrt{\frac{(\Sigma X_a^2 - [(\Sigma X_a)^2/N_a]) + (\Sigma X_b^2 - [(\Sigma X_b)^2/N_b])}{(N_a - 1) + (N_b - 1)}\left(\frac{1}{N_a} + \frac{1}{N_b}\right)}$$

This looks absolutely ghastly. In fact, it is quite simple to substitute the various values of X and N into the formula – you need only follow the worked example on page 51. There is really nothing more than a couple of standard deviations.

Where we are using a *related samples* design (that is, repeated measures or matched subjects) life is much easier. We take the difference (d) between the scores of the subject (or the matched pair) under the two conditions. If subject 1 scores X_a under condition A, and X_b under condition, B, then:

$$d_1 = (X_a - X_b)$$

Using these differences in a related-samples design:

$$t = \bar{d} \div \sqrt{\frac{\Sigma d^2 - [(\Sigma d)^2/N]}{N(N-1)}}$$

Simply substitute the d and N values and calculate t. Follow the worked example on page 78.

When you have found the value of t for your results, Table C will give you the probability of the null hypothesis. Unlike the Normal distribution, the t-distribution changes slightly with different sample sizes. It is necessary to look in Table C under the appropriate 'degrees of freedom'. The degrees of freedom (df) are determined by the sample size:

$$\text{For independent samples:} \quad (df) = (N_a - 1) + (N_b - 1)$$
$$\text{For related samples:} \quad (df) = (N - 1)$$

Note: If you are using a matched-subjects design, N is the number of matched pairs.

One- or two-tailed tests (see a fuller discussion on page 68)

Table C gives the probabilities of t values for a *two-tailed test*. This is appropriate where the hypothesis does not predict which sample mean will be bigger.

For a one-tailed test, the probabilities in Table C must be *halved*, as only one tail of the distribution is considered. So, values of t in the $p = 0.1$ column will be significant at the 5% level ($p = 0.05$), for a one-tailed test.

Example:

In Table C, with six degrees of freedom, $p = 0.05$ when t is greater than 2.447. This is a two-tailed test. For a one-tailed test, $p = 0.05$ when t is greater than 1.943 (by looking in the $p = 0.1$ column for six degrees of freedom).

Remember, a one-tailed test is only significant if the differences are in the predicted direction. Even vast differences in the other direction will not support your hypothesis. On balance, it is safer to use a two-tailed test unless there are compelling reasons to predict the direction of the difference between two groups.

T-test – independent samples: procedure

The computation of t requires little more than finding the variance (standard deviation squared) of the two groups. Steps 1–6 are identical to method 2 for the standard deviation (p. 50).

(Check the assumptions of the t-test, page 80)

Step no.	Result of step	What to do
1a	ΣX_a	Add together all the individual scores of the first group.
2a	$(\Sigma X_a)^2$	Square (1).
3a	$\dfrac{(\Sigma X_a)^2}{N_a}$	Divide (2) by the number of scores in the first group.
4a	X_a^2	Square each score in the first group.
5a	ΣX_a^2	Add all (4).
6a	$\Sigma X_a^2 - \dfrac{(\Sigma X_a)^2}{N_a}$	Subtract (3) from (5).
7a	$\dfrac{X_a}{N_a} = \bar{X}_a$	Divide (1) by the number of scores in the first group to find the mean.

This procedure is now repeated for the scores of the second group (steps 1b–7b).

8	$\left[\Sigma X_a^2 - \dfrac{(\Sigma X_a)^2}{N_a} \right] + \left[\Sigma X_b^2 - \dfrac{(\Sigma X_b)^2}{N_b} \right]$	Add (6a) and (6b).
9	$(N_a - 1) + (N_b - 1)$	Find the total number of scores in both groups minus 2.

T-test – independent samples: worked example

The results are taken from E 11. Two groups of subjects are asked to estimate the height (over 5 ft) of a man. One group thinks he is a professor (P group), the other thinks he is an unemployed labourer (U group).

The samples are not obviously either non-normal or of widely differing dispersion. (To check this, see F-test, worked example.)

The first group – P group

Subject no.	Score (X_a)	**4a** Squared score (X_a^2)
1	10	100
2	9	81
3	8	64
4	10	100
5	8	64
6	$7\frac{1}{2}$	56.25
7	9	81
8	9	81
9	$8\frac{1}{2}$	72.25

$\overline{9} = N$ **1a** $\overline{79}$ **5a** $\overline{699.5}$ **7a** $\dfrac{79}{9} = 8.778$

2a $79^2 = 6241$ **3a** $\dfrac{6241}{9} = 693.44444$

6a $699.5 - 693.4444 = 6.0556$

The second group – U group

Subject no.	Score (X_b)	**4b** Squared score (X_b^2)
1	$5\frac{1}{2}$	30.25
2	7	49
3	8	64
4	8	64
5	6	36
6	8	64
7	8	64
8	6	36
9	$8\frac{1}{2}$	72.25

$\overline{9} = N_b$ **1b** $\overline{65}$ **5b** $\overline{479.5}$ **7b** $\dfrac{65}{9} = 7.222$

2b $65^2 = 4225$ **3b** $\dfrac{4225}{9} = 469.444$

6b $479.5 - 469.444 = 10.0556$

The hard work has now been done.

8 $6.0556 + 10.0556 = 16.112$

9 $(9-1) + (9-1) = 16$

Step no.	Result of step	What to do
10	$$\dfrac{\left[\Sigma X_a^2 - \dfrac{(\Sigma X_a)^2}{N_a}\right] + \left[\Sigma X_b^2 - \dfrac{(\Sigma X_b)^2}{N_b}\right]}{(N_a - 1) + (N_b - 1)}$$	Divide (8) by (9).
11	$\left(\dfrac{1}{N_a} + \dfrac{1}{N_b}\right)$	Add the reciprocals of the numbers of scores in each group.
12		Multiply (10) by (11).
13		Find the square root of (12).
	$$\sqrt{\dfrac{\left[\Sigma X_a^2 - \dfrac{(\Sigma X_a)^2}{N_a}\right] + \left[\Sigma X_b^2 - \dfrac{(\Sigma X_b)^2}{N_b}\right]}{(N_a - 1) + (N_b - 1)} \times \left(\dfrac{1}{N_a} + \dfrac{1}{N_b}\right)}$$	
14	$(\bar{X}_a - \bar{X}_b)$	Take (7b) from (7a).
		Divide (14) by (13).
15	$$\overset{t}{(\bar{X}_a - \bar{X}_b)} \Big/ \sqrt{\dfrac{\left[\Sigma X_a^2 - \dfrac{(\Sigma X_a)^2}{N_a}\right] + \left[\Sigma X_b^2 - \dfrac{(\Sigma X_b)^2}{N_b}\right]}{(N_a - 1) + (N_b - 1)} \times \left(\dfrac{1}{N_a} + \dfrac{1}{N_b}\right)}$$	
16		Find the probability of this value of t, with (step 9) $(N_a - 1) + (N_b - 1)$ degrees of freedom. Refer to Table C.
17		Interpret this result in terms of the experimental hypothesis.
18		Pat yourself on the back.

10 $\dfrac{16.1112}{16} = 1.0069$

11 $\dfrac{1}{9} + \dfrac{1}{9} = 0.2222$

12 $1.0069 \times 012222 = 0.2237$

13 $\sqrt{0.2237} = 0.4730$

14 $8.778 - 7.222 = 1.556$

15 $\dfrac{1.556}{0.4730} = 3.29 = t$

16   From Table C, with 16 degrees of freedom (from step 9), this value of t lies between $p = 0.01$ and $p = 0.001$. The difference between the mean scores of the P group and the U group is highly significant ($p = 0.01$).

17   We can reject the null hypothesis that the difference between the two groups is due to random errors alone. Knowledge of a man's occupation does effect our estimation of his height.

Note: If you are using a calculator, and let's hope you are, it is worthwhile looking to see where the writing and keying of large figures can be avoided by accumulating calculations in a memory. For example, for each subject in turn enter X, enter it into the first memory, square X, enter this into the second memory. In this way ΣX and ΣX^2 are accumulated in the two memories to be recalled and used without being written down and re-entered. The whole calculation can be done in the calculator.

T-test – related samples: procedure
(Check the assumptions of the t-test, page 80.)

Step no.	Result of step	What to do
1	$(X_a - X_b) = d$	Find the difference, with direction ($+$ or $-$) for each pair of scores.
2	Σd	Add all the individual differences (1).
3	$(\Sigma d)^2$	Square (2).
4	$\dfrac{(\Sigma d)^2}{N}$	Divide (3) by the number of pairs of scores.
5	d^2	Square each difference.
6	Σd^2	Add all (5).
7	$\Sigma d^2 - \dfrac{(\Sigma d)^2}{N}$	Subtract (4) from (6).
8	$N(N-1)$	Multiply the number of pairs by 'the number minus 1'.
9	$\dfrac{\Sigma d^2 - [(\Sigma d)^2/N]}{N(N-1)}$	Divide (7) by (8).
10	$\sqrt{\dfrac{\Sigma d^2 - [(\Sigma d)^2/N]}{N(N-1)}}$	Find the square root of (9).
11	$\dfrac{\Sigma d}{N} = \bar{d}$	Divide (2) by the number of pairs to find the mean difference.
12	$\bar{d} \div \sqrt{\dfrac{\Sigma d^2 - [(\Sigma d)^2/N]}{N(N-1)}} = t$	Divide (11) by (10) to find t.
13		Find the probability of this value of t in Table C, with $(N-1)$ degrees of freedom.
14		Interpret this result in terms of the experimental hypothesis.

T-test – related samples: worked example

These results are taken from E 14. In this repeated-measures design each 'subject' is a pair of subjects: we measure the behaviour of the pair. The behaviour measured is their disagreement in perception. This is measured directly by the area (in mm²) enclosed by a chart recorder trace. The two conditions are whether or not the pair are allowed to communicate with each other. The hypothesis states that communication will affect the amount of disagreement.

Pair no.	Disagreement in mm²		**1**	**5**
	Not communicating (X_b)	Communicating (X_a)	Difference (d)	Squared difference (d^2)
1	124	279	−155	24025
2	340	371	23	529
3	923	703	220	48400
4	629	254	375	140625
5	414	228	186	34596
6	90	256	−166	27556
7	387	122	256	70225
8	393	330	63	3969
9	399	367	32	1024
10	501	306	195	38025
11	384	309	75	5625
12	386	450	−64	4096
12 = N			**2** 1040	**6** 398695

3 $1040^2 = 1081600$ **4** $\dfrac{1081600}{12} = 90133.33$

7 $398695 - 90133.33 = 308561.66$

8 $12(12-1) = 132$

9 $\dfrac{308561.66}{132} = 2337.6$

10 $\sqrt{2337.6} = 48.35$

11 $\dfrac{1040}{12} = 86.67$

12 $\dfrac{86.67}{48.35} = 1.79 = t$

13   From Table C, with 11 degrees of freedom, the 5% level of significance requires a t-value of 2.201. Our result is some way below this and hence not significant.

14   We cannot reject the null hypothesis that the observed differences in disagreement could be the result of random error alone. We cannot with any certainty state that communication affects the amount of disagreement in perception in this particular experiment. (See page 254 for details of the experiment.)

Notes on the use of a calculator are similar to those in the other example t-test. If the calculator has a memory it is much easier to find (d) and then (d^2) for each pair in turn. The sum of the squared differences ($\Sigma\, d^2$) will accumulate in the memory.

Assumptions of the t-test

All significance tests make some assumptions about the populations from which the samples are drawn.

The t-test assumes that the population (if they really are different) from which the two samples are drawn are Normally distributed and have the same variance (standard deviation squared, p. 46). In fact, it is unlikely that any two populations are perfectly normal and have exactly the same variance. Besides, all we know of *our* populations are the two small samples. The chances are that we will violate the assumptions of the t-test. Does this matter?

Happily, the t-test is very robust. This means that it suffers quite large violations of its assumptions without becoming unreliable. But it is a good idea to know what liberties we can afford to take.

Normality?

We do not have to be *certain* that the populations are Normal; it is enough that they are not obviously non-Normal. A good look at the sample scores can be enough. Do they cluster round the mean with scores close to the mean being more common than extreme scores? Are the median and mean reasonably close, i.e. is the distribution symmetrical about the mean? There may be theoretical reasons for doubting the normality of the population (see 11b for an example). If you are in serious doubt it is possible to check the normality of the sample scores using a chi-squared test of goodness of fit. It is a little tedious. The scores must be divided into intervals. The expected frequencies in these intervals are calculated from the areas under the standard Normal curve in the intervals. A worked example of such a test is given on page 37. We can use the t-test if there is no significant difference between the observed and expected frequencies; that is, if we are not reasonably certain that the scores are *not* normally distributed.

Same variance?

Again, we must check that there is no obvious difference in the variances of the two samples. Where there are equal numbers in the samples this can be done by taking a close look at the scores. Do they have roughly the same range? Is the deviation about the mean obviously different in the two samples?

This is much more difficult to judge where there are large differences in sample size. In this situation it is as well to check for a large difference in variance statistically, using an F-test (p. 82). This is really no sweat at all; all you need is the variance (σ^2) of each sample and you will be computing this as part of the t-test anyway. Look at the t-formula on page 71, having found the two variances and carried out the F-test, you only have to substitute the values of the two variances into the formula and you have the t-statistic.

Again, as the t-test is quite robust, it is only necessary to assure yourself that it is *not* reasonably certain the variances are different.

If it appears that you cannot use a t-test it is a very simple matter to convert the continuous variable – the scores – into rank-ordered data and use either the Mann-Whitney or Wilcoxon test (p. 90). Neither of these make the assumptions of the t-test – and they are a lot easier to compute if no calculator is handy. Their advantages and disadvantages will be discussed later when we look at the tests.

The advice here is to use the t-test unless you obviously cannot. It uses *all* the information you have collected and so is a powerful test.

The F-test

(CD – one variable discrete, with two conditions; one variable continuous, with reasonably Normal distribution)

Normal distributions can only differ in two ways, the means and the standard deviations. The t-test looks at differences in the means of the two groups; the F-test looks at differences in the standard deviation. In fact, it uses the square of the standard deviation – the variance (p. 46).

The F-test can be used on the same data as the t-test and the two are complementary. The t-test can only be used if the difference in variance is not significant. The F-test is used to check this. If the variances *are* found to differ significantly, the F-test has provided a significant difference between the samples.

There are occasions when the variance is the only difference between two samples. For example, IQ tests are balanced to eliminate sex preferences for different types of problem. This ensures that the *means* of male and female scores are the same, usually standardized to 100. However, we may (and do) find a difference in variance between these two distributions [intelligence].

25. The distribution of IQ in males and females. The difference in variance is exaggerated.

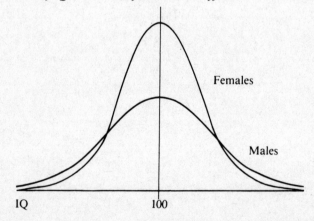

The F-test is embarrassingly simple. When you have found the variance of each sample, the F-statistic is just the number of times one variance is larger than the other.

$$F = \frac{\text{Larger variance}}{\text{Smaller variance}} = \frac{\sigma_L^2}{\sigma_S^2}$$

Whether or not the result reflects a significant difference will depend on the sizes of the two samples: that is, the degrees of freedom in the two samples of scores. As usual the degrees of freedom for each sample are (sample size − 1):

If the sample with the larger variance (σ_L) has a size of N_L, then

$$df_L = (N_L - 1)$$

and

$$df_S = (N_S - 1)$$

These two degrees of freedom are found at the top and side of Table D: their cross-reference gives the value of F significant at the 5% level for a two-tailed test.

F-test: procedure
The F-test is most commonly used to check the assumption of the t-test, that both sets of scores have similar standard deviation.

Step no.	Result	What to do
1a	$\dfrac{\Sigma X_a^2 - [(\Sigma X_a)^2/N_a]}{(N_a - 1)} = \sigma_a^2$	Find the *variance* of one set of scores using method 2 for standard deviation (p. 50).

Note: You will do this in the t-test anyway. The upper half of this formula is the same as steps 1a–6a in the t-test: independent samples.

1b	$\dfrac{\Sigma X_b^2 - [(\Sigma X_b)^2/N_b]}{(N_b - 1)} = \sigma_b^2$	Find the variance of the other set of scores.

2	$\dfrac{\sigma_L{}^2}{\sigma_S{}^2} = F$	Divide the larger of (1a) and (1b) by the smaller to find F.

3	In Table D, find the cross-reference of $df_L(N_L - 1)$ and $df_s(N_s - 1)$. N_L and N_S are the sample sizes of the scores with the larger and smaller variances. If the observed value of F exceeds the table value, there is a 5% significant difference between the variances.

4	If significant, interpret this result in terms of the experimental hypothesis. If not significant, carry on with the t-test. Steps 1–6 of the t-test have already been calculated in the F-test. Whatever the result your work is not wasted.

F-test: worked example

The results are taken from E11. These were used in the worked example of the t-test: independent samples. The F-test is often used to check the assumptions of such a test. The two tests are complementary and use virtually the same calculations.

P group scores

Subject no.	Score (X_a)
1	10
2	9
3	8
4	10
5	8
6	$7\frac{1}{2}$
7	9
8	9
9	$8\frac{1}{2}$
$9 = N_a$	

The variance of this set of scores is calculated from the worked example of the t-test: independent subjects, step 6a.

$$\text{Variance } (\sigma_a^2) = \frac{(\text{Step 6a})}{(N_a - 1)} = \frac{6.0556}{8} = 0.7569 \quad \textbf{1a}$$

U group scores

Subject no.	Score (X_b)
1	$5\frac{1}{2}$
2	7
3	8
4	8
5	6
6	8
7	8
8	6
9	$8\frac{1}{2}$
$9 = N_b$	From the t-test, step 6b

$$\text{Variance } (\sigma_b^2) = \frac{(\text{Step 6b})}{(N_b - 1)} = \frac{10.0556}{8} = 1.2569 \quad \textbf{1b}$$

2 The U group scores have the larger variance.

$$F = \frac{1.2569}{0.7569} = 1.66$$

3 $N_L = 9$, $N_S = 9$

The cross-reference of df_L and df_S in Table D is $F = 4.43$.

The observed value of F (1.66) does not exceed the table value; there is no significant difference between the variances of the two sets of scores.

4 We can carry out the t-test.

Sign test

(CD – one variable discrete, with two conditions; one variable continuous, related samples only)
Examples: D 1, 2; E 5, 16

This quick and simple test can only be used with related samples, that is, repeated-measures or matched-subjects designs. In these designs each subject or matched pair appears under both conditions of the independent variable. The score under one condition is compared with the score under the other condition. Any difference between these two scores may be the result of an experimental effect or random error.

The null hypothesis states that the difference is caused by random error *alone*. What does this null hypothesis predict?

A subject scores X_a under condition A, and X_b under condition B (don't they always?). The difference in the scores, X_a-X_b, may be positive or negative. If such differences are due to random error alone we would expect as many positive as negative differences. The probability of a negative difference is the same as the probability of a positive difference:

$$p(-)=p(+)$$

There is a third possibility: the difference between the two scores could be zero. If we reject all such subjects (or matched pairs) then *all* differences must be either positive or negative.

$$p(-)+p(+)=1 \quad \text{and, so,} \quad p(-)=\tfrac{1}{2} \text{ and } p(+)=\tfrac{1}{2}$$

Now these are exactly the same as the probabilities of a tossed coin landing heads or tails. As we found on page 12, we can calculate the probability of any combination of heads and tails in a number of throws; in exactly the same way we can calculate the probability of any combination of positive and negative differences.

Happily, we don't have to. The significance of combinations of positive and negative differences can be found in Table E.

Sign test: procedure

Step no.	What to do
1	Look at the difference between each subject's (or matched pair's) scores under the two conditions. Record the direction of the difference. Reject all subjects with no difference.
2	Find the total number of differences (T).
3	Find the number of the less frequent sign (L).
4	In Table E, find the cross-reference of T and the required significance level, p. The table gives the critical level of L for a two-tailed test. The result is significant if the observed L is equal to or less than the table value.
5	Interpret the result in terms of the experimental hypothesis.

As you can see, the sign test is very quick and simple – because it uses very little information. It uses only the direction of any differences but not the amount; consequently it is not very powerful. The experimental effect must be quite large to be picked up by the sign test.

It can be very useful in some circumstances. It can give a quick indication of significance. If the sign test narrowly misses significance it is well worth carrying on with the more powerful, and time-consuming, Wilcoxon or t-test.

Where the experimental effect is obviously large and the sample size is large it may be sufficient for your purposes to find a significant difference with the sign test without wading through the t-test merely to find more significance. The Wilcoxon test (p. 98) gives a good compromise between these two; simpler than the t-test and much more powerful than the sign test.

Sign test: worked example

These results come from E 10. Subjects were interviewed by the experimenter. The dependent variable was the amount of time the subjects looked at the experimenter's face in one minute. The independent variable was the distance between the subject and the experimenter. The order of these two conditions was counterbalanced between subjects. The hypothesis is that the eye contact will be greater in the longer distance condition.

Subject no.	Time spent in eye contact during one minute of interview		**1** Direction of difference $(-$ or $+)$
	Long distance (X_a)	Short distance (X_b)	$(X_a - X_b)$
1	55.6	36.7	+
2	47.3	50.5	−
3	58.3	49.6	+
4	50.4	47.0	+
5	38.9	43.5	−
6	58.1	45.7	+
7	58.4	43.0	+
8	57.8	55.3	+
9	46.3	54.8	−
10	53.9	44.3	+
11	56.9	37.2	+
12	56.1	50.0	+
13	53.3	45.8	+
14	55.7	58.3	−
15	41.9	37.4	+

Total number $15 = T$ **2**

The less frequent sign is 'minus', of which there are $4 = L$ **3**

4   From Table E, the result is significant at the 5% level (p = 0.05) if L is 3 or less. The observed value of L is 4. This is not significant at the 5% level.

5   We cannot conclude that eye contact is affected by distance.

Note: In fact, we had a theoretical reason for predicting the direction of the differences found in the experiment and this specific prediction was made in the hypothesis. We are entitled to use a one-tailed test (p. 14 and p. 68). For a one-tailed test, the significance levels in Table E are halved. So, cross-reference T = 15 and p = 0.1. The critical value of L is still 3. Our result still fails to reach 5% significance. Remember, the sign test is not very powerful. It is well worth subjecting these scores to further analysis. The same set of scores is used in the worked example of the Wilcoxon test (large samples) on page 100. Compare the results.

Mann–Whitney and Wilcoxon tests

(RD – one variable discrete, with two conditions; one variable in rank order)
Examples: D 1, 5; E 5, 6, 11, 12

These two tests deal with a variable measured in rank order. The variable may be measured this way for simplicity: it is easier to see the order in which runners cross a winning line than to time each runner separately.

More commonly, however, rank-order measures are obtained from continuous measures because those continuous measures are unsuitable for a t-test. The t-test makes certain assumptions about the characteristics of populations of scores (p. 80): that they are normally distributed with the same standard deviation.

Parameters and parametric tests

The characteristics of a population are called **parameters**. They are things such as the mean, the standard deviation and the shape of the distribution and so on. We rarely, if ever, know the parameters of a population. They are estimated from the characteristics of the sample. The characteristics of a sample are called **statistics**. Tests that rely on assumptions about the parameters of the population are termed **parametric tests**. We have admitted in our look at the t-test that probably no naturally occurring population is perfectly Normal in distribution. Many are approximately so and we can use a parametric test, the t-test, on these populations. Sometimes, however, it is obvious that we cannot make the assumptions of the parametric tests; the standard deviations of the two samples may be wildly different or the distributions far from Normal. In this case we must use a **non-parametric** test that does not make these assumptions about the populations.

The Mann–Whitney and Wilcoxon tests are both non-parametric tests using rank-ordered data.

The Mann–Whitney test

This test looks for differences between two independent sets of scores and corresponds to the t-test for independent samples. Let's compare the way these two tests work.

You are about to gamble on the outcome of a mouse race. The novice mice are waiting in the stalls. Just before they come under starter's orders you glimpse a shifty-looking character who sidles up and gives five of the mice one or two crumbs, which they eat with gusto. Something in the angle of his narrow-brimmed trilby hat tells you this is not the blameless gesture of goodwill towards small creatures that it appears. Unfortunately, you are unable to take advantage of this situation as you don't know whether the 'crumbs' will have the effect of speeding the mice up or slowing them down. As often happens when one discovers a fraud – but cannot use it – you righteously denounce the shifty character. He protests that a few crumbs wouldn't affect the mice and besides he was several miles away at the time. The matter can be resolved by observing the mice.

We have a familiar situation. There are two groups of mice: five 'doctored' mice (D), five plain mice (P). The experimental hypothesis is that there is a significant difference in running speed between these two groups, but we cannot predict the direction of this difference. The null hypothesis is that any difference is due to random error alone.

You could run the race, time each mouse, obtain the mean time for each group and, using a t-test, assess the significance of any difference between the group means.

The racetrack does not have the wherewithal for precision timing. You can record the *order* in which the mice passed the post. Assuming the null hypothesis, the order in which they pass the post is random. You will be very dubious if the doctored mice take the first five places – or the last five places. In the event, the mice cross the line in the following order:

$$D\ D\ D\ P\ D\ D\ P\ P\ P\ P$$

The shifty character shrugs; it could happen by chance. True, but how likely is this null hypothesis? The ranks of the doctored mice are:

$$1, 2, 3, 5 \text{ and } 6$$

The sum of these ranks is 17. What is the probability of getting a rank sum of 17 or less when there is no real difference between the groups? As usual, we will reject the null hypothesis if this probability is less than 0.05.

If the null hypothesis is true, each order is as likely as any other. What is the probability of any one order occurring? There are two ways to tackle this.

We can treat any one order as a sequence of events, each with an individual probability. The probability of the whole sequence is the product of the individual probabilities (see page 12).

Take our order (we could use any order):

$$D\ D\ D\ P\ D\ D\ P\ P\ P\ P$$

We can consider the race as pulling the mice, randomly, out of a bag containing all the starters.

First pull: The probability of pulling a D mouse from a bag containing 5 D and 5 P mice is:

$$\frac{\text{(No. of D mice)}}{\text{(Total no. of mice)}} = \frac{5}{10}$$

Second pull: The probability of pulling a D mouse from a bag now containing 4 D and 5 P mice is $\frac{4}{9}$

Third pull: The probability of pulling a D mouse from a bag now containing 3 D and 5 P mice is $\frac{3}{8}$

Fourth pull: The probability of pulling a P mouse from the bag now containing 2 D and 5 P mice is $\frac{5}{7}$

The probabilities of D mice on the fifth and sixth pulls are

$$\frac{2}{6} \text{ and } \frac{1}{5}$$

The probability of pulling out P mice on each of the remaining pulls is 1, as there are only plain mice left in the bag. So, the probability of our order is:

$$\frac{5}{10} \cdot \frac{4}{9} \cdot \frac{3}{8} \cdot \frac{5}{7} \cdot \frac{2}{6} \cdot \frac{1}{5} \cdot 1.1.1.1 = \frac{1}{252}$$

This will be the same for all orders.

Now, how many of these 252 orders have a rank sum for D mice of 17 or less? You can find this quite easily by trial and error. The smallest rank sum for the 5 D mice is:

$$1+2+3+4+5 = 15$$

The next smallest is:

$$1+2+3+4+6 = 16$$

There are two rank orders which give a rank sum of 17:

$$1+2+3+4+7 = 17$$

and $$1+2+3+5+6 = 17 \text{ (the observed order)}$$

There are thus 4 orders with a rank sum of 17 or less. The probability of getting one *or* another of these 4 orders is:

$$\frac{1}{252} + \frac{1}{252} + \frac{1}{252} + \frac{1}{252} = 0.0159$$

This is the probability of getting a rank sum of 17 or less for D mice.

But, we need a two-tailed test. We are not sure whether the shifty character was stimulating or nobbling the mice. The hypothesis does not predict the direction of the difference; we would have been just as suspicious had the order been reversed.

The probability of getting a rank sum of 17 or less for either D mice or P mice is:

$$0.0159 + 0.0159 = 0.0318$$

This is still below the 0.05 probability of the 5% significance level. We can reject the null hypothesis – the mice were doped.

It is quite possible, but very tedious, to calculate the probability of any rank order for any two samples. It is also unnecessary. The Mann-Whitney test uses these calculations. The significant rank sum will increase as the sample sizes increase. This is embodied in the Mann-Whitney statistic, U.

$$U = N_a N_b + \frac{N_a(N_a + 1)}{2} - T$$

N_a and N_b are the sizes of the two samples, A and B. A is the smaller sample (if they are the same size either can be group A). T is the sum of the ranks in group A.

So, for our mice:

$$U = 5 \times 5 + \frac{5 \times 6}{2} - 17 = 23$$

A second statistic, U', is found.

$$U' = N_a N_b - U$$

We will use the smaller of U and U'. (I grant you that these statistics U and U' look rather arbitrary and complex. They are not. You could quite easily work out that the smallest possible value of T is:

$$\frac{N_a(N_a + 1)}{2}$$

and that the largest possible value is:

$$N_a N_b + \frac{N_a(N_a + 1)}{2}$$

U and U' then are simply the differences between the observed rank sum (T) and the greatest possible and least possible values of T.)

For our mice, $U = 23$ and $U' = 25 - 23 = 2$. We use the U' value of 2. Significant U values are found in Table F, by the cross-reference of the two sample sizes. There is a significant difference between the two samples if the observed U (or U') value is smaller than the table value. Follow the worked example.

Where large samples are used (in this case, over 20) the distribution of U becomes approximately Normal. By expressing the observed U value as a standard score we can use the area under the standard Normal curve to give a probability (p. 64).

We have just seen that the difference between the greatest and least possible value of T is: $N_a N_b$. The mean of the distribution of U is half way between these two extremes, that is,

$$\frac{N_a N_b}{2}$$

The standard deviation of the distribution is:

$$\sqrt{\frac{N_a N_b (N_a + N_b + 1)}{12}}$$

The standard score for any observed value of U is thus:

$$z = U - \frac{N_a N_b}{2} \bigg/ \sqrt{\frac{N_a N_b (N_a + N_b + 1)}{12}}$$

The probability of any standard score can be found from Table B. For a two-tailed test there is a significant difference if the standard score is greater than 1.96 (see page 70).

Mann-Whitney test: procedure

Step no.	What to do

1   Rank all the scores in the two groups of scores.

If two or more scores tie, they each take the *mean* rank of the tied ranks. So, if the 3rd, 4th and 5th scores are the same, each takes the rank

$$\frac{3+4+5}{3} = 4.$$

2   Take the smaller of the two groups; this is group A. If they are the same size, either can be group A. The other group is group B.

3   Find T, the sum of the ranks of group A.

4   Find U, where $U = N_a N_b + \dfrac{N_a(N_a + 1)}{2} - T$.

5   Find U', where $U' = N_a N_b - U$.

6   Take the smaller of U and U'.

7   In Table F, find the cross-reference of N_a and N_b. There is a significant difference between the groups if (6) is equal to or less than the table value of U.

8   Interpret this result in terms of the experimental hypothesis.

Mann–Whitney test: worked example

These scores come from D 3, using a single subject-design. Darts were thrown at the bull of a dartboard using either the preferred or non-preferred hand. The distance of each dart from the centre of the bull was recorded. A t-test was not used as there is reason to suspect that there is a considerable difference in variance between the two sets of scores: the non-preferred hand is more erratic. The hypothesis is that the preferred hand darts land closer to the bull.

Distance of dart from centre of bull (cm):

Preferred hand			Non-preferred hand		
Score	Rank	1	Score	Rank	1
0.4	2.5		5.4	17.5	
5.4	17.5		2.5	8	
2.6	9		2.1	7	
3.4	11		0.4	2.5	
12.5	23		4.1	12	
5.3	16		9.2	22	
5.2	15		0.3	1	
12.6	24		2.0	6	
16.5	25		4.9	14	
1.3	4		1.5	5	
6.4	20		3.1	10	
5.6	19		7.2	21	
16.6	26		4.4	13	
				139	3

2 The non-preferred hand scores were taken as group A.
   $N_a = 13$, $N_b = 13$.

3 Sum of ranks for group A is $139 = T$.

4 $U = 13.13 + \dfrac{13(13+1)}{2} - 139 = 169 + 91 - 139 = 121$.

5 $U' = 169 - 121 = 48$.

6 $U' = 48$ is the smaller and is taken as the Mann–Whitney statistic.

7 In Table F the cross-reference of the two sample sizes is 45. The observed U value is larger than the table value. The results fall just short of significance.

8 We cannot reject the null hypothesis that the difference between the scores of the two hands is due to random chance alone.

Note: In fact, the experimental hypothesis does predict the direction of the difference and so we are justified in using a one-tailed test. In this case the results *are* significant at the 5% level. It might be better just to increase the sample size.

The Wilcoxon test

The Wilcoxon is the non-parametric equivalent of the t-test for correlated samples. It has similarities with the sign test and the Mann-Whitney. It looks at the rank order of differences between pairs of scores. Each subject (or matched pair) scores X_a under condition A and X_b under condition B. If there was no real difference between the two conditions we would expect the difference between the scores $(X_a - X_b)$ to be negative as many times as positive. This is the basis of the sign test (p. 86).

Moreover, we would expect there to be the same amount of negative difference as positive difference. That is, if the differences are rank ordered, we would expect the sum of the ranks of positive differences to be more or less the same as the sum of the ranks of negative differences. Now this is like the Mann-Whitney test; comparing the rank sums of two groups (positive differences and negative differences).

The test is very simple. The differences $(X_a - X_b)$ are rank ordered by magnitude and the direction, plus or minus, noted. The sum of ranks of the less frequent sign is found – T. This is exactly the same as the T in the Mann-Whitney test. This observed value of T is compared with the significant value of T in Table G for the appropriate number of subjects (or matched pairs). There is a significant difference between the experimental conditions if the observed value of T is *smaller* than the table value. Follow the worked example.

The distribution of the statistic T also approximates to normality when the sample size is large (over 10 for a Wilcoxon test). The mean of this distribution is:

$$\frac{N(N+1)}{4}$$

(For what it is worth, this again is common sense. It is halfway between the least possible value of T, that is, zero, and the greatest possible value, that is, the sum of all the ranks. This is:

$$\frac{N(N+1)}{2}$$

The mean of these two values is

$$\frac{N(N+1)}{4}$$

All statistical tests are common sense once you spot what is going on.)

The standard deviation for T is:

$$\sqrt{\frac{N(N+1)(2N+1)}{24}}$$

And so any particular T value can be expressed as a standard score:

$$Z = T - \frac{N(N+1)}{4} \bigg/ \sqrt{\frac{N(N+1)(2N+1)}{24}}$$

The probability of this standard score (or greater) can be found by using the area under the standard Normal curve in Table B in the usual way (pp. 64 and 70).

For a two-tailed test, there is 5% significance if the standard score is greater than 1.96.

Wilcoxon test: procedure

Step no.	Result of step	What to do
1	$(X_a - X_b)$	Find the difference, with direction ($+$ or $-$) for each pair of scores.
2	$\left| X_a - X_b \right|$	Rank these differences, ignoring the direction. The smallest difference is ranked 1. Ties are treated in the same way as in the Mann-Whitney test.
3	T	Find the sum of ranks for the less frequent sign ($+$ or $-$).
3a	(for sample sizes, under 10 and, optionally, up to 30) Refer to table G to find the significant T value for the appropriate sample size. Results are significant if the observed T value is smaller than the table value.	
4	(for sample sizes over 10) $$\frac{N(N+1)}{4}$$	Find the mean of the T distribution. N is the number of subjects (or matched pairs).
5	$T - \dfrac{N(N+1)}{4}$	Take (4) from (3) (ignore the sign).
6	$$\sqrt{\frac{N(N+1)(2N+1)}{24}}$$	Find the standard deviation of the T distribution.
7	$T - \dfrac{N(N-1)}{4} \Big/ \sqrt{\dfrac{N(N+1)(2N+1)}{24}}$ $= z$	Divide (5) by (6). This is T expressed as a standard score.

Wilcoxon test: worked example

The results tested here are the same as those used in the worked example of the sign test (p. 88). The sign test did not reveal a significant difference between the amount of eye contact at long range and at short range in E 10. The Wilcoxon test uses more information and hence has greater power.

Subject no.	Time spent in eye contact during one minute of interview Long distance (X_a)	Short distance (X_b)	**1** Difference ($X_a - X_b$)	**2** Rank order of difference
1	55.6	36.7	18.9	14
2	47.3	50.5	−3.2	3 (−)
3	58.3	49.6	8.7	10
4	50.4	47.0	3.4	4
5	38.9	43.5	−4.6	6 (−)
6	58.1	45.7	12.4	12
7	58.4	43.0	15.4	13
8	57.8	55.3	2.5	1
9	46.3	54.8	−8.5	9 (−)
10	53.9	44.3	9.6	11
11	56.9	37.2	19.7	15
12	56.1	50.0	6.1	7
13	53.3	45.8	7.5	8
14	55.7	58.3	−2.6	2 (−)
15	41.9	37.4	4.5	5

3   T = (for negative differences) $2 + 3 + 6 + 9 = 20$.

3a   The T value for the 5% significance level is 25 (from Table G, N = 15). The observed T is smaller than this. There is a significant difference between the conditions.
or

4   Mean of T is $\dfrac{15(15+1)}{4} = 60$

5 $20 - 60 = -40$ (ignore the sign)

6 $\dfrac{15(15+1)(30+1)}{24} = 310 = 17.607$

7 $\dfrac{40}{17.607} = 2.272 = z$

Step no.	What to do

8

In Table B, find the probability of a z-score greater than observed by finding:

$$0.5 - \text{(area under the standard Normal curve)} \times 2$$

for a two-tailed test. Or:

$$0.5 - \text{(area under the standard Normal curve)}$$

for a one-tailed test.

9

Interpret this result in terms of the experimental hypothesis.

8   From Table B, the area under the curve between the mean and a standard score of 2.272 is:

$$0.4884$$

For a two-tailed test, $p = 2(0.5 - 0.48840) = 0.023$.
There is a significant difference between the conditions. In fact, we knew this as the z-score was greater than 1.96. However, we have now found the actual probability of the null hypothesis.

9   We can reject the null hypothesis that the differences in the amount of eye contact observed in long-range and short-range interviews is due to random errors alone. Eye contact is affected by the proximity of the two people.

Note 1: This is a good example of the superior power of the Wilcoxon test compared with the sign test.

Note 2: To save time and effort it is a good plan to find the significant value of T in Table G before you start ranking the differences. As ranking proceeds you can tot up the ranks of the less frequent sign. If this tally exceeds the significant value you can abandon further ranking – your results are not significant.

Parametric or non-parametric?

Except on the rare occasions when observations are made in rank order, the ranked data used in these two non-parametric tests are derived from continuous measurements. This has to be done if the continuous measurements are not suitable for the parametric t-test. Even when a parametric test could be used, the Mann-Whitney and Wilcoxon tests are an alternative to the t-tests. Where there is this choice we can look at the advantages and disadvantages of the parametric and non-parametric tests (and perhaps allow personal preference the casting vote).

The important differences between the tests stem from differences in the amount of information held by ranked and continuous measurements. The t-test, using more information, is more powerful than its non-parametric counterpart. This will be important if the experimental effect is weak.

On the other hand, in order to deal with all this information, the t-test is forced to make assumptions about the measurements. And although the t-test is robust, that is, it is still reliable when the assumptions are stretched a bit, it is not unbreakable. When the assumptions are obviously violated the parametric t-test cannot be used.

The non-parametric tests are not restricted by these assumptions. However, they pay for their wider application with a loss of power. Which to use? When the experimental effect appears large, and the scores look normal, it doesn't much matter. When the experimental effect (if any) is small, use the more powerful t-tests unless the parametric assumptions look dubious, then you must play safe with a non-parametric test.

There is another consideration, more prosaic but, perhaps, more decisive. The differences in information content result in differences in mathematical complexity. The t-test requires more operations, with all manner of sigmas and squares and so forth. In small samples the non-parametric tests need only the simplest calculations and the ranking of scores. But, the operations of the t-test can all be quickly and simply performed inside a simple calculator with a memory. The non-parametric tests require ranking. This cannot be done with a calculator and, if the samples are large, can be plenty tedious.

Where you have a choice between parametric and non-parametric tests and a calculator, I advise using the parametric t-test. If no calculator is handy use the simpler non-parametric test. If significance is narrowly missed you can try the t-test later.

I repeat: there is no virtue in heroically wading through figures and log tables. Let your fingers do the walking – get a calculator.

Correlation

The chi-squared test was used to assess the association of two discrete variables; for example, is driving speed (over or under 30 m.p.h.) associated with the sex of the driver? A correlation measures the association between two continuous variables.

Consider an experiment, similar to the chi-squared example, to assess the association between engine size and driving speed. The 2×2 contingency table will look like this:

26. *The 2×2 contingency table for driving speed and engine size (fictitious data)*

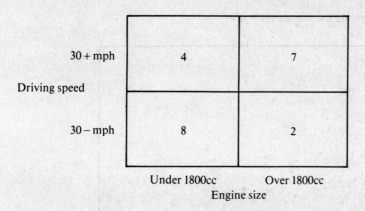

We could use a great deal more of the information collected if both variables were recorded continuously. The actual driving speed and engine size of each observation is recorded. These observations can be displayed as points on a scattergram: engine size is given by the horizontal position of the point, speed by the vertical position of the point. An observation of a car of 1575 c.c. travelling at 26 m.p.h. is recorded in figure 27.

27. Scattergram of driving speed and engine size

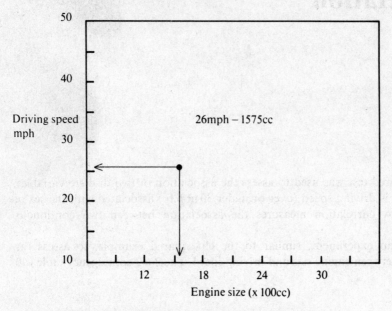

And a fictitious sample of 20 observations could look like this:

28. Scattergram of driving speed and engine size

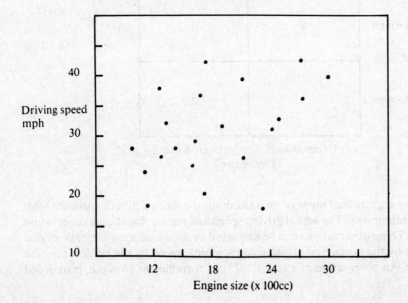

By drawing divisions at 30 m.p.h. and 1800 c.c. we will produce the contingency table for the chi-squared test:

29. (compare with fig. 26)

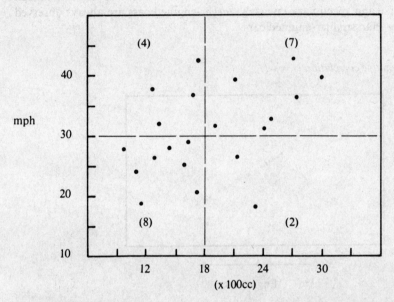

The measure of the association between the two continuous variables is the correlation coefficient (symbolized by the letter r). This can take values from -1 to $+1$.

A correlation of $+1$ (perfect positive correlation) between speed and engine size would mean that cars with *larger* engine sizes are always observed driving *faster*

30. Perfect positive correlation (r = + 1)

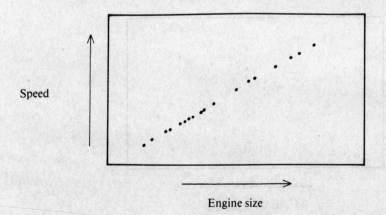

than cars with smaller engine sizes. The observed speed and engine size vary together. Displayed on a scattergram, perfect positive correlation would appear as in figure 30.

A perfect negative correlation ($r = -1$) between engine size and speed would mean that engine size and speed vary inversely; *larger*-engined cars are always observed driving *slower* than smaller-engined cars.

31. Perfect negative correlation ($r = -1$)

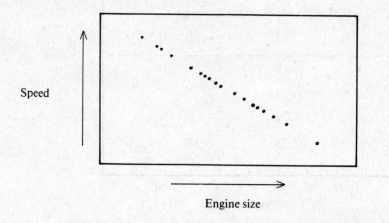

Speed

Engine size

If there is no relationship between engine size and speed the correlation coefficient is 0.

32. No correlation ($r = 0$)

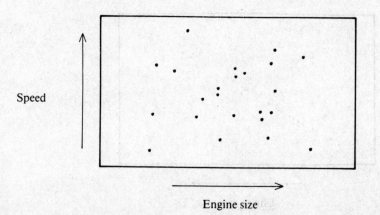

Speed

Engine size

A correlation coefficient of 0 (or near it) does not necessarily mean that there is *no* relationship between the variables. It means that there is no monotonic relationship between them. A monotonic relationship is one in which, as one variable increases, the second variable *consistently* increases (as in figure 30) or *consistently* decreases (as in figure 31). It is fairly common to find a 'U-shaped' relationship between two variables. Figure 33 shows the relationship between the performance on a particular test and the arousal of the subject.

33. U-shaped relationship between arousal and performance on a particular task

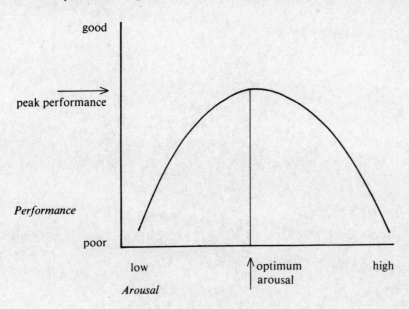

Performance is poor when the arousal is very low; the subject is drowsy or even asleep. Performance improves as the arousal increases, and the subject becomes more alert, to reach a peak performance. As arousal increases still further the performance becomes worse: the subject is petrified with fear. Other instances of this U-shaped relationship between arousal and performance may spring to mind. There is a *positive* correlation between arousal and performance for low values of arousal; a *negative* correlation between the two variables for high values of arousal. The correlation between the two variables overall will be very small as the curve is *non-monotonic*. A correlation, then, measures the monotonicity of a relationship between two variables.

The inevitable presence of random error makes correlation coefficients of 1 or −1 very rare. Having found the correlation coefficient between two variables, we must then take into account sample size and so forth to assess the significance of this observed correlation.

Coefficients of correlation can be found in various ways. We shall look at two: rank-order correlation and product-moment correlation.

Rank-order correlation

(RR – both variables rank ordered)
Examples: D 3; E 4, 19

The principle behind finding the rank-order correlation is very simple. It is popularly supposed that there is a relationship between stupidity and the tendency not to come in out of the rain. We can measure this relationship. 'Stupidity' will be measured by the number of errors on a particular test and the 'tendency not to come in out of the rain' by the amount of water a person absorbs before seeking shelter.

The scores on the two variables are found for each subject and these scores are ranked. There will be a perfect positive correlation if the subject ranked first in stupidity was also the wettest, and the subject ranked second in stupidity was the second wettest, and so on. Correlation will be high if the difference between the subject's ranks on the two tests is small. This is the principle behind rank-order correlation.

We can find this difference in ranks for the two tests (D) for each subject. As usual, we are not interested in the direction of the difference, only in the amount. We can ignore the direction by squaring each difference in ranks, D^2. The mean of these values can be found for all the subjects:

$$\frac{\Sigma D^2}{N}$$

There is perfect correlation $(r = 1)$ when there is *no* difference between ranks: that is, when

$$\frac{\Sigma D^2}{N} = 0$$

And so, logically,
$$r = 1 - \frac{\Sigma D^2}{N}$$

(The correlation coefficient is 1 when there are no rank differences.)

The actual formula for the correlation coefficient is similar to this but is structured so that $r = -1$ when there is maximum difference between ranks for all the subjects (i.e. when there is perfect negative correlation).

$$r = 1 - \frac{6}{(N^2 - 1)} \cdot \frac{\Sigma D^2}{N}$$

Rank-order correlation: procedure

Step no.	Result	What to do
1		For each variable, rank the subjects' scores, bearing in mind the form of the experimental hypothesis. For example, in the worked example one variable is 'errors in maze learning'. The subject with the greatest number of errors is given rank 1. The hypothesis could have stated the variable as 'maze-learning skill'. In this case the subject with the greatest number of errors would be ranked last. Look at the operational definition of the hypothesis.
2	D	For each subject, find the difference between the ranks on the two tests.
3	D^2	Square each (2).
4	ΣD^2	Add all (3).
5	$\dfrac{6\Sigma D^2}{(N^2-1)N}$	Divide $6 \times (4)$ by $(N^2-1)N$, where N is the number of subjects (or observations).
6	$1-\dfrac{6\Sigma D^2}{(N^2-1)N}$ $=r$	Take (5) from 1 to find the rank-order coefficient of correlation.

(If two or more scores tie, each takes the mean of the tied ranks. Thus scores tying for ranks 2 and 3 both take 2.5. The rank-order correlation is unreliable if there is a high proportion of ties between ranks – use the product-moment correlation.)

Rank-order correlation: worked example

These scores are taken from E 4. Subjects were given a general IQ test. Their performance on this is correlated against the number of errors each subject scored when learning a maze to a set criterion.

Subject no.	Errors in maze learning Score	Rank 1	IQ Score	Rank 1′	2 Difference in rank (D)	3 Difference squared (D²)
1	39	6	107	11	5	25
2	51	4.5	109	9	4.5	20.25
3	25	8	114	6	2	4
4	18	9	119	4	5	25
5	88	1	111	8	7	49
6	31	7	124	2	5	25
7	65	2	113	7	5	25
8	6	11	126	1	10	100
9	16	10	117	5	5	25
10	51	4.5	122	3	1.5	2.25
11	56	3	108	11	7	49

4   349.5

5 $\dfrac{6(349.5)}{(120)11} = 1.589$

6 $1 - 1.589 = -0.589 = r.$

There is a correlation of -0.589 between errors in maze-learning and IQ. In other words, the higher the IQ, the fewer the errors.

Note: If we had correlated IQ and maze learning *skill*, by assigning rank 1 to the *lowest* number of errors, we would have found a *positive* correlation.

Compare this result with the product-moment correlation using the same set of scores.

Product-moment correlation

(CC – both variables continuous)
Examples: D 3; E 4, 14, 19

The product-moment correlation coefficient uses more information than rank-order correlation. Rank order does not specify the amount by which, say, the fourth score on a test exceeds the fifth, merely that it does exceed it.

In the following two scattergrams there is perfect positive rank-order correlation:

34.   r (rank order) = + 1

Score X

Score Y

The two variables in figures 34 and 35 have a rank-order correlation of + 1.
Every observation has the same *rank* on both variables.

In the second scattergram, however, the association of the two variables is closer. The difference is apparent because the scattergram uses the actual scores of each variable. So does the product-moment correlation. This gives it the power to distinguish finer differences in correlation.

The rationale behind the product-moment correlation is a little different from that of rank-order correlation but still straightforward. Let us look a little closer at the scores of the subjects, wreathed in vacuous grins, as the rain pours down. Each subject has a score for wetness (Y) and for stupidity (X).

35.   r (rank order) = +1

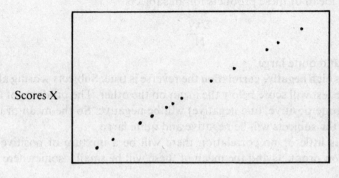

Scores X

Scores Y

The scores in this second scattergram show a closer association between the two variables. The observations lie along a straight line.

Subject no.	Stupidity (X) Errors on test	Wetness (Y) Grams of water
1	38	8
2	25	17
3	15	12
4	10	4
5	2	9
	Total 100 X̄ = 20	Total 50 Ȳ = 10

We find the mean score of each test. We can then find the deviation from the mean of each subject's scores on the two tests. Deviations from the mean are usually symbolized by lower-case letters, thus:

$$(X - \bar{X}) = x \quad \text{and} \quad (Y - \bar{Y}) = y$$

For subject 2, the deviation from mean stupidity, is $(25 - 20) = 5$: the deviation from mean wetness is $(17 - 10) = 7$. The product of these two deviations, xy, is 35.

For subject 1, the deviations are 18 and -2. The product is -36.
For subject 4, the deviations are -10 and -6. The product is $+60$.

Where there is **high positive correlation** subjects scoring above the mean on one test will score above the mean on the other test – the product of their deviations is positive. And subjects scoring below the mean on one test will also score below the mean on the other test – the product of these two negative deviations is also positive. So, the mean of these products for all subjects,

$$\frac{\Sigma\,xy}{N}$$

will be positive and quite large.

Where there is **high negative correlation** the reverse is true. Subjects scoring above the mean on one test will score below the mean on the other. The products of these two deviations (one positive, one negative) will be negative. So the mean of these products for all the subjects will be negative and quite large.

Where there is little or no correlation there will be a mixture of positive and negative deviation products and the mean of these will be small – somewhere near zero.

The actual size of each deviation will depend on the standard deviation of the scores for that test (this is, after all, exactly what the standard deviation measures). To avoid this problem the deviations are expressed as *standard scores* by dividing each deviation by the standard deviation of scores on that test:

$$\frac{x}{\sigma_x} \quad \text{and} \quad \frac{y}{\sigma_y}$$

Each product of standard scores is thus:

$$\frac{xy}{\sigma_x \cdot \sigma_y}$$

The mean of these values for all the subjects in the sample is the correlation:

$$r = \frac{\Sigma(XY/\sigma_x \cdot \sigma_y)}{N}$$

or, as σ_x and σ_y don't change:

$$r = \frac{\Sigma\,xy}{\sigma_x \cdot \sigma_y \cdot N}$$

By using standard scores instead of actual deviations from the mean we ensure that perfect positive correlation is $+1$ and perfect negative correlation is -1.

A truly horrifying moment can be had by expressing all the bits in this formula in terms of actual scores. The standard deviations are expanded by using the first method of finding standard deviation (p. 49). This method uses the deviation of each score from the mean, and we have to find that anyway (x and y).

$$r = \frac{\Sigma\,(X-\bar{X})(Y-\bar{Y})}{N\left\{\sqrt{\dfrac{\Sigma\,(X-\bar{X})^2}{(N-1)}}\right\}\left\{\sqrt{\dfrac{\Sigma\,(Y-\bar{Y})^2}{(N-1)}}\right\}}$$

Simply substitute the various values of X and Y, each subject's score on the two variables, and the value of N, the number of subjects.

Follow the worked example.

Product-moment correlation: procedure

Step no.	Result of step	What to do
1a	ΣX	Add together all the individual scores on one variable.
2a	$\dfrac{\Sigma X}{N} = \bar{X}$	Divide (1) by the number of observations to give the mean score.
3a	$(X - \bar{X})$	For each subject, find the deviation from the mean (2), with the direction + or −.
4a	$(X - \bar{X})^2$	Square each (3).
5a	$\Sigma (X - \bar{X})^2$	Add all (4).
6a	$\dfrac{\Sigma (X - \bar{X})^2}{(N-1)}$	Divide (5) by $(N-1)$.
7a	$\sqrt{\dfrac{\Sigma (X - \bar{X})^2}{(N-1)}} = \sigma_x$	Find the square root of (6) to give the standard deviation of the scores.

This procedure is now repeated for the scores of the second variable (steps 1b–7b).

8	$(X - \bar{X})(Y - \bar{Y})$	For each subject, multiply (3a) and (3b). Pay attention to the sign, + or −.
9	$\Sigma (X - \bar{X})(Y - \bar{Y})$	Add all (8).

Product-moment correlation: worked example

These results are the same as those used in the worked example of rank order correlation, taken from E 4.

Subject no.	Score (X)	Errors in maze learning Deviation **3a** $(X - \bar{X})$	Square deviation **4a** $(X - \bar{X})^2$
1	39	−1.55	2.4025
2	51	10.45	109.2025
3	25	−15.55	241.8025
4	18	−22.55	508.5025
5	88	47.45	2251.5025
6	31	−9.55	91.2025
7	65	24.45	597.8025
8	6	−34.55	1193.7025
9	16	−24.55	602.7025
10	51	10.45	109.2025
11	56	15.45	238.7025
1a	446		**5a** 5946.7275

2a $\quad \dfrac{446}{11} = 40.55$

6a $\quad \dfrac{5946.7275}{10} = 594.67275$

7a $\quad \sqrt{594.67275} = 24.386$

Subject no.	Score	IQ Deviation **3b**	Squared deviation **4b**	**8** Deviation product
1	107	−8.45	71.4025	13.0975
2	109	−6.45	41.6025	−67.4025
3	114	−1.45	2.1025	22.5475
4	119	3.55	12.6025	−80.0525
5	111	−4.45	19.8025	−211.1525
6	124	8.55	73.1025	−81.6525
7	113	−2.45	6.0025	−59.9025
8	126	10.55	111.3025	−364.5025
9	117	1.55	2.4025	−38.0525
10	122	6.55	42.9025	68.4475
11	108	−7.45	55.5025	−115.1025
1b	1270		**5b** 438.7275	**9** −913.7275

2b $\quad \dfrac{1270}{11} = 115.45$

6b $\quad \dfrac{438.7275}{10} = 43.87275$

7b $\quad \sqrt{43.87275} = 6.624$

Step no.	Result of step	What to do
10	$N(\sigma_x)(\sigma_y)$	Multiply N by (7a) and (7b).
11	$$\frac{\Sigma(X-\bar{X})(Y-\bar{Y})}{N(\sigma_x)(\sigma_y)}$$ or: r	Divide (9) by (10) to give the product-moment correlation.

10   11(6.624) (24.386)=1776.8615

11 $\dfrac{-913.7275}{1776.8615} = -0.514 = r$

Note: As usual, where a calculator is available, you are advised to work across the steps for each subject, letting ΣX and $\Sigma(X-\bar{X})^2$ accumulate in the memories.

The value of the product-moment correlation coefficient here (r = −0.514) should be compared with that of the rank-order coefficient worked example, (r = −0.589).

   The rank-order correlation is higher than the product-moment correlation. The reason for this can be seen by looking again at figure 34. The rank-order correlation in figure 34 is +1, the product-moment correlation would be somewhat below this as the correlation is clearly not perfect when the actual scores of the subjects are used.

Significance of a correlation coefficient

The correlation coefficient, however derived, measures the association between the two variables in the sample scores. We do not know whether this correlation is due to a real relationship between the variables or simply the result of random error in the variables. There is usually *some* correlation between any two variables by chance alone. This may be quite large if the sample size is small. For example, if there is a sample of only two observations, then a rank-order correlation will give a coefficient of either -1 or $+1$ by chance alone. As usual we must find the probability of getting the observed correlation with the sample size on the basis of the null hypothesis – that there is no real relationship between the variables.

If you have followed the reasoning behind some of the other significance tests in this book the process will be familiar.

In the worked example of product-moment correlation there is an observed correlation coefficient of -0.0514, with a sample size of 11. What is the probability of this observed coefficient being due to random error alone? We can simulate the null hypothesis. Each observation in the sample of eleven is made by pairing two scores. One score is randomly drawn from, say, the population of IQ scores; the other is randomly drawn from, say, the population of car speeds in the high street. We could take eleven such pairings and calculate the correlation between car speed and IQ in this sample. Any correlation will be due to random error alone as the pairs of scores were drawn up randomly. Any correlation is likely to be fairly small, either side of zero.

By repeating this process many times we could build up a distribution of these correlation coefficients. The mean of this distribution will be zero; as there is no relationship between the variables this is the most likely value for their correlation.

We can find the standard deviation of this distribution. Using this, we can express the observed correlation ($r = -0.514$) as a standard score and hence find the probability of that standard score (or greater) using the area under the standard Normal curve.

Well, of course, all this is not necessary as we can derive the standard deviation of r theoretically:

$$\text{Standard deviation of } r = \sqrt{\frac{(1-r^2)}{(N-2)}}$$

Curiously, the distribution of r is not Normal but closely approximate to the t-distribution used in the t-test. As there, we will find t, the equivalent of a standard score

$$t = r \bigg/ \sqrt{\frac{(1-r^2)}{(N-2)}}$$

The probability of the observed t-value is found in Table C by selecting the appropriate *degrees of freedom* $(N-1)$.

If the t-value is larger than the table value at the 5% significance level $(p = 0.05)$ then the observed correlation is significant. That is, it is unlikely that the observed correlation is due to random error alone: there is a significant association between the variables.

Follow the worked example.

Significance of correlation: procedure

Step no	Result of step	What to do
1	r	Find the correlation between two variables from N observations, using either the rank-order or product-moment method.
2	$(1-r^2)$	Square (1) and subtract from 1.
3	$\dfrac{(1-r^2)}{(N-2)}$	Divide (2) by (number of observations -2).
4	$\sqrt{\dfrac{(1-r^2)}{(N-2)}}$	Take the square root of (3).
5	$r \Big/ \sqrt{\dfrac{(1-r^2)}{(N-2)}}$ $=t$	Divide (1) by (4) to find t.
6		Find the probability of this value of t with $X\,(N-1)$ degrees of freedom. Refer to Table C.
7		Interpret this result in terms of the experimental variables.

Significance of correlation: worked example

The correlation coefficient used in this example is the product-moment correlation of IQ and maze-learning errors found in the worked example, page 121, based on E4.

1   The product-moment correlation of IQ and maze errors is computed on page 123.

$$r = -0.514$$

2     $(1 - 0.514^2) = 1 - 0.26196 = 0.735804$

3     $\dfrac{0.735804}{9} = 0.081756$

4     $\sqrt{0.081756} = 0.28593$

5     $\dfrac{0.514}{0.28593} = 1.798$

6   The t-value for the 5% significance level, with 10 degrees of freedom, is $t = 2.228$. The observed value of t is some way below this. We cannot reject the null hypothesis that the observed correlation was due to random error alone.

7   Although there is some negative correlation observed between IQ and maze-learning errors, we cannot be 95% certain that this is not due to random error.

Note: We *could* have used the rank-order correlation coefficient for the same set of scores (p. 114), $r = -0.589$. In this case the t-value would have been $t = 2.187$. This is very close to significance – but we know that rank-order correlations give *over-estimates* of the correlation between variables. This problem is discussed in the following section.

Product-moment or rank order?

Practical considerations first. There is a clear difference in the ease of calculating these two statistics: the rank-order method can virtually be done in your head, the product-moment method really needs a calculator – or a lot of time.

Perversely, there is a danger in using the rank-order method. As we saw in figures 34 and 35, and in the two worked examples, the rank-order method gives an *over-estimate* of the correlation of variables. This is important when the significance of the coefficient is found. A rank-order coefficient of correlation may reach significance where the more accurate product-moment coefficient, derived from the same scores, does not (see the note on the previous page). By using a rank-order correlation we are more likely to decide that there is an experimental effect when, in fact, there is none. This is a type 1 error drawing a false association between events (p. 13). This is what scientists are anxious to avoid.

The advice here is to try a rank-order correlation first. If the coefficient is not significant you need go no further. If it is significant, particularly if it is only just significant, then it is safer to go back and compute the product-moment coefficient.

There are two more points to bear in mind. The rank-order correlation shares a problem with all ranking tests: they become unreliable if there is a high proportion of ties in the ranking. In this case the solution is very simple – use the product-moment method.

In some experiments it is convenient to collect the scores in rank orders. For example, where subjects are asked to arrange a list of stimuli by personal preference, ranking may be more natural than awarding points on some arbitrary scale. In this case rank-order correlation is the only choice.

Planning the experiment

An outline of the experiment is beginning to emerge. The hypothesis suggests a relationship between two sorts of events, the variables. These are defined by the way they will be measured in the experiment. This measurement of the variables in turn suggests the type of statistical analysis to be used. We can now proceed to the detailed planning of the experiment. A fair amount of the planning will have been done in deciding how the variables are to be measured but we can always modify these decisions as we hammer out a detailed, practicable plan. This plan consists of the answers to two questions:

1 What, *exactly*, are you going to do? (the design)

2 To whom, *exactly*, are you going to do it? (the subjects)

The choice of design and subjects is obviously closely related: what you are going to do depends to some extent on whom you intend to do it to, and vice versa. However, we will consider the two questions separately.

The design

The various statistical tests are intended to detect relationships between the experimental variables. As we have seen, all the tests make assumptions about the data and the tests are only valid if these assumptions can be made. The design of the experiment must ensure that this is the case.

Independence of observations
The statistical tests assume that the observations or scores on a variable are independent of one another. Exactly how this independence is ensured will depend on the experiment. Let's look at the problem in a few examples. We must check that one observation does not influence another.

Example:
In E 18, the speed of cars coming down a street is observed. These observations can only be considered independent if the cars are not in sight of one another. A following car may well have to slow down if the car in front is crawling along; the car in front may well speed up under the influence of the following car, engine revving, apparently trying to climb up his exhaust pipe. We cannot be sure for either car that the speed is not affected by the speed of the other.
Solution:
Discard all observations when two cars travelling in the same direction are in sight of one another.

Example:
In D 1, subjects mark the perceived mid-point of the horizontal line in the two figures:

36.

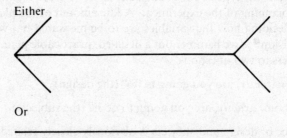

We cannot be sure that subjects' perceived mid-points are independent if they watch each other mark the mid-point or, even worse, if any trace of another subject's mark can be seen on the figure.
Solution:
Figures are duplicated and a new pair is given to each subject.

In this repeated-measures design the subject must see one other mid-point being marked, his own, on the first figure. To minimize this danger, the first figure is removed before the second is presented. The first judgement of mid-point may still influence the second – an *order effect* (p. 9). If the two figures are always presented in the same order this will produce a *constant error*.

Solution:
The order of presentation is randomized or counterbalanced.

Check the independence of observations in your experiment and change the design if necessary. Some dependence may be unavoidable in repeated-measures or single-subject designs (e.g. an order effect). Check that the effect is small and cannot produce a constant error or change to an independent-subjects or matched-subjects design.

Constant errors

These must be eliminated. Order effect can be dealt with by counterbalancing as in the example opposite. Other constant errors can come from the experimenter himself.

The experimenter is looking for, and expects, a difference between the two experimental conditions. He may unconsciously (or consciously) influence the subject by small signs: a sigh of disappointment, or a grin of approval if the subject behaves as expected. Of course, the experimenter strives to treat all subjects in exactly the same way. **Standardized instructions** to the subject can be read from a prepared script and the whole experiment made as automatic as possible to minimize the risk of subtly influencing the subjects. These **experimenter effects** are avoided if the experimenter is unaware to which experimental condition he belongs. He can hand over the running of the experiment to a colleague who has no expectations of the results. This is known, for obvious reasons, as a **blind technique.**

A similar problem can arise if the subject has expectations of the 'correct' result and behaves accordingly. A well-known example of this is the **placebo effect.**

Example:
The subject is given a placebo, an inert substance disguised as a pill. He believes it to be an active drug. The subject's reactions to the placebo are often similar to his reactions to the real drug. When testing any drug the problem is to distinguish the real effect of the active ingredients from the placebo effect.
Solution:
Administer the drug and a placebo identical in appearance to two groups of subjects. The subjects are unaware which pill they have taken. Any difference in the reactions of the two groups must be the effect of the active ingredients of the drug. This is another blind technique. Ideally, the experimenter measuring the subjects' reactions is also unaware which pill has been taken. This then is a **double-blind technique.**
Note:
Can the subject's expectations unconsciously affect his behaviour? This question is investigated experimentally in E 11 and E 17. An experiment by Schachter and Singer (1962) [perception of emotion] provides a classic demonstration of the subtle effects of subject expectations.

Another precaution against such effects is the use of **naive subjects.**

Example

In D 1 the mid-point of the horizontal line in the Muller–Lyer figure is usually perceived to the right of the actual mid-point (see figure 36). Subjects who are familiar with such illusions may 'allow' for the illusion and mark a point to the left of their perceived mid-point. In this case the constant error will counteract the experimental effect.

Solution:

Use subjects naive to this experiment: that is, unfamiliar with the ways of visual illusions.

In many cases subjects can guess the purpose and hence the expected result of the experiment. It may be necessary to mislead the subject about the experiment in order to conceal what behaviour you are observing.

Example:

In E 10 the dependent variable is the amount of eye contact during an interview between the experimenter and the subject. The independent variable is the distance between them. It is important that subjects are unaware that eye contact is being measured. How can we explain the observers watching both the experimenter and the subject?

Solution:

The subject is told that the interview is a preliminary to the actual experiment. The distance between subject and interviewer is varied by using different seating arrangements, supposedly to suit the tape-recording of the experiment. The observers are holding dummy microphones and are 'checking for sound levels'. As soon as measurements have been taken the subject is told of the deception.

The moral and practical problems of such deception are considered in the next chapter dealing with subjects.

The relative importance of any of these order, experimenter or placebo effects will depend on the experiment you are designing. Check that all possible sources of constant errors are eliminated by counterbalancing, blind techniques and using naive subjects.

Random errors – to control or not to control?

Before we can consider what to do about the random errors in our design we must consider whether random errors are a bad thing. What do they do? Random errors *obscure* an experimental effect. On the other hand, real life is full of random variation. If our experiments are to tell us anything about how people really behave we must make the experiment as close to real life as possible – and that includes countless random variations. This is a real dilemma that bedevils the social sciences.

Consider this fictitious example:

> A scientist is investigating sex differences in driving safety; specifically he wants to see if there is any sexual difference in the speed of reaction when braking the car in an emergency. He can approach the problem in two ways:
>
> 1 He leaps out in front of cars and times how long it takes them to stop. They are given no warning to make the situation as real as possible. The scientist finds that there is considerable variation in stopping times because there are many random variables. There is variation in the condition of the roads, the cars, the lighting and weather and so on. There is considerable variation in the drivers: their ages, health, eyesight, strength of push on the brake pedal, alertness, and whether they care about the lunatic leaping in front of them. All this variation obscures any sexual difference in reaction time. He finds no significant difference.
>
> 2 He can attempt to control these variables. The experiment is carried out at the laboratory in a sound-proof booth, under constant lighting and temperature and using accurate reaction timers. Under these carefully controlled, and artificial conditions a small but significant difference is found.

Notice that neither design allows him to say much about sexual differences in emergency braking. In the first design he found no significant difference and so he cannot decide whether there is no experimental effect or an experimental effect is obscured by all the random error.

In the second design he found an experimental effect, but under such artificial conditions that he may not be justified in generalizing his findings to real driving conditions.

At least the second design allows him to establish a relationship, even if of rather restricted use. On the other hand the control of all these variables is an expensive and time-consuming business; if the laboratory equipment were not available he would have no choice.

Of course his dilemma would be resolved if the experimental effect were large enough to give significant results in the real-life conditions.

The moral of this tale is to try wherever possible to investigate *large* experimental effects. This will allow you to get significant results without the need for complex control of random variables. In turn it will be easier to apply your findings to the behaviour of ordinary people in the real world.

How can you know that an experimental effect will be large *before* the experiment is carried out? You can't. Of course, some effects are likely to be larger than others but 'there is no logically rigorous method of generating useful hypotheses' (p. 4). The answer is to carry out a **pilot experiment.**

Pilot experiments

You have a rough outline of the experiment, the experimental variables and how they might be measured. You have eliminated all constant errors. Now carry out a small-scale version of the experiment. Are the procedures practicable? This is the time to iron out practical details of the measurements, instructions to subjects and so on. Carry out a suitable analysis on the results of the pilot study.

Are the results significant? If so, you can carry on with a full-scale experiment with reasonable confidence. If not, you must decide what to do.

You may suspect that there is *no* experimental effect. In this case you can either abandon the whole thing or carry on with the experiment and be content to establish the rather watery fact that you are *not* 95% certain that there is an experimental effect.

Note: You will *not* be able to state that you are 95% certain that there is *no* effect. You may suspect that there *is* an experimental effect, but that the particular design you have chosen does not reveal it. This can be the result of a **floor** or **ceiling** effect.

Floor and ceiling effects

In E 4 one experimental variable is the subject's performance on an IQ test. The subjects are given, say, thirty questions to answer in half an hour. The difficulty of these questions must be suited to the ability of the subjects. If they are too difficult no subject will be able to answer any question; all subjects will score the same – zero. This is the same as a pile of sand would score. Clearly something is wrong: the subjects all have different mental abilities and all are brighter than the pile of sand. This is a floor effect. (An extreme and ludicrous example of such an effect might occur in the BBC quiz programme, 'Mastermind'. Here the pile of sand could well win by having the lowest number of 'passes'.)

A ceiling effect occurs if the questions are too easy. All the questions are answered correctly by all the subjects who thus all get the same score – 100 per cent (except, of course, the pile of sand). The IQ test, or any other task, must be appropriate to the range of abilities of the subjects.

The second experimental variable in E 4 is the performance on a maze devised by the experimenter. Floor and ceiling effects are avoided by adjusting the number of decisions in the maze if necessary after the pilot experiment.

You may suspect from the pilot study that there is an effect although this is obscured by random error. There are two solutions:

1   Increase the sample size.
    Any experimental effects on the dependent variable will accumulate as the
    sample size increases; the experimental effect is always in the same direction.
    The effects of random errors on the dependent variable will tend to cancel
    themselves out as the sample increases; being random, some will act in one
    direction, some in the other. You may recall in the case of the shifty

character's coin (p. 13) we could not reject the null hypothesis of a fair coin with a sample size of four tosses. When the sample size was increased to eight tosses it was clear that the coin was crooked.

As the sample size increases, any experimental effect becomes easier to recognize among the mass of random variation. This recognition of an effect is the job of the significance tests. All tests take into account the sample size used.

2 Control the random variables.
By controlling some of the more important variables in the experiment the amount of random error is reduced, making it easier to recognize an experimental effect: that is, the results can reach significance.

Note: For those who like that sort of thing, you can see that both these tactics aim to reduce the dispersion (the standard deviation) of the scores.

$$\text{Standard deviation } (\sigma) = \sqrt{\frac{x^2}{N}}$$

σ gets smaller as N, the sample size, increases. This is the first tactic.

σ gets smaller as x gets smaller (x is the deviation from the mean – the result of random error). This is the second tactic.

It is impossible and undesirable to remove all random errors, but it may be possible to control the major sources of error without elaborate equipment.

Subject variables can be reduced by using *single-subject* (p. 10), *repeated-measures* (p. 8), or *matched-subjects* designs (p. 9). Bear in mind the dangers of order effects with the first two of these. Subject variables can also be reduced by using subjects of one sex, or in a particular age range and so forth, if you suspect that these variables are an important source of error. The subject's motivation can be a source of enormous variation. Is he dropping off with boredom? It is good designing to keep subjects interested, particularly if you ever want to use them again.

Stimulus variables can be controlled. The lighting, noise levels, duration of presentation, in fact any number of variables *could* be controlled. Whether it is profitable to do so will depend on:

their effect on the experimental variables,
the simplicity of controlling them,
the size of the experimental effect.

We can see how these decisions are put into practice by taking a closer look at a couple of examples.

Example:

D 1 (p. 162). A quick pilot study reveals that the experimental effect is large. The majority of the subjects place the perceived mid-point of the arrowed figure to the right of the perceived mid-point of the plain horizontal line (see figure 1).

When the two figures are presented separately there is no evidence of an order effect: we are safe in using a repeated-measures design – but the order of presentation is counterbalanced just to be sure. Each subject marks the mid-point on both figures and the difference between these is measured.

By using duplicated stimuli we control any random variation in the figures and, incidentally, avoid the chore of drawing dozens of figures by hand. The control of other variables is probably unnecessary as long as common sense keeps them within reasonable limits. Subjects should view the figures at approximately the same distance, say, normal reading distance, around 40 cm. The lighting and the subjects' eyesight should be adequate for the task. These last three points can be covered by giving the subjects written instructions. If these can be read, eyesight, lighting and distance can be assumed to be adequate. These standard instructions are also a simple precaution against any experimenter effect.

The choice of statistical analysis is also part of the design. What are the alternatives? the dependent variable is continuous (the position of the perceived mid-points measured from the left of the figure). The independent variable is discrete (which figure is presented). With this combination of variables (CD) we refer to the flow chart on page 20. The repeated-measures design gives two possibilities:

1   A t-test for related samples. Can we make the assumptions of the t-test? The pilot results will give some idea of this.

2   A sign test. This is very simple but not very powerful. The results of the pilot study will indicate whether the experimental effect is large enough to reach significance on a sign test.

As an alternative, the differences in subjects' scores can be ranked. This will give the opportunity to use a non-parametric test.

3   The Wilcoxon test. If we cannot make the assumptions of the t-test the Wilcoxon test is a more powerful alternative to the sign test.

The number of subjects will be a consideration in selecting a test.

Because we have avoided the rigorous controls of laboratory conditions the actual testing of each subject is quick and simple. We can use large numbers of subjects and test them where we find them.

We have answered the first question in the plan: 'What, exactly, are you going to do?' To whom, exactly, you are going to do it, that is, the selection of subjects, is to be considered in the next chapter.

The simplicity of this design stems from the large experimental effect we found in the pilot study and the ease of taking the measurements. It is not always so simple, particularly if we want to study some 'naturally occurring' behaviour.

Example:
E 18 (car speed and sex of driver). A quick pilot study reveals that the experimental effect, if any, is likely to be small. If we are to get significant results we must attempt to reduce the number of variables affecting the driving speeds. Let's consider some of these.

Congestion: we have already looked at this when considering the independence of observations. We will use only cars travelling alone down the street. We must select a quiet road at a quiet time (a country lane?) Congestion of pedestrians may affect driving speeds. All observations should be made at the same time of day, in the same spot and perhaps on the same day of the week – or where there are no pedestrians (a country lane?) A modification to the original idea is emerging.

The weather may affect the drivers' speeds. We will make observations only when the road is dry. This is an excellent excuse to avoid standing out in the rain.

The experimenter must take care to remain out of sight of the driver when the speed measurement is made. The sight of someone with a clipboard recording the speed of his car is enough to make any driver pause and influence his speed.

Subject variables: we cannot use a repeated-measures design here. We could attempt a matched-pairs design by matching men and women driving the same model of car. Any other subject variables would be difficult to match; there is a limit to the amount of information to be gleaned from a subject speeding past at 30 m.p.h. This matching will drastically reduce the number of observations made. We must consider the advantages of matching against the loss of observations. On balance, an independent-subjects design is preferable. We have a choice of two tests:

1 A t-test for independent samples. As usual we must check that the assumptions of this parametric test are not violated. Or the observations of speed can be ranked.

2 A Mann-Whitney test. This will be used if the assumptions of the t-test cannot be made. Ranking the observations involves a loss of information. This leads to a difference in power between the two tests. With a small experimental effect we need all the power we can get to reach significance. The t-test is preferable if possible.

The control of other variables is difficult under these natural conditions. We must try to increase the significance of the results by making a large number of observations. If the pilot study is discouraging we might consider a radical change of design or hypothesis, or carry on and establish that the effect is, at most, not significant.

So far, the aim of the design has been to detect an experimental effect, a relationship between the two experimental variables. The design will also determine how such a relationship can be interpreted.

Causality

Some hypotheses suggest that the relationship between the variables is **causal.** That is, a change in one variable causes a change in the other. Such a causal relationship can only be established in designs where the experimenter manipulates one variable (the independent variable) and looks for *consequent* changes in the other variable (the dependent variable). We will refer to such designs as **causal designs.**

Note: Strictly speaking, these are called experiments [experimental methods]. However, the term 'experiment' is often used loosely to refer to scientific investigations in general, particularly in the laboratory, when there may be no manipulation of either variable. I have used 'experiment' in this way throughout this book to avoid confusion when referring to 'the experimenter', 'experimental variables' and 'experimental effects' when there is no manipulation of variables.

Causal designs

In causal designs the experimenter usually makes the independent variable discrete with two values, the two experimental conditions.

Example:
In D 1 the independent variable is the figure presented to the subject. The hypothesis is that the position of the perceived mid-point *depends* on the presence or absence of the arrow-heads.

Example:
In E 11 subjects are asked to estimate the height of a person with whom they have been chatting. Some subjects believe the person is a professor, others believe he is an unemployed labourer. The hypothesis is that the subjects' estimation depends on which occupation they believe the person to have. This is the independent variable the experimenter manipulates.

Non-causal designs
The experimenter does not manipulate either of the experimental variables but simply observes their value for each subject.

Note: This design is commonly referred to as a correlation (correlation methods) because the variables are often both continuous and a correlation is found between them. It is quite possible, however, to have a *causal* design in which both variables are measured continuously and their correlation is found as long as one of those variables is manipulated by the experimenter. To avoid this confusion I use the term 'non-causal' for a design in which neither variable is manipulated, and hence no causal relationship can be established.

Example:
In E 4 the experimenter observes the performance of each subject on a maze-learning task and an IQ test. If a significant correlation is found between these we cannot claim that IQ and maze learning are causally related. Changes in both could be caused by changes in a third variable – perhaps motivation.

Example:
In D 2 the experimenter observes each subject's preferred way of folding arms and clasping fingers. Both of these are discrete variables. A chi-squared test is used to find any significant relationship. This is a non-causal design that does not use a correlation.

Causal or non-causal design?
In practice the choice between a causal or non-causal design will often be decided by the nature of the experimental variables – whether either can be manipulated. Where a choice is possible a causal design is chosen; the results tell us more about the variables – not just *that* they are related but *how* they are related. Against this great advantage we must weigh the disadvantages of manipulating one of the variables. This manipulation is artificial and may only be possible in artificial conditions, perhaps in the laboratory. We may not be justified in generalizing findings under such artificial conditions to everyday behaviour.

It is sometimes possible to avoid artificial conditions and use a causal design in a natural setting, the subjects unaware that they are taking part in an experiment. This is splendid. But beware: people take a dim view of anyone observing their behaviour, let alone manipulating it. Your moral rights and obligations as experimenters are considered in the next chapter. E 9 is an example of such a **field experiment.**

A reasonable compromise between the artifices of the laboratory and the uncontrollable variation in everyday life is suggested in I 1, studies in schools. In this situation a certain amount of control of the subjects, the children, is quite normal.

The manipulation of an independent variable may be impossible for a variety of reasons:

1 Theoretically impossible. Some variables, particularly *state* variables, cannot be manipulated. The variables of sex, heredity, intelligence and personality are more or less fixed for each subject.

2 Practically impossible. Where an independent variable could, in theory, be manipulated, it may be impossible to do so with limited resources. E 20 examines the relationship between the behaviour of cows and the weather. Short of housing a herd of cows in a hermetically sealed vessel, it is impossible to manipulate their weather. A non-causal design is chosen. The age of a subject is theoretically easy to manipulate – but it does involve a very long wait.

3 Morally impossible. Even when it is practically quite simple to manipulate a variable, it may be morally unacceptable (and possibly illegal). It has not been established that smoking is causally related to lung cancer in humans. It is possible to design a suitable experiment to do so.

    Take two groups of children. The independent variable – smoking – is manipulated by preventing one group from smoking and forcing the other group to smoke. The experimenter observes the incidence of lung cancer in the two groups. Such an experiment is morally unacceptable.

    Where manipulation is impossible with human subjects it may be possible to use animals. This is commonly done to avoid (often unsuccessfully) moral problems. For example, animals are used to test new drugs. Such legal and moral questions are considered in the next chapter on subjects.

If for some reason the experimenter cannot manipulate one of the experimental variables he must simply observe their value for each subject. This has its advantages. The moral and practical problems of manipulating a variable are side-stepped. The observations can often be made simply and quickly under natural conditions. In these circumstances subjects can often be unaware they are subjects at all (e.g. E 9 and E 18). It may be possible to dispense with meeting the subjects altogether if the information about them is available in some other way.

Example:
Sex differences in the age of first marriage can be investigated by collecting information from official records or local newspapers.

Alternatively, this sort of simple concise information could, of course, be collected by asking a subject the question 'How old were you when you got married?' This is the basis of the **survey.**

The survey

This is simply a method of observing the variables in a large number of subjects by using their verbal reports. This can speed things up. It is quicker to ask of a subject 'Do you ever eat cornflakes?' than to haunt his house every morning observing his breakfast.

We can also ask questions about the subject's experiences, beliefs and other internal events that may not be apparent in his (non-verbal) behaviour. I suspect the only way of discovering if a man believes in God is to ask him: it is rarely apparent in his behaviour.

Of course he may lie. Strictly speaking, a survey will only be observing verbal behaviour. This may be a long way from the behaviour you are interested in. This flexibility of language presents another problem: the infinite variety of possible answers to a question must somehow be constrained to values on a continuous variable or a small number of discrete choices, to allow statistical analysis.

Example:

The *open-ended* question 'What do you think of the present Government?' will produce a variety of replies, some very long, others short and pithy but none identical to any other. How can we describe the observations of this variable?

Alternatively, the experimenter may ask the *forced-choice* question 'What do you think of the present Government?'

Approve ☐   Disapprove ☐   (Tick one box)

The answers will form a straightforward discrete variable but may not accurately represent the subjects' feelings. The majority of subjects will not simply 'approve' or 'disapprove' without some qualification.

A compromise between these two extremes is to provide a larger number of response choices or to divide the range between approval and disapproval into, say, a 10-point scale. When approval = 10 and disapproval = 0, the subject who has grave reservations about the government but on balance approves may give a response of 6. These questions can be given in two ways: by **interview** or **questionnaire.**

Interviews

The experimenter interviews the subjects, asking the questions and recording the answers. The flexibility of verbal behaviour can give rise to a large experimenter effect. What the subject answers may be influenced by his feelings towards the experimenter.

Don't go asking people if they believe in God while wearing a dog collar.

Questionnaires

The experimenter delivers written questions to the subjects who fill in the answers and return them to the experimenter. This will, hopefully, reduce the experimenter effect, but take care that the question does not give a clue of the expected result or the experimenter's feelings.

'Do you still believe in God?' hints that perhaps you should have grown out of this by now. A questionnaire will use forced-choice questions. Take care that the response options give the subjects a reasonable choice. A market research question about the taste of a new soup can be biased to give a favourable result if the possible responses are limited to:

Superb ☐   Very tasty ☐   Pleasant ☐   Unpalatable ☐

The soup is unlikely to be unpalatable but that only leaves favourable responses.

More accuracy is possible in an interview. The experimenter can allow the subject to respond freely and then translate the answer, with suitable probing, into the most appropriate category. In an **unstructured** interview the experimenter's questions are not predetermined but follow from the subject's answers in a natural, conversational way. This may allow a rich picture of the subject's opinions and attitudes to emerge but prevent any subsequent analysis. Keep any questions simple.

The choice between interview and questionnaire may be determined by your resources. Interviews take time, usually about three times as long as you think they will take. A pilot study is recommended to check how long you will need and how many subjects you need to unearth the experimental effect you suspect. A large number of questionnaires can be delivered and returned very quickly. This is the greatest advantage of the questionnaire. It is also its greatest disadvantage: not all the questionnaires will be returned – perhaps very few. These few will not be a random sample of those who received a questionnaire but a very particular group of subjects – the sort that return questionnaires. They form a **biased sample** (p. 148).

Example:
300 questionnaires, each of 950 questions, are sent out without a return envelope or postage. Only 17 completed questionnaires are returned. This will be a very biased sample of people who have enough spare time and inclination to wrap them up and post them back to the experimenter. An odd bunch altogether. No conclusions about people in general could be drawn from their answers.

Solution:
Keep the questionnaire short and simple; explain the purpose where possible and make its return as painless as possible, perhaps by collection.

The interview can avoid such problems by interviewing all the people in a chosen sample. (The techniques of sampling are covered in the following chapter.) A compromise between interviews and questionnaires can be made by using subjects in groups (e.g. a class of students in a common room) explaining the questionnaire and collecting the completed questionnaire there and then.

Although surveys are usually part of a non-causal design, this is not necessarily so. A survey is just one way of taking observations.

Non-quantitative designs

So far we have only considered designs that produce quantitative data. This data is analysed statistically to test some hypothesis that the experimenter has in mind. Where possible a causal design is used to establish cause and effect between two variables.

When we looked at surveys it was pointed out that, in order to produce quantitative data, we must sacrifice much of the richness of individuals' opinions, feelings and behaviour by asking structured, forced-choice questions. Similarly, the other designs covered in this book can only look at a small, isolated part of a subject's behaviour: much of the richness of human behaviour and experience is sacrificed. You may feel that this sacrifice is too great. It is quite possible to observe behaviour without the restrictions of quantification and many studies do just this.

These may be *case studies* dealing with the behaviour and experience of one or two subjects in great depth. Gregory and Wallace (1963) looked at the perceptions and feelings of a man recovering his sight after many years of blindness [perception: deprivation studies].

It would be impossible, in a purely quantitative description, to capture the richness and nuances of social behaviour in the family of chimpanzees described in Van Lawick-Goodall's study *In the Shadow of Man*. And yet such studies are a valuable part of our psychological knowledge. Such studies are difficult, not least in their interpretation. A taste of the difficulties can be found in I 2. They are also rather time-consuming and so unsuitable for the comparatively little time you will be able to devote to each practical investigation.

Finally

Beware of over-elaborate designs. It is better to complete a modest experiment, with the possibility of subsequent elaboration, than to have to abandon an over-ambitious project. Each experiment in Part II contains suggestions for further elaboration.

Beware of elaborate equipment. Careful designing can avoid the need for expensive and fickle apparatus.

Example:
A playing card can be categorized by suit (red or black), or by number (odd or even). Do these decisions take the same time? A laboratory design might use a

tachistoscope. This presents a stimulus, one card, and accurately measures the time before a response is made by the subject pressing the appropriate button (say, red or black). The experiment can be tackled without a tachistoscope. The subject is asked to sort a whole pack of cards into two piles (say, red or black). The time taken to sort the whole pack can be measured on an ordinary stopwatch.

For a shining example of such elegance of design, see the experiment by Held and Hein (1963) [perception: deprivation studies].

Examiners love elegant designs.

You have decided exactly what you are going to do. We can now consider to whom you are going to do it – the subjects.

References

Gregory, R.L. and Wallace, J.G. (1963), 'Recovery from early blindness: a case study', *Exp. Psychol. Soc. Monogr.*, *No. 2*, Cambridge
Held, R. and Hein, A. (1963), 'Movement-produced stimulation in the development of visually guided behaviour', *J. Comp. and Phys. Psychol.*, vol. 56, 607–13
Van Lawick-Goodall, J. (1971), *In the Shadow of Man*, Collins (also available in paperback by Fontana Books)

Subjects

If you are interested in the behaviour of tree-frogs, then tree-frogs must be your subjects. If you are interested in the behaviour of new-born humans your subject will be new-born humans. You must obviously choose your hypothesis and design with the subjects in mind: it is pointless thinking long and deep about tree-frogs if you don't have any. My advice is to use humans – we've got lots of those.

Human subjects

Humans are plentiful. You can hardly help observing them and hypotheses about their behaviour spring readily to mind. We know more about humans than any other animal; we humans are terribly interesting, if only to ourselves. Human subjects have great practical advantages over other species.

Humans do not have to be fed, watered or cleaned out. They are very cheap. They often come in handy groups. They are pitifully simple to motivate: no bags of rewards or painful punishments, just tell them it's an experiment and off they go. Instructions and procedures can be explained verbally. Humans are quick to learn and show an enormous range of behaviours. Therein also lie their disadvantages.

Rapid learning can lead to large order effects. Being human, they are every bit as smart as the experimenter; they will have hypotheses and expectations about their behaviour. It is difficult these days to find subjects naive about anything. It may be necessary to mislead your subjects. This should be avoided if possible. First, unless you are a good liar, they will see through your deception and your results will be ruined. Secondly, people are suspicious of psychologists as it is; deceiving them will not help win their trust. Thirdly, it may be that, had they known exactly what you were doing, they would not have agreed to be a subject. This is morally unacceptable.

As a guide, if there is *any* suspicion that the experimental procedure could be considered in *any* way unpleasant or embarrassing then the subject *must* be fully informed. If the experiment requires that the subject be misled then you *must* be satisfied that the experiment could not cause *any* discomfort to the subject.

If these conditions cannot be met the experiment must be abandoned. Do not rely on your judgement of discomfort. Consult older and wiser heads. If in doubt – forget the experiment.

Moral problems of this sort are most common in causal designs where the experimenter must manipulate the subject in some way. This manipulation may be trivial, as in E 1 and E 17. More significant manipulation must have the subject's consent. If the subjects are children it will be necessary to get the consent of the parents *as well*. The children themselves might agree to take part in an experiment on tooth decay by stuffing themselves with sweets; their parents might object. (I have been accused of 'dealing with the devil' by the parent of a nineteen-year-old subject after a simple experiment using hypnosis.)

Care of subjects
Look after your subjects. You may need them again. Keep them as informed as possible both before and after the experiment. Tell them the results and your conclusions, bearing as bravely as possible the inevitable question, 'What does that tell you about me?'

Don't keep them hanging about unnecessarily. Any bugs in the design should have been ironed out in the pilot study.

If you have misled your subjects you should put them in the picture as soon as possible, explaining why it was necessary. If any information should remain confidential between yourself and the subject (e.g. the choice of friends in a sociogram, I 1a) make sure it does. In the same way you must assume that people would prefer to keep their score on various measures – IQ, personality, even a simple skilled task – to themselves. Your subjects are allowing you to study them and their behaviour. This is very trusting of them. Thank them (and sign them up for the next experiment).

Animal subjects

Animal subjects are used for two reasons: if the experimenter is interested in the behaviour of that animal; or if the experimenter cannot use human subjects for some reason. The second reason will not concern us much as relative beginners. Animals are commonly used when it is morally impossible to use human subjects. This is not always satisfactory. Some people would argue that animals and humans have the same moral rights – but humans can do something about it. The experiments that use animals in this way tend to require elaborate equipment (e.g. surgical modification as the IV [ablation techniques]) or a lot of time (e.g. rearing conditions as the IV [socialization: child-rearing techniques]). These experiments can establish causal relationships, impossible with human subjects, but generalizing these animal results to human behaviour is problematical.

It is perfectly reasonable to investigate animal behaviour for its own sake. Common sense will dictate which animals and which hypotheses to look at. Use animals already kept for some other purpose: in a zoo, a farm or the biology department. Keeping animals yourself for a short experiment is not a good idea. The behaviour of pets is often so weird as to tell you little of any use. Observe someone else's animals and formulate a worthwhile hypothesis. What experiments are possible will depend on your resources. There are also laws about what you can do to animals in the cause of education and science.

Whichever species you choose as subjects, you cannot test every member, you must select a sample.

Sampling

In D 1 we wish to test the perception of the Muller–Lyer figure in humans. We cannot test all humans; we must take a sample. Who? The t-test assumes that the sample is drawn randomly from the whole population – a random sample.

> Note: Strictly speaking, the population is the population of all possible scores on the test. As we get one score from each subject, this is the same as the population of humans.

If the results of D 1 are to be used to make statements about the perception of humans, the sample of subjects must be a random sample of the population of humans.

Random samples
In a random sample of a population each member of the population has an equal chance of being selected.

Example:
Select a random sample of 10 from the population of 400 students in a college. Place the names of all the students in a hat, shuffle them about and draw out 10 names. Each student has an equal chance of being selected.

Example:
Select a random sample of 100 households from the population of households in Banbury. Where do we get a list of households – the telephone directory? No. Many households in Banbury are not on the phone; they would have no chance of being selected. Selection from the phone book will give you a biased sample: phone subscribers may be wealthier, or lazier, than other householders.

Selecting a random sample of the population of humans is clearly impossible in practice. We can tackle the problem the other way round. In the second example overleaf, we might run our experiment on subjects selected from the phone directory. Any results will then apply to the population of which our sample was a random sample, that is, phone subscribers. In practice this is what is done. In D 1 we might select a random sample of 50 from the population of students at a college. The results of the experiment can safely be applied to all students of that college. We will probably be safe in generalizing the results of other British students unless we suspect that our college students are not representative of students in general in their visual perception (if, say, the college is an art college). We would be less sure of applying the results to all adults in Britain (age might affect visual perception), still less to adults of all cultures. The sample of college students might form a very biased sample of human adults.

As you can see, random sampling is an ideal that is rarely achieved. Subjects are all too often a self-selected group of volunteers, or a class of students – psychology students at that. This cannot be helped. However, the sample used will affect the conclusions that can be drawn from the results. The method of selecting the sample must be reported when the experiment is written up. Any reader can then judge for himself the bias of the sample.

Randomization

The subjects are selected. It may be necessary to allocate them to conditions of the independent variable.

Example:
In E 11, subjects are allocated either to the P group, and told one story, or to the U group, and told a different story. Which group a subject joins will be random with the proviso that there are equal numbers in each group. A coin is tossed for each subject; if the coin lands 'heads' he will join the P group. This is done until one group has half the sample size, the remaining subjects go to the other group.

Subject no.	Coin toss	Experimental group (U or P)
1	H	P
2	T	U
3	H	P
4	H	P
5	T	U
6	H	P
7	All remaining subjects	U
8	go to the U group.	U

Such simple randomizing techniques are used throughout the experiment. In repeated-measures designs, the order of the conditions is randomized to prevent constant errors.

Example:
In E 10 the subject is interviewed at two distances, the two conditions of the IV. The order of these conditions is decided on the toss of a coin for each subject. Alternatively the order could be *counterbalanced.*

Example:
In E 16, the subject performs under three conditions. He judges the television viewing preferences of:
(A)   someone he likes
(B)   someone he dislikes
(C)   himself.
The order of these three judgements must be randomized. The three conditions can be picked from a hat. Or, if you prefer something a little more scientific, the order can be decided on the roll of a die. First, allocate the faces of the die to the three experimental conditions:

Die face	Experimental condition
1 or 2	(A)
3 or 4	(B)
5 or 6	(C)

Roll the die. The first roll gives a 5, condition (C). The second roll gives a 2, condition (A), and hence the third condition is (B).

Note: If the second roll had given a 6 or another 5 it would have been ignored.

Repeat this procedure for each subject.

If you prefer something more scientific still, use the table of random numbers, Table H.

Random-number tables
Table H contains a string of digits produced by a computer. Start at any point in the table (close your eyes and stab with the finger). The table can be read in any direction – up, down, left or right. The probability of any digit or combination of digits occurring at any point in the table is equal; the numbers are random.
   With ingenuity the table can be used for any randomization task. In the example above we allocate the three experimental conditions to the digits 1, 2 and 3. Starting

at any point, we look for the order in which these digits occur. My chosen bit of Table H reads:

$$6\ 5\ 0\ 4\ 9\ 3\ 8\ 1\ 8\ 6\ 5\ldots$$

Number 3 (condition C) occurs first, 1 (condition A) occurs second and hence condition B must be third.

The same procedure can be used for selecting from any number of alternatives:

Example:
We wish to select a sample of four subjects from a population of 76. Each member of the population is given a number from 01 to 76. Each of these pairs of digits is equally likely to occur in Table H. Starting at any old point the digits are read off in pairs, say:

33 46 82 **28 08** 74 35   and so on

The first four numbers in our population are selected as the random sample.

Remember: The role of randomization is to eliminate any constant errors from the design.

The experiment is planned. What you are going to do, how and to whom. Now go and do it.

Reporting the experiment

You have carried out the experiment, thanked the subjects, sat down and analysed the results. What for? We will gloss over the mundane reasons of examination requirements. The experiment has revealed, or confirmed, or discovered the lack of, some relationship between events in the world. You have increased the sum of human knowledge. Terrific. You must now share this with a waiting world by reporting the experiment.

I must break it to you that the world will not be very interested. You will be talking to only a few fellow psychologists. Bear this in mind.

Style

Up to now your psychology writing will probably have been confined to answering questions in essay form. Whoever asked these questions already knew the answers; your task was to display your knowledge and understanding of the issues – you were to show off. Your reader was assumed to be an intelligent layman who would need the psychological issues explained in some detail.

The situation is quite different in the write-up of the experiment. As a working psychologist you are informing others of your findings. This is *new* knowledge. Your task is not to show off but to inform, as precisely – and concisely – as possible. To make this easier most experimental reports follow a standard pattern. This is not compulsory but it is a convention that works well for both the writer and the reader. The headed sections allow the reader to find particular bits of information quickly; they also form a logical structure for the writer and a checklist of essential points.

Before you write up your first practical have a look at some examples in a psychology journal or collection of papers. [examinations: format of practical reports].

The structure of the report

This is a framework, not a cage. Although most experiments will fit such a structure, it may be modified to suit a particular investigation, a case-study for example.

Given below is the conventional order of sections. I do not suggest they should be *written* in this order. The 'method' section might well be written before the final analysis of the results while all the details are fresh in the mind. The title and abstract are usually written last. It is a good idea to write up the experiment as soon as possible, before enthusiasm flags.

1 Title
Make this as specific as possible. A reader should be able to tell from the title if the experiment is likely to interest him. This is best done by making the title some statement of the experimental hypothesis. Example: E 18, 'Sex differences in driving speeds'. This experiment will be of interest to anyone studying sex differences in behaviour or factors affecting driving speeds. Both variables are in the title.

2 Abstract
This is a brief summary, one short paragraph, of the experiment and its findings. This will allow the reader, attracted by the title, to judge whether he need read further. He will want to know the essentials of the design, subjects and method, the results (whether or not significant) and any major conclusions. Keep it brief.

3 Introduction
This will give the background of your experiment, the problem you are tackling. This background will often consist of other experiments or theories tackling the same problem in various ways. These should be mentioned if they have some direct bearing on your experiment. They may, for example, predict a particular outcome to your experiment or use the same techniques in a different setting.

You may have done a considerable amount of reading around your problem. There is a natural temptation to display all this knowledge, relevant or not, as in a psychology essay. This should be resisted. Remember, your reader is a psychologist. He will be familiar with psychological terms and concepts and the general background of psychological knowledge. He may need information specific to your experiment to understand exactly the problem you are tackling.

Your experiment may be so original, or bizarre, that there is little or no background of experiments or theory. More likely you have simply been unable to find any. This is unavoidable if you do not have access to a university library. No matter. Explain the rationale behind the experiment in terms of the observations that led to your hypothesis. These often make the most interesting experiments.

The introduction should lead the reader to a statement of the experimental hypothesis.

4 Method

This section tells the reader exactly what you did. This will allow him to assess the results. Obviously it is impossible, and unnecessary, to include details of all the conditions of the experiment: the weather, what you had for breakfast, and so on. The criterion will be that a reader should be able to reproduce your experimental results. You *must* be satisfied that any conditions you omit had little or no effect on the results. It is unlikely that the breakfast of the experimenter affects the subject's behaviour; the weather may do so, as in E 18, on driving speeds. In this case the weather must be considered in the method. The method is usually divided under several headings.

(a) Design

Is the design causal or non-causal? The independent and dependent variables (or experimental variables) will be operationally defined with their method of measurement and any manipulation by the experimenter. Which subjects design was used – single subject, repeated measures, matched subjects or independent subjects? This section will describe the steps taken to remove constant errors (allocation of subjects to conditions, randomization, counterbalancing, placebos, etc.) and the control of any other variables.

(b) Subjects

How many subjects were used, how were they selected and from what population? It is essential that these details are given for the reader to assess the usefulness of the results. There is always a temptation to gild these accounts a little: four friends of the experimenter become ' a random sample of four'. Resist this, or better still don't use your friends.

Were the subjects naive? Were they misled? You must also report if any subjects were rejected from the original sample for whatever reason (if, for example, they spotted your deception).

(c) Apparatus and materials

The reader should be able to reproduce these exactly. Any commercially manufactured equipment (closed-circuit TV cameras, tape recorders, etc.) should be identified by the make and model number. If the equipment has been specially built for the experiment, details of the construction and function should be given (in an appendix if these are lengthy). The experimental set-up of equipment is best explained with a clearly labelled diagram.

Any stimuli used must be carefully defined with the details of presentation. For a visual stimulus give the distance, illumination, colour, etc. Where this varies from subject to subject you can give the broad range of conditions.

Examples of any stimuli in the form of word-lists, visual patterns, IQ and personality tests, etc., should be included, perhaps in an appendix.

(d)   Procedure

This section describes the step-by-step procedure of running the experiment. It will include the standard instructions given to the subjects and any rewards or punishments handed out. Any problems encountered in the experiment, and their solution, should be covered here.

Finally, this section is the place for anything that might affect the results that did not fit conveniently into any other section. Could the reader reproduce your experiment?

5 Results

These should be displayed as clearly as possible. This can be done in a number of ways: histograms, graphs, or tables of figures. Each should be understandable without searching in the surrounding text. If the means of two sets of scores are to be compared, these should be given below the scores. Report the type of statistical test used and the outcome. There is no need to show the details of the statistical tests, your reader will be well aware how to do a t-test, or whatever. (You may; however, wish to show off – just a little – to an examiner reading your report. It will help both of you to include the statistical analysis as an appendix at the end of the report.)

Was the test significant – if so, how significant? Give the probability of the null hypothesis. This outcome must then be interpreted in terms of the experimental hypothesis. This is the last step given in each of the worked examples.

This statement about the experimental hypothesis is the result of the experiment.

6 Discussion

You can consider what the results mean. What light do they throw on the theories discussed in the introduction? What is their relationship to other experiments in the same field? These questions will have been considered when you were designing the experiment. In a well-designed experiment the results should be unequivocal. A significant result means that there is a relationship between the experimental variables – provided there are no constant errors. If the results are not significant, is this because there is no experimental effect – or was an effect obscured by random error? You will have done your best to remove these doubts in the design but no design is perfect. Now is the time for a little self-flagellation. Identify any sources of error and their likely effect, with suggestions for improvement. Consider the subjects that circumstances forced on you. Does a small, biased sample restrict the usefulness of the results? Don't gloss over these design faults – your reader won't.

Finally, you will discuss the questions raised by your results and, perhaps, suggest experiments that could answer them. You could even do them yourself.

7 References

The reader may not be familiar with the previous experiments and theories mentioned in the introduction and discussion. This last section lists the sources of all this information. The references are to the authors and are listed alphabetically with the journal or book in which they appeared. The conventional format for each reference is:

(*a*) *for a paper in a journal:*
Author or authors
Date
Title of the paper (usually in inverted commas)
Name of the journal (this is often abbreviated)
Volume number of the journal
Page numbers

Example: Harlow, H. F. and Harlow, M. K. (1962), 'Social deprivation in monkeys', *Scientific American*, vol. 207, pp. 137–46.

(*b*) *for a book or chapter in a book:*
Author or authors
Date
Title of the book
Publisher
Page numbers, or chapter if necessary

Example: Lorenz, K. (1966), *On Aggression*, Methuen

Endless examples of these and minor variations will be found at the end of any book or journal article. You may wish to refer to other sources: TV programmes, films or newspapers. Try to shape the reference in a similar way and make it clear.

8 Appendices

This is the place for examples of any experimental materials that could not be fitted neatly into the text: word-lists, personality and IQ tests, construction details of special equipment and the details of the statistical tests. These might not be included in a psychological journal where space is pressing but you can afford the space. You have done all the work in these and you might as well use them. The reader can ignore them if he wishes.

All this is best typed and presented in a ring-backed folder. Typing does not add one jot or tittle to the value of the experiment but it does bring a certain professional air to the whole thing. (Could this be the birth of another experiment? – and so it goes on.)

Part II

Introduction

This part of the book is a collection of suggestions of hypotheses and experiments to test them. I hope it will soon prove completely redundant as you stumble across your own problems, formulate hypotheses and design suitable experiments. That is the aim of the book. The suggestions are divided into three sections, on the very rough basis of the time and effort needed for each.

1 Demonstrations

These can be done very quickly, perhaps in a matter of minutes, with little or no apparatus. They can be used for demonstrating and practising the various procedures of design and analysis covered in Part I. It is worth trying them out and using the results in the appropriate statistical test. Like any other experiment, each quick demonstration will raise other questions and hypotheses that can be tested, perhaps in a longer experiment. One or two such variations and elaborations are suggested for each demonstration.

2 Experiments

These are rather meatier than the demonstrations. In most cases they will take longer to set up and run; in some cases you will need to build or get hold of specialized apparatus. Most of this apparatus will be found in any college. If a piece of apparatus is not available it is always possible to get round the problem by changing the type of measurements taken or the design of the experiment.

Any of the suggestions in this section would be suitable for an A-level practical notebook. Each experiment has suggestions for variation and elaboration. A series of these can be followed up to form a more extensive study of a particular problem.

3 Investigations

This section looks at a couple of larger-scale studies: animal behaviour in zoos and developmental studies in schools. In both cases arrangements must be made beforehand with the zoo or school. Once there, it is worth making the most of the situation and carrying out a series of related experiments. With your limitations of time this is probably best done by a series of experimenters working on separate aspects of the behaviour and pooling the findings. Alternatively, arrangements could be made for a single experimenter to visit the school or zoo regularly over some time.

Of course, it is quite possible to tackle just one part of these suggested investigations as a single experiment.

Using the suggestions

The format of the suggested experiments roughly follows that of the experimental report (p. 152) with one or two differences.

The problem
This section is equivalent to the introduction of an experimental report. However, it is only intended to guide the reader to the general area of psychology involved. It is up to the reader to ferret around in the reading to find more detailed information and to decide what is relevant. This guidance is given in various ways. Where possible there is a reference to the associated textbook, *Understanding Psychology*. This reference is by the index heading in that book, enclosed in square brackets thus [perception: deprivation studies]. In this way the reference can be used with most general textbooks by using either the index or the contents. Ideally it should be used with at least two such textbooks: different authors will tackle the same problem in different ways.

There may also be a reference to a particular book or paper. These are often to be found in most general textbooks; look in their bibliography sections. The sources of all the references are given at the end of each experiment.

University libraries have other ways of tracking down lines of similar experiments through collections of abstracts, ordered by subject, and citation indexes. It is worthwhile getting the librarian to instruct you in the use of these.

Don't get bogged down in all of this. You have limited time, use it for the experiment. You will not be expected to produce the definitive review of work around the problem. You will be expected to understand what problem the experiment is designed to answer. The section ends with a statement of the experimental hypothesis.

A method
This follows the format of the experimental report, translating the hypothesis into practical details. Remember, the suggested experiment is one way to test the hypothesis; it is not the only way or even the best way. This suggested method can be used in several ways. It can be used as a step-by-step recipe for the experiment. You can simply follow the steps of the design, apparatus and procedure to get the results. Such slavish copying will not, of course, impress an examiner, who will be looking for originality, amongst other things, in your work.

The method can be used as an introduction to a series of experiments related to the suggested one. They will all share similar problems, perhaps use the same or similar apparatus and measurements. Some variations are suggested after each experiment, others will occur to you as you carry out the experiment.

The suggested method can be used as an example of all the bits and pieces covered in Part I. Go through the various parts of the method following how the hypothesis is translated into a detailed practicable experiment, taking account of errors, floor and ceiling effects, experimenter effects and so on.

Results and analysis
This section covers the collecting of the results and the selection of a suitable statistical test. There is usually a choice of tests with some guidance.

Variations
After each experiment there are two or three variations and elaborations. Some are given in detail, others just pose a question and leave the reader to formulate his own experiment.

In many designs the experimenter controls certain variables because he suspects that they may have a significant effect on the experimental variables. One obvious variation is to test this suspicion. Some variations can be done at the same time as the original experiment, for example, by collecting additional information from the subjects. It is worth thinking long and hard *before* you carry out an experiment whether you may need some other information later. On the one hand you don't want to have to gather a fresh lot of subjects and run the whole experiment again for one slight, but interesting, variation. On the other hand there is a tendency to collect reams of information on the off-chance that it might be useful at some time. This is irritating for the subjects and potentially confusing for you. The solution is to plan carefully the experiment and any obvious variations beforehand. As a further precaution, always get the subject's name and some sort of address. If the subject is a student his course number or department is usually enough to find him again in case an interesting variation occurs to you later on.

D 1   Measuring a visual illusion

The problem

Some research in visual perception suggests that a visual stimulus is detected by the receptors in the retina and subsequently coded in terms of the elements or parts of the stimulus; that is, the edges, corners, straight lines and so on. (See Hubel and Wiesel (1962) [physiological psychology: visual perception].) Other studies emphasize that we perceive in terms of meaningful wholes rather than in elements or parts [Gestalt psychology: perception]. These views are not necessarily antagonistic. However, we could ask to what extent it is possible to attend to just one part of a visual stimulus and ignore the rest if we wished.

In these two drawings the horizontal line is exactly the same length. The only difference is the addition of the arrow-heads.

37.

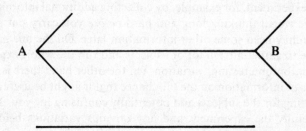

Is it possible to ignore these when judging the mid-point of the horizontal line?

The experimental hypothesis is that there is a difference in the perceived mid-point of the two horizontal lines.

A method

a) Design

Causal: The independent stimulus is the presence or absence of the arrow-heads on the figure. The experimenter can easily manipulate this variable and look for a consequent change in the dependent variable.

The dependent variable is the position of the perceived mid-point marked on the figure by the subject.

A repeated-measures design can be used. The order of presentation of the two figures is counterbalanced or randomized to avoid constant errors.

It may be that the subjects are inclined to perceive the mid-point, say, to the left in either figure. The direction of the arrow-heads should be randomized between subjects. The measurements of the mid-point will always be taken from the same end, say, the 'sharp' end, A. When A is to the left in the figure the position of the perceived mid-point in both figures is measured from the left.

b) Subjects

The main restriction is that their eyesight should be adequate for the task. You can satisfy yourself on this by giving them written instructions. This will also minimize any experimenter effect. There is evidence that the size of some visual illusions changes with age. Subjects could be restricted to a broad age-range, say, 15–45 years old. It is always safer to avoid subjects familiar with visual illusions.

c) Apparatus

This consists of the two figures, a straight line and the arrow figure derived from the Muller–Lyer visual illusion. The horizontal line of both figures is the same length. The figures are duplicated and a fresh pair presented to each subject.

Written instructions can also be duplicated.

d) Procedure

Each subject is given the written instructions. This will give you some idea of his normal reading distance. One figure is then presented at the same distance and the subject marks the mid-point of the horizontal line ignoring the arrow-heads (if any). The figure is removed and the procedure is repeated with the second figure. Subjects should not see anyone else's response.

The subject should, of course, be prevented from any means of measuring the mid-point, by marking off lengths on his pencil and so on.

Results

The positions of the perceived mid-points are measured from the same end of both figures. The difference (with sign) between these two measures is taken (d). This statistic is used in the statistical test.

Analysis (variables CD)
A t-test for related samples, a sign test or a Wilcoxon test can be used. A sign test is probably adequate for large sample sizes.

Variations

1 One variation of this experiment is explored in E 1. This experiment looks at one hypothesis put forward to account for the Muller–Lyer illusion.

2 I mentioned that the size of the illusion may change with age. This is explored in a developmental investigation in schools, I 1c.

3 This experiment can also be used to investigate conformity. This is explored in E 15.

References

Hubel, D.H. and Wiesel, T.N. (1962), 'Receptive fields, binocular interaction and functional architecture in the cat's visual cortex', *J. Physiol.*, vol. 160, 106–54

Index guide: visual illusions; perception; Gestalt psychology

Arm folding

	Right	Left
Right		
Left		

Hand preference

Hand clasping

	Right	Left
Right		
Left		

Hand preference

After a little experience, a glance at the frequencies in such a contingency table will tell you if it is worth carrying on with the chi-squared test.

2 At what age are these preferences established? You will need to have access to children at various ages, in a nursery school or a playgroup. You must come up with an operational definition of an *established* preference. With your children it may be sufficient to ask them to try the other position; they may be unable to do this without help.

D 3   Accuracy in dart throwing with the preferred and non-preferred hand

The problem

Most people prefer to use a particular hand for skilled tasks, e.g. writing or dealing cards. This preference includes much larger actions: throwing a ball or holding a tennis racket. Certainly doing any of these tasks with the non-preferred hand *feels* very clumsy – but is there a large difference in performance between the two hands? Many people will claim that they cannot throw a dart with the non-preferred hand, let alone aim the thing. We can test this hypothesis that there is a difference in accuracy of dart throwing between the two hands.

A method

a) Design

Non-casual: We cannot manipulate which of the two hands is preferred, one of the experimental variables. The other variable is the accuracy of the throw measured as the distance the dart lands from the target aimed at.

One difficulty in this experiment is that the subject has very strong expectations of the results – that is why he prefers one hand to the other for dart throwing. It is important that the subjects are attempting to be as accurate as possible with both hands. One solution is to test groups of subjects, all using the same hand, preferred or non-preferred, in a competition. Ideally the subject should be unaware of the result of each throw to ensure independence. This may be unnecessary if each subject in a group of, say, five throws only one dart on each turn. This will minimize any readjustment of aim from one throw to the next.

A repeated-measures design is used. Each subject makes ten throws with one hand; the mean of these ten scores is taken as the score for that hand.

b) Subjects

An obvious source of variation in the scores is the dart throwing experience of the subjects. All of this will be with the preferred hand. It is possible to restrict the sample to subjects of similar dart-throwing experience. Perhaps a better solution is to use an unfamiliar throwing height and distance; the target could be at a height of 5 feet and a distance of 7 feet. This will negate much of the skill acquired through long practice.

c) Apparatus
A target and some darts; a dartboard is not essential. A piece of paper, with a central target spot, fixed to a pin-board will give a permanent record of the throws. This could be replaced after each subject has thrown one dart, to minimize any adjustment of aim on the basis of the previous throw.

d) Procedure
Several subjects are asked to take part in a dart-throwing competition using first, say, the non-preferred hand (this order will be counterbalanced for the next group). Each subject throws one dart at the target spot. The hole made by the dart is marked with the subject's initials. After all the subjects have thrown, the paper is replaced. This procedure is repeated until each subject has had ten throws.

   The whole procedure is repeated with the other hand.

Results

For each subject: the experimenter measures the distance of each throw (i.e. the hole made by the dart) from the target, for the non-preferred hand. The mean of these distances is the non-preferred hand score. The preferred hand score is found in the same way. The difference (with sign) between these two scores is the statistic (d) used in the statistical test.

Analysis (variables CD)
A sign test or a Wilcoxon test (if the differences are ranked) is suitable. There is some reason to believe that there is a considerable difference in the variance of scores of either hand. You may not be able to use the parametric t-test.

Variations

1   Much of the difference in the scores with the preferred hand will be the result of different amounts of practice. There should be little or no difference in practice with the non-preferred hand.

   There could be a transfer of skill from one hand to the other. Is there a relationship between scores on the preferred hand and on the non-preferred hand? That is, do subjects who throw well with one hand throw well with the other? The same scores can be used to detect any correlation between the dart-throwing skill of the two hands.

38. *Scattergram of dart throwing accuracy for the preferred and non-preferred hand.*

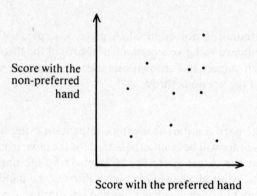

Score with the non-preferred hand

Score with the preferred hand

A rank-order or product-moment correlation is found between the scores on both hands. Is this significant? Any such correlation could be the result of subject differences in hand and eye coordination affecting the dart throwing of both hands.

2 There are many other skills that require good hand and eye coordination. In some of these the subject cannot always *choose* which hand to use. For example, when catching a ball with one hand. Is there a difference in performance between hands on such a task? Is the clumsy feel of the non-preferred hand the result of differences in practice or a real difference in potential?

Index guide: skill; hand preference

D 4   Decision times in a card-sorting task

The problem

Many tasks consist of responding appropriately to a stimulus. When driving a car the driver sees an amber traffic light. He must decide on an appropriate response – to dash through it or slow down – and then make the response. In this case the decision will be based on many variables: the other traffic, the presence of a policeman, the car's speed, the condition of the car and the road, how late he is and so on. Psychologists interested in these mental processes often use the speed of making such a decision to investigate the processes involved. The task is usually fairly simple to reduce the number of variables and allow these to be controlled. The technique is to present the subject with a stimulus, say a playing card. The subject decides whether the card is, say, red or black and makes an appropriate response. The experimenter can now vary the required response in some way whilst keeping the decision the same. Any difference in the subject's reaction time, from the presentation of the stimulus until the response is completed, must be the result of the difference in the response.

Similarly, the experimenter changes the decision keeping the response the same. Now the differences in the reaction time are the result of differences in the type of decision, the internal processes, required by the task.

In the laboratory the stimulus is presented by a tachistoscope which can accurately time the period between presentation and response. An alternative and cheaper technique is to accumulate a series of such presentations, decisions and responses, measuring the time for the whole series with an ordinary stopwatch. This technique will be used to investigate differences in deciding whether a playing card is 'red or black' and 'odd or even'.

The hypothesis is that the time taken to sort the pack of cards into two piles will depend on the decision required.

A method

a) Design
Causal: The independent variable is the decision required in the card sorting. In one condition the subject sorts the cards into red cards and black cards. In the other condition he sorts the cards into odd numbers and even numbers.

You can use a repeated-measures or single-subject design. Ideally a combination of the two is used. A single subject performs both card-sorting tasks several times. There are likely to be some order effects as the subject becomes more skilled in handling the cards; the order of the two sorting tasks is counterbalanced or randomized. He performs equal numbers of both tasks and the mean sorting time under both conditions is found. You can take the results of this single subject and look for a significant difference in the means, using a t-test for independent samples.

In a repeated-measures design each subject performs under both conditions of the IV. In this experiment we can use the mean score of the subject under each condition. The difference between these means is found for each subject and used in the t-test for related samples.

b) Subjects
There are no special restrictions. I suppose the ability to shuffle cards without getting them all over the floor is a useful qualification.

c) Apparatus
A pack of playing cards. Remove all the picture cards, the tens and the nines, leaving the ace to eight of each suit.

You will need some form of stopwatch. The shrewd reader will have discovered that I am all in favour of modern calculators. Many of these have sophisticated stopwatch functions; these will serve the purpose nicely.

d) Procedure
The pack of 32 cards is well shuffled. The subject holds the pack face down in one hand and takes one card at a time with the other. He looks at the card, decides whether it is red or black and places it on the table in front of him, red cards to the right and black cards to the left. He picks the next card from the pack and so on. The experimenter measures the time taken to sort the whole pack.

The subject is asked to sort the whole pack as quickly as he can, making no mistakes. It is important that the same instructions are given to each subject. The performance may vary with the emphasis placed on speed or avoiding mistakes (see variation 4).

The procedure is exactly the same for the other condition. Odd cards are placed to the left, even cards to the right. Each subject sorts the pack several times under each condition.

Results

Find the mean sorting time for each subject under the two conditions. The difference between these two means (d) is the statistic used in the statistical test.

Analysis (variables CD)

Use a t-test for related samples. Alternatively the differences (d) can be ranked and used in a Wilcoxon test. A quick idea of the significance will be given by the sign test.

Variations

There must be thousands of variations on this simple card-sorting experiment. The problem is to decide which variations can gradually unravel the variables affecting the speed of sorting. In these variations one line of investigation is followed; many other hypotheses can be followed in the same way.

1 In the original experiment the decisions for each of the 32 cards were either of colour (black or red) or of number (odd or even). In either case the set of possible stimuli was the same, the 32 cards in the pack. There is a difference when we consider the features the subject uses to sort the cards. When sorting by colour there are only two possibilities, red or black. When sorting by number there are eight possibilities, the numbers one to eight. Is this discrepancy the cause of the differences in sorting time?

In this variation both conditions require the subject to sort by number. In one condition the subject sorts odds and evens as before. In the other condition he sorts 'four and under' and 'five and over'. As the same feature is used in both conditions we might predict that sorting times will be the same. Is this the case?

2 We will assume that you find a difference in sorting time in the first variation. Why? A possible hypothesis is the different requirements for accuracy in distinguishing the numbers. For example, a number 2 is turned up. Under the 'odds and evens' condition the numbers either side of number 2 fall into a different category in the sorting task. A general impression of the number from a first glance at the spots is not enough. In the other condition the numbers either side of number 2 fall into the same category in the sorting task; a general impression, 'lowish' or 'highish', may be sufficient except in the case of numbers 4 and 5.

We can test this hypothesis. The experimenter uses two identical packs. From these he makes up two experimental packs of 32 cards each. One contains the numbers 1, 2, 7 and 8; the other contains the numbers 3, 4, 5 and 6. The task is to sort both packs into '4 and under' and '5 and over'.

The hypothesis predicts faster sorting times with the first pack. Is this the case?

3   In the experiment and its variations above the pack of cards is sorted into two equal piles. The probability of any one card being of one particular sort is more or less 0.5. Does this probability affect the sorting speed?

In this variation the proportion of reds in the pack is varied; the subject is told the proportion on any trial. The experimenter is looking for a relationship between sorting speed and the proportion of reds in the pack. This proportion can be varied from 1 (all reds) to 0 (no reds).

The relationship, if any, between this proportion and sorting speeds will not be monotonic. We will expect the fastest speeds to be for proportions around 1 and 0 with slower times in between. A simple correlation is unsuitable for measuring this relationship. The experimenter gets round this problem by considering the proportion of reds in the pack in two ranges: from 1 to 0.5, and from 0.5 to 0. Each range is correlated with sorting speed.

4   It was suggested in the original experiment that the instructions to the subject could give rise to variation in the sorting speed by emphasizing the need for speed or avoiding mistakes. The subjects may be able to 'trade' speed for accuracy. This can be tested by varying the instructions to the subjects. In one condition the subjects are instructed: 'Go as fast as you can and try not to make any mistakes.' In the other condition they are instructed: 'Go as fast as you can but make absolutely sure you make no mistakes.' Will this difference in instructions produce different sorting speeds? In this case an independent-subjects design or a matched-subjects design must be used.

Index guide: reaction time; choice reaction time; information theory

D 5　Sex differences in numerical and linguistic abilities

The problem

The differences between men and women are a perennial source of interest to men and women. Sex differences in *non*-sexual behaviour have been the cause of endless argument, particularly in recent decades. Traditionally men and women have behaved differently, taken different roles in the family, done different jobs and so on. Are these differences in behaviour the result of socialization alone or of innate differences in ability? Men have supposed themselves superior in logical thought; the vast majority of mathematicians and philosophers have been men. This could be the result of a monopoly of education and opportunity. Perhaps, but then we might expect a similar dominance in all intellectual pursuits. This is not the case: women have always held a prominent place in literature. These differences in career may or may not be based on differences in potential.

Many tests have been designed to measure intellectual abilities, the various IQ tests being the best known and widely used [intelligence: testing]. IQ tests are designed to measure reasoning ability in various forms: linguistic, numerical, visual/spatial, etc., and sex differences have been found in these abilities. Typically, males score higher in numerical ability, females score higher in linguistic ability. This experiment examines these differences.

Most A-level and degree courses require certain entry qualifications, usually in terms of O- or A-level passes. This is very handy. We will assume that all the students on such a course fall into a broad ability range; within this range we can look for differences in the performance on two simple tests. Linguistic ability we shall measure (and so operationally define) by performance on a form of the Wisconsin Verbal Fluency test. Numerical ability is measured by the speed of counting backwards in sevens from some arbitrary number. These tests rely on the *use* of the numbers or words rather than mathematical or linguistic knowledge. In effect we have two experiments: sex differences in numerical ability, and in linguistic ability.

The experimental hypotheses are that females will score higher than males on linguistic tests, males will score higher on numerical tests.

A method

a) Design

Non-causal: One experimental variable is the sex of the subject. The other is the subject's performance on either the linguistic or the numerical test.

An independent-subjects design is used: subjects can hardly be male and female (see 'Subjects').

b) Subjects

Ideally the subjects should be of similar overall intelligence. For the purpose of this simple experiment a group of students on some course is used, assuming you have some handy. The course entry qualifications will restrict the range of overall abilities somewhat. In a more elaborate experiment a matched-subjects design could be used, male and female subjects being matched by IQ.

c) Apparatus

For linguistic ability: Each subject needs a sheet of paper and a pencil. The experimenter needs a clock.

For numerical ability: The experimenter needs a stopwatch (a clock with a second hand will do at a pinch) *or* as for linguistic ability.

d) Procedure

Linguistic ability: The subjects are tested all together provided they can be trusted not to cheat. The experimenter explains that they will be given a letter of the alphabet. The task is to write down as many four-letter words, beginning with this letter, as possible in, say, four minutes. There should be no proper names; a small dictionary can be used to judge the validity of any dubious slang. Two words that sound alike can be used but a word that has two meanings cannot be used twice. A three-letter noun plus 's' to form a plural cannot be used but a part of a verb ending in 's' can. So, 'asks' is allowed but 'ants' is not; 'bats' or 'dogs' can be used as they are parts of verbs as well.

The experimenter starts the clock as he gives the letter to the subjects (popular consonants, m, b, p, t, etc., are the best).

At the end of four minutes the subjects can check each other's lists for repetitions – surprisingly easy to make – and dubious words. The score is the number of words the subject lists.

Numerical ability: Each subject is asked to count aloud, backwards in sevens. So, if the subject starts at 398, he counts '391, 384, 377' and so on. A different three-digit number is taken from the table of random numbers for each subject. He is asked to count twenty numbers as quickly as possible; his score is the time taken to do this. The experimenter checks for mistakes (if he can keep up).

If there is a large number of subjects and time is limited they can be tested together. They are all asked to count backwards, quietly, from some three-digit number for, say, 100 seconds. At each number in the sequence they make a pencil stroke on a piece of paper; the score is the number of strokes they record in 100 seconds. Again, they must be trusted not to cheat.

Results

The scores are collected and the mean score for males and females is calculated for each test.

Analysis (variables CD)

A t-test for independent samples can be used to look for a significant sex difference in the mean scores on either test. Alternatively, the scores can be ranked and the non-parametric Mann-Whitney test used. Note that in the first version of the numerical test a *low* score shows high numerical ability. In the second version high scores show high ability, as in the linguistic test.

Variations

1   In some courses (e.g. Psychology A-level) the entry qualifications may not stipulate the subject of the O-level passes. A quick analysis of O-level successes and failures may reveal a sex difference. In this case the numerical and linguistic abilities are measured discretely; a chi-squared test is used to test the association of sex and specific ability.

  For linguistic ability:

39.   English O-level

	Passed	Failed
Males		
Females		

  For numerical ability:

                    Maths O-level

	Passed	Failed
Males		
Females		

If a large number of subjects have both English and Maths O-level then the grades of their passes can be compared. All subjects are asked to record in which subject, Maths or English, they got the higher grade. Subjects with equal grades are discarded:

40.

Higher O-level grade

	Maths	English
Males		
Females		

2 Life is unfair. Although there may be some differences in specific abilities it often appears that individuals who are depressingly good in one subject are also depressingly good in others. Is this true for performance on the linguistic and numerical tests used in this experiment? Each subject performs both tests and the scores are compared. Remember that an association of ability in the two tests will result in a *negative* correlation if the first version of the numerical test is used.

Index guide: sex differences; intelligence tests; numerical ability; linguistic ability

D 6 Associations of number and colour

The problem

Some people associate particular colours with numbers, particularly the first few integers. For example, I imagine the number four to be brown; I am prepared to admit that it might be seen as red but I cannot understand how anyone could see it as green or blue. There are two questions we can ask: does everyone have these associations? Among the people who do, is there any agreement on which number has which colour? Both questions can be examined in a quick demonstration. A subject is asked to assign a colour to each of the first seven integers. The subject will find some difficulty doing this if he has no associations between colour and number – the task makes no sense. The hypothesis is that among people who can carry out this task there is a regular association between particular colours and numbers.

A method

a) Design
Non-causal: One experimental variable is the numbers the subject is given. The other experimental variable is the colour he associates with each number. An independent-subjects design is used.

b) Subjects
Initially there are no restrictions. Some subjects may report that they have no associations between number and colour.

c) Apparatus
An instruction sheet is given to each subject. This will include the list of colours. For seven integers I suggest the seven colours: black, white, brown, red, green, yellow, blue.

The number of colours and integers will depend on the number of subjects available – see 'Results and analysis'.

d) Procedure

The experiment can be run as a questionnaire but it may be simpler to use a group of subjects and collect their responses then and there. Under each number the subject writes the most appropriate colour selected from the list. No colour is to be used twice. The experimenter collects the score sheets.

Results and analysis (variables DD)

Each colour is considered separately. For example, red could be associated with the numbers in the following distribution:

Integer	1	2	3	4	5	6	7	total
No. of associations with red	0	5	7	3	8	4	1	28

The null hypothesis predicts that red will be equally associated with all seven integers. The expected value for each integer will be $28/7 = 4$. A chi-squared test of goodness of fit is used. For safety the expected value should not be less than 5 for any contingency. This experiment, then, requires $(5 \times 7 =)$ 35 subjects. The number of integers and colours can be reduced if there are fewer subjects.

The associations of the other colours are treated in the same way.

Variations

1 A similar experiment can investigate associations of colour and days of the week. Where subjects associate colours with days of the week *and* numbers, is the sequence of colours the same for the days and the numbers?

2 Are any of the subjects aware of the origins of their own colour associations? Such introspections are a legitimate and valuable, if non-quantitative, part of psychological investigation.

Index guide: colour associations

D 7 Meaning in short-term memory of words

The problem

The ability to store and recall information over short periods, less than a minute or so, depends on many factors [short-term memory]. These factors are not necessarily the same as those affecting longer-term storage [long-term memory]. This quick experiment looks at one variable in short-term memory, the semantic organization of the items to be remembered. This is a well-established factor in long-term memory (for example, see Bower, Clarke, Lesgold and Winzenz, 1969).

In this experiment the subject is asked to memorize a list of 10 words. In one condition the 10 words are arranged in a sentence, in the other condition they are ordered randomly. The hypothesis is that more words will be remembered in the first condition.

A method

a) Design

Causal: The independent variable is the order of the words in the list, whether random or forming an intelligible sentence. The dependent variable is the subject's memory of the words in the list. This can be measured in three ways.

1 In **ordered recall** only words recalled in their original order are scored as correct.

2 In **free recall** the words can be recalled in any order.

3 In **recognition** the subject is taken through a list of, say, 30 words. The subject states whether each word was in the original list.

Any of these methods can be used. I suggest that the results of all three measurements are compared. For the sake of this demonstration I will use free-recall measurements.

A repeated-measures design cannot be used as the order effect, using the same 10 words, would be enormous. Use an independent or matched-subjects design.

b) Subjects
There are no special restrictions. Half the subjects are given the words as a sentence, half as a random list.

c) Apparatus
The list of words can be taken from any non-technical book. Find a ten-letter sentence with no repeated words. The order is randomized using the random number tables; assign a number to each word and note the order in which the numbers occur in the table.

Some form of stopwatch is used to time the period between perception and recall.

d) Procedure
The experiment is explained to the subject. He will be given a list of 10 words to study for five seconds. The list is removed and the subject counts backwards in 3s from some three-digit number for 30 seconds. The counting is done aloud to prevent the subject repeating the words to himself. The experimenter then asks the subject to recall any of the words from the list. The storage interval (30 seconds) can be altered to avoid any floor or ceiling effects (p. 134).

Results and analysis (variables CD)

The mean score of subjects under the two conditions is calculated. A t-test for independent samples is used to find the significance of the difference in the means.

Variations

1   We have used one measure of memory – free recall. We could argue that more words are recalled from the sentence because the sentence structure aids the recall itself rather than the actual storage of the items. If this is so we might expect the difference to lessen or disappear using the *recognition* measurement.

2   Is there any pattern to the words that are forgotten in the random list? There are several possibilities. The position of the word in the list may affect the ability to remember that word. Are words best remembered at the beginning, middle or end of the list? The type of word itself may be important. Are nouns and verbs easier to remember than common conjunctions?

References

Bower, G.H., Clarke, M.C., Lesgold, A.M. and Winzenz, D. (1969), 'Hierarchical retrieval schemes in recall of categorized word lists', *J. Verbal Learning and Verbal Behaviour*, vol. 8, 323–43

Index guide: long-term memory; short-term memory; meaning; recall

D 8 Estimating distances: close to home and distant

The problem

I was brought up in Hertfordshire, some 25 miles from London. It seemed a long way. I moved north with my job and found that my perspectives of distance had changed; my old home seemed very close to London. This does not appear to be just the result of growing up in a place. I consistently underestimate the distance between two places if they are both some distance away. As a simple example, how long is the Red Sea? You might be surprised at the answer. This interesting question of our perception of geography relative to ourselves is considered by Gould and White in their book *Mental Maps* (1974).

The hypothesis for this experiment is simple: a person's concept of distance changes as the distance from the person increases. The subject is asked to estimate two distances:

1 The distance between two towns close to his own home.
2 The distance between two towns, both more than 150 miles from his home but in the British Isles.

A method

a) Design

Causal: The independent variable is the distance of the pair of towns from the subject's home. In the first condition, close to home, one of the two towns can be the home town of the subject. In the second condition, distant towns in the British Isles, the distance between the two towns should be similar to the first condition. The dependent variable is the subject's estimate of the distance between each pair of towns.

A repeated-measures design is used.

b) Subjects

There are no special restrictions. The subjects should have at least some idea of where the towns are. For the sake of this demonstration it will be simple if all the subjects come from the same home town or area so that the same four towns can be used throughout the experiment.

c) Apparatus

A road atlas in the form of several maps covering the British Isles is ideal. The experimenter can point out the positions of the two distant towns without allowing a direct comparison with the two near towns.

d) Procedure

The subject is asked to estimate the distance, *in a straight line*, between a pair of towns. The order of the two pairs is counterbalanced. The experimenter checks that the subject knows where the two near towns are. He points out the position of the two distant towns on a map that does not cover either of the near towns.

Results

Find the percentage error, with sign, for each estimate. Give underestimates a minus sign. For each subject, find the difference, with sign, between these percentage errors for the distant and near towns. This is the statistic d used in the analysis.

Analysis (variables CD)

A Wilcoxon test or a sign test can be used. It might be safer to avoid a t-test as there is likely to be a considerable difference in the variances of estimates in the near and distant conditions.

Variations

1   The experiment can be extended by including distances between places in other continents, for example, between towns in the USA. Again these should be pointed out on a map by the experimenter. Use as large a scale map as possible to avoid the distortions of the map projection. On the other hand you could ask subjects to estimate distances within their home town.

2   Are these cognitive distances affected by political or physical barriers? That is, do distances within one country appear less than distances crossing a border? This border can be physical or political. Paris, for example, is closer to both Amsterdam and Bristol than it is to Bordeaux or Brest. Is it so in our mental

maps? When investigating this problem, beware of asking the direct question, 'Which is closer to Paris – Bristol or Bordeaux?' In the experience of many people the *least* likely answer is often correct in such a conundrum. Ask for estimates of distances, possibly mixing the two you are interested in among several you are not.

You could compare the results of such an experiment against one asking the direct question, 'Which is closer . . .?' This may reveal the lure of the paradox mentioned above.

References

Gould, P. and White, R. (1974), *Mental Maps*, Penguin Books

D 9   Occupational status

The problem

Most human societies, and many animal societies, have an unequal distribution of status among the members. That is, individuals in the society are given different amounts of respect and prestige by the others in the society. An individual's status will be determined by many factors depending on the society in question. In a group of pig-tailed monkeys the important determinants of status are age and sex. The highest status individual in this group is usually an old male. He may lose this position when ill-health or old age allows a stronger pig-tailed monkey to challenge successfully for this position. Strength and courage, then, are other factors.

In humans the determinants of social status can vary from one society to another. They can be relatively simple as in the hereditary caste system of India where an individual's social status was largely determined by the status of his parents. They can be a subtle mixture of wealth, parentage, education, behaviour and several other ingredients.

Social status is an elusive quality. In the end it is determined by how we regard and behave towards one another. The 'rules' determining social status are carried in our heads. The experiment looks at one possible factor affecting social status in modern British society – an individual's occupation.

The hypothesis is that people can assign status positions to individuals about whom only one thing is known – their job. The subject is asked to rank various occupations according to social status. If the task makes sense to the subject we will suspect that occupation is a factor in social status. The hypothesis also suggests that the subjects will order the occupations similarly.

A method

a)   Design
Causal: The independent variable is the occupation of the imaginary person. We will use six different occupations (see 'Results and analysis'), for example: shop

assistant, plumber, teacher, doctor, building labourer, postman. The order of these six occupations is randomized using the random number tables.

The dependent variable is the subject's ordering of these occupations. A repeated-measures design is used; that is, all the subjects are asked to order all six occupations.

b) Subjects
There are no special restrictions. There is always a danger of biased sampling when using a small sample. In a quick demonstration you cannot hope to get anything like a representative sample. You will need at least thirty subjects if six occupations are used (see 'Results and analysis').

c) Apparatus
A response sheet for each subject.

d) Procedure
The experimenter gives each subject the list of occupations (this can be done as a group to save time). The subject is asked to order the occupations by social status, giving rank 1 to the occupation with the highest status.

Note whether any of the subjects find the task nonsensical.

Results and analysis (variables DD)

Treat each occupation separately. Record the frequency of the various ranks for that occupation. This is compared to the frequency expected on the null hypothesis, using chi-squared as a test of goodness of fit. If the six occupations were ranked randomly, the expected frequency in each rank would be:

$$\frac{\text{Total number of observations (i.e. subjects)}}{\text{Number of ranks}}$$

The chi-squared test is unreliable if the expected frequency in any rank falls below 5. So, you will need at least thirty subjects for six occupations. If you don't have thirty subjects, reduce the number of occupations. The other occupations are treated in the same way. Do the subjects agree significantly on the order of status in the six occupations? Compare their overall order with the Registrar General's classification of occupations.

Variations

1   The six occupations used in the experiment are fairly well established. A new occupation must find its niche in the status ladder we clutter our heads with. We might expect a greater variation in status positions given to, say, a pop star or a professional sportsman (e.g. a tennis player). Both of these are occupations of relatively young people. Does their status position depend on the age of the subject ordering the list? A list of occupations containing one or both of these occupations is given to two groups of subjects, one of subjects below 25 years of age, the other of subjects over 40 years of age. A chi-squared test is used to look for an association between age and the assigning of status to youthful occupations.

2   There are many other factors associated with status in our society (see also E 11).

References

The Registrar General's classification of occupations can be found in most general textbooks of sociology.

Index guide: status; social class; occupational status

D 10   Extra-sensory perception

The problem

In recent years there has been much research into the supposedly supernatural powers of human brains. Certainly, brains are staggering enough in dealing with the normal processes of perception, memory, imagination and so forth. These processes have one great limitation: they are only available to the owner of the brain. Normally we can only receive information about these thought processes of other minds through the physical senses of vision, hearing, touch, etc. Many people have claimed, however, that these thought processes can be transmitted and received directly from one mind to another – so-called extra-sensory perception (ESP). One person looks at, say, a playing card; a second person becomes aware of the card the first is perceiving. If this sounds unlikely (and it does to me) it is worth considering how radio and television transmission might appear to someone from the last century. If such extra-sensory perception is possible the potential is staggering.

In this simple experiment we can test the hypothesis that a visual perception by one subject is available to a second subject. The first subject tosses a coin and observes the result. The second subject, unable to see the coin or the other subject, must guess the result of each toss of the coin.

A method

a)   Design

Non-causal: One of the experimental variables is the first subject's (the transmitter's) perception of the coin face. The other experimental variable is the second subject's (the receiver's) guess – or perception – of the same coin face.

A single-subject design is used. One pair of subjects is used for a large number of trials.

49911

b) Subjects
There are no special restrictions. The experimenter must rely on the integrity of the subjects: there is much opportunity for skulduggery in all ESP experiments. If ESP does occur it may well be that there are good and bad receivers and transmitters, or that a particular pair of subjects will succeed where either paired with another subject will fail. I haven't the slightest notion what would constitute a potentially successful pair. Perhaps subjects should choose their own partners.

c) Apparatus
An ordinary coin is tossed by the transmitter. Both subjects have a score sheet for recording their perceptions.

d) Procedure
The subjects sit back to back. The transmitter tosses a coin in the air calling 'Now'. He catches the coin and concentrates on the coin face for five seconds. The receiver records his guess of the coin face on his score sheet and calls 'Ready'. The transmitter then records the coin face on his score sheet. This is done after the receiver to prevent the receiver hearing any difference in the strokes of the transmitter's pencil. The transmitter calls 'Now' and tosses the coin for a second trial. The experimental effect, if any, is likely to be very small. A large number of trials can be run with each pair.

Results and analysis (variables DD)

The coin face recorded by the transmitter and the receiver for each trial can be compared in a 2×2 chi-squared test of association.

	Transmitter's perception	
	Heads	Tails
Receiver's guess — Heads		
Receiver's guess — Tails		

Alternatively, each trial can be scored as 'same' or 'different' if the subjects' coin faces agree or not. These scores are then compared to chance scores using chi-squared as a test of goodness of fit or a sign test. The hypothesis predicts that there will be more 'same' scores than 'different' scores and so a one-tailed test can be used.

The real value of this demonstration lies in considering the significance level used in the statistical tests. If twenty pairs of subjects are used we might expect at least one pair to score above the 5% (one in twenty) significance level by chance alone. The significance level is arbitrary. We may wish to set a higher significance level before accepting the phenomenon of ESP.

Variations

1 If the demonstration gives no evidence of ESP we might ask what prompts the receiver to call one face or the other. The result of each toss of the coin is random. The probability of a head occurring after a run of, say, four heads is still 0.5. However, there may be a tendency in the receiver to balance the number of heads and tails reported. This will be detected in a tendency to alternate responses, with few sequences of the same face being reported. Is this prediction supported or does the receiver show a bias to one face or pattern of faces? The frequency of sequences of heads or tails in the receiver's guesses can be compared with the expected frequencies of such sequences using chi-squared as a test of goodness of fit.

Index guide: parapsychology; extra-sensory perception

E 1   Testing a theory of visual illusion

The problem

The Muller–Lyer figures are a familiar visual illusion:

41.

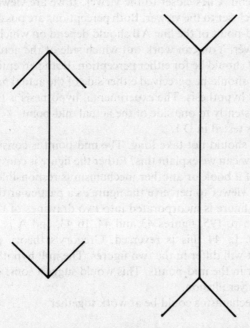

The two vertical lines are the same length although the left one appears much smaller. One theory put forward to account for this illusion, by Gregory (1966) in his book *Eye and Brain*, suggests that the two figures are interpreted by the perceptual system as three-dimensional objects [perception: set in hypothesis testing]. The left-hand figure is seen as the *outside* corner of an object (e.g. a building):

the vertical line is the nearest part to the viewer. The right-hand figure is seen as the *inside* corner of an object (e.g. a room): the vertical line is the farthest part from the viewer. The two equal lines are seen as being at different distances from the viewer and hence are perceived as having different lengths through the mechanism of perceptual constancies.

How does this theory cope with the modified Muller-Lyer figure used in D 1 (figure 37). This could be perceived as, say, an open book. If we are viewing the

42.

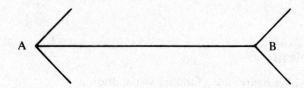

inside of the book, end A lies closer to the viewer. If we are viewing the *outside* of the book, end B lies closer to the viewer. Both perceptions are possible. The position of the perceived mid-point of the line AB should depend on which end is perceived as closer to the viewer. You can work out which side of the actual mid-point the perceived mid-point should lie for either perception. Both perceptions seem equally likely so mid-points should be perceived either side of the actual mid-point. We will take this as the null hypothesis. The experimental hypothesis is that the perceived mid-point lies consistently to one side of the actual mid-point.

This hypothesis is tested in D 1.

Carry out D 1; it should not take long. The mid-point is consistently perceived nearer to end B. How can we explain this? Either the figure is consistently perceived as, say, the *inside* of a book or another mechanism is responsible for the illusion.

We can force the viewer to perceive the figure as a particular three-dimensional interpretation. The figure is incorporated into two drawings of three-dimensional objects as shown on p. 195, figures 43 and 44. In 43, end A is further from the viewer than end B. In 44 this is reversed. Gregory's theory predicts that the perceived mid-point will differ in the two figures. The null hypothesis is that there will be no difference in the mid-points. This would suggest some other mechanism causes the Muller-Lyer illusion.

Of course, two mechanisms could be at work together.

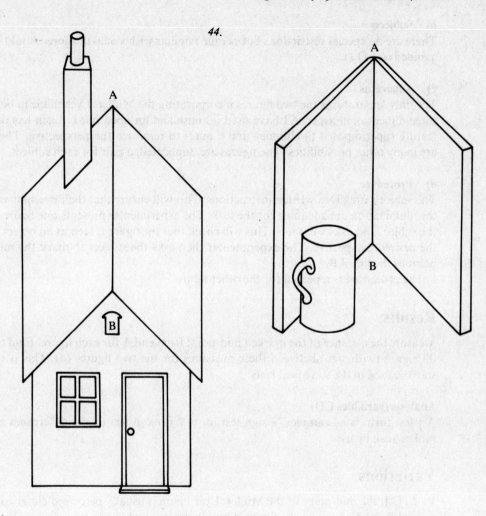

A method

a) Design

Causal: The independent variable is the figure presented to the subject. The dependent variable is the position of the perceived mid-point of the line AB on either figure. The position is always measured from the same end.

A repeated-measures design is suitable but, as usual, you should assess the size of any order effect in a pilot study and counterbalance or randomize the order of presentation to prevent constant errors.

b) Subjects
There are no special restrictions but people familiar with visual illusions should be avoided (see D 1).

c) Apparatus
The only apparatus is the two figures incorporating the Muller–Lyer shape in both three-dimensional aspects. I have used a house and an open book. Each has one feature superimposed (a chimney and a mug) to reinforce the perspective. There are many other possibilities. The figures are duplicated, a pair for each subject.

d) Procedure
The subjects are given written instructions. This will ensure that their eyesight and the illumination are adequate for the task. The experimenter presents one figure to the subject and asks what it is. This will check that the figure is seen as an object in the desired perspective. The experimenter then asks the subject to mark the mid-point of the line AB.

    The procedure is repeated for the other figure.

Results

Measure the distance of the marked mid-point from end A for each figure. Find the difference (with sign) between these measures for the two figures (d). This is the statistic used in the statistical tests.

Analysis (variables CD)
A t-test for related samples, a sign test, or a Wilcoxon test (if the differences are ranked) can be used.

Variations

1   In D 1, the mid-point of the Muller–Lyer figure is usually perceived closer to end B. Is this because the figure is usually interpreted in one way, as, say, the inside of a book?

      If you study the following figure

45.

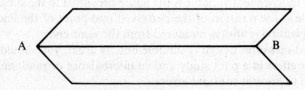

it occasionally appears to switch from one perception, say the inside of a book, to the other, the outside of a book. We could measure the amount of time a subject has either perception.

The subject is asked to look at the centre of the figure. The experimenter explains that the figure can be perceived as a three-dimensional object in two ways and checks that the subject does so. The amount of time the subject has each perception can be measured with two electric clocks connected to a power supply via a two-pole switch.

46.

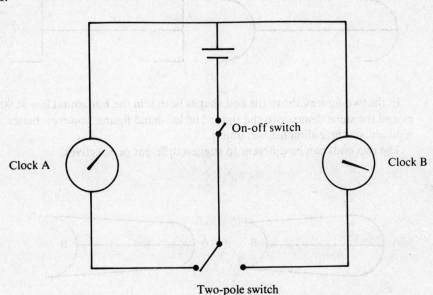

Two-pole switch

The subject is instructed to push the switch to the right when he has one perception and to the left for the other perception. The experimenter switches on the power supply and the clocks record the total amount of time spent in each perception over one minute, when the experimenter switches off the power supply.

The subject is then asked to mark the centre of the line AB (as in D 1).

The perspective theory predicts that subjects who mark the mid-point closer to B will perceive the figure predominantly as, say, the inside of a book; subjects who mark the mid-point closer to A should perceive the figure predominantly as the outside of a book. This prediction can be tested using a chi-squared analysis.

Take care that the clock you choose will start when the power is switched on; many electric clocks need a nudge. You can devise other ways of measuring the predominance of a particular perception.

2 There are endless possibilities to investigate this Muller–Lyer figure. What is the effect of varying the angle of the arrow-heads, or the size of the arrow-heads? You are not restricted to arrow-heads. Similar additions to a simple line can be used to test the perspective hypothesis.

47.

In the two figures above the end shapes both join the horizontal line at 90° and extend the same distance to the right. The left-hand figure, however, better represents a three-dimensional object.

The two ends can be different to suggest different perspectives.

48.

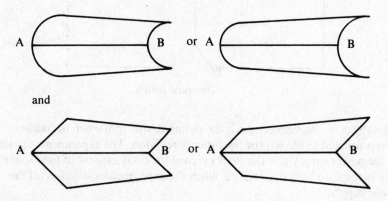

This is similar to the original experiment. The subject is asked to mark the mid-point of both figures. If A is seen as closer in the left-hand figure and B closer in the right-hand figure, the perceived mid-points should differ. Check which end does appear nearer in the figures.

3 The same techniques can be tried with other illusions.

References

Gregory, R.L. (1966), *Eye and Brain: the Psychology of Seeing*, Weidenfeld and Nicolson

Index guide: perception; visual illusions; size constancy

E 2 Coping with a displacement of the visual field

The problem

One of the classic problems in perceptual psychology is the nature–nurture debate. That is, do we have to learn to perceive [perception: nature/nurture]? One approach to this problem is to alter the perceptual apparatus of the subject and see whether he can learn to adjust to this change [perception: readjustment studies]. Several studies using human subjects have used prisms, filters and mirrors to alter their visual perceptions (e.g. Kohler, 1962; Stratton, 1897). K.U. Smith and W.M. Smith (1962) used a television camera and monitor to displace the visual field of their subjects. These researchers were interested in whether the subjects could learn to readjust their visual systems. This learning, if it takes place at all, can take a considerable time. Humans can, however, cope with these bizarre alterations in their vision almost straight away. This experiment looks at the tactics they use to do this before any significant readjustment of the visual system can take place.

The subject's visual field is altered using the closed-circuit TV camera and monitor arrangement suggested in E 17, variation 2. By placing the TV monitor on its side or upside down, the visual field is rotated through 90° or 180°. How does the subject cope with this displacement if he is asked to draw a straight line between two points? The subject has two sources of information about the position of his hand and where it is going. First, he can feel the position of his hand and its movement; this is proprioceptive or muscular feedback. Second, he can see the position of his hand and its movement; this is visual feedback. Normally the information from these two sources coincides. In this experiment these two sources of information disagree by 90° or 180°. The hypothesis is that the subject's performance will depend on the amount of displacement of the visual field.

A method

a) Design

Causal: The independent variable is the amount of visual displacement of the visual field – 0°, 90° or 180°. The dependent variable is the subject's performance in drawing a straight line between two points. This can be measured by the total area between the subject's trace and the straight line between the two points.

A repeated-measures design is used. The order of the three displacements is randomized to avoid any constant errors.

b) Subjects

There are no special restrictions.

c) Apparatus

The closed-circuit TV and monitor as in figure 70 (p. 274). In a simpler arrangement the subject looks at the monitor in front of him and draws the line with his hand out to the side. A screen prevents him glancing at his hand.

A piece of paper is placed in the view of the camera. The two dots, the start and the finish, are marked on this. The line between them is at 45° to the horizontal on the monitor screen. Measuring the subject's performance is made a lot easier if a faint graph paper is used.

d) Procedure

The subject is shown the apparatus. He is asked to place his hand on the paper and to look down at it. He sees his hand in the monitor. He is given a pencil and the point of this is placed on the start dot by the experimenter. The subject is shown the position of the second dot. He is asked to try and draw a straight line to this dot without taking his pencil off the paper. The line should be as smooth as possible and the subject is encouraged to keep going once he has started drawing. When he reaches the second dot the subject is asked what he thought had been done to his visual field. The experimenter removes the paper and records the amount of visual displacement. The subject is asked to turn away as the monitor is rotated for a different displacement. A new sheet of paper is placed under the camera and a second trial is run. Each subject has one trial under each rotation of the monitor.

Results

On each record sheet the experimenter draws the straight line between the two dots. The subject's score is the area between this line and the subject's trace. This involves the tedious task of counting the squares on the graph paper. Each subject will now have a score for each of the three displacements; these are considered in pairs. The hypothesis is concerned with the difference between the 90° and the 180° scores. Find this difference, with sign, for each subject. This is the statistic d used in the analysis.

Analysis (variables CD)
A t-test for related samples, a Wilcoxon or a sign test can be used. Comparisons of the 0° and 90°, and of the 0° and 180° scores are made in the same way. In these cases the assumptions of equal variance of the parametric test might be a little strained – use another test. You can also analyse the subject's ability to spot the sort of displacement used. Is this awareness of the displacement associated with relatively good performance?

Variations

1   You may notice in the 90° displacement trials that the subjects' traces are predominantly to one side of the straight line between the dots. This may give some clue to the subjects' tactics in coping with the displacement. A simple variation can establish this bias. Each subject is tested under two conditions: the visual field is rotated 90° clockwise and anticlockwise. The subject's tendency to stray to, say, the left of the straight line is measured under both conditions. This is calculated as: (area under the trace to the left of the line) – (area under the trace to the right of the line). What differences can we predict? Under the 90° clockwise displacement the relative positions of the two dots is shown in figure 49.

The subject sees the dot B to the left. He moves his pencil to the left but *sees* his hand move down the paper. If he compromises between the two sources of information his trace will strike off to the right of the correct line. Under the opposite displacement his compromise course is to the left of the line. Is this hypothesis of compromise supported by the subject's behaviour?

2   The original experiment considered only three positions of the visual field. In a larger-scale experiment the independent variable could be continuous, the camera being rotated by a few degrees between trials. The results of such an experiment are best displayed on a graph of angle of displacement against the subject's performance. A correlation between these two variables is unsatisfactory – the results of the original experiment suggest that the relationship is not monotonic.

49.

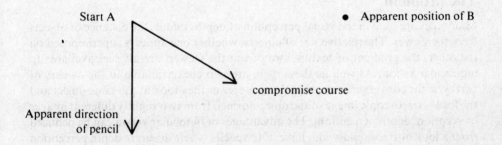

References

Kohler, I. (1962), 'Experiments with goggles', *Sci. Amer.*, vol. 206, 62

Smith, K.U. and Smith, W.M. (1962), *Perception and Motion: an Analysis of Space-structured Behavior*, Saunders

Stratton, G.M. (1897), 'Vision without inversion of the retinal image', *Psychol. Rev.*, vol. 4, 341

Index guide: perception; displacement of visual field; nature/nurture

E 3   Binocular vision in depth perception

The problem

Many cues are used in the visual perception of depth, that is, the distance of objects from the viewer. The relative size of objects, whether one appears superimposed on the other, the gradient of texture away from the viewer, are all cues available to monocular vision. As well as these there are two cues available to the owners of two eyes: the convergence angle of the two eyes as they look at the same object and the fused stereoscopic image of the object formed from two slightly different images [perception: depth perception]. The advantages of binocular vision can be deduced from a look at the animals who have it. In species where accurate depth perception is important, both eyes face forward and can converge on an object. Arboreal monkeys and birds of prey share this trait with the cats and many other predators.

This quick experiment compares the subject's accuracy in judging depth using monocular and binocular vision.

A method

a)   Design
Causal: The independent variable is the number of eyes the subject uses in judging the distance of an object. The dependent variable is the accuracy of that judgement. This is measured as the difference between the actual distance of the object and the subject's attempt to match the distance.

A repeated-measures design is used.

b)   Subjects
Subjects should have normal or corrected vision.

c)   Apparatus
The apparatus is shown in figure 50.

50.

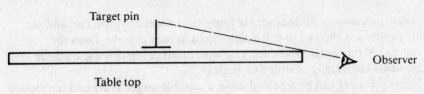

Target pin

Table top

Observer

The target consists of a large pin stuck through a small disc of cardboard. This is fixed onto a sheet of graph paper. The graph paper can be moved on the table top to position the pin at three distances, 30, 35 or 40 cm, from the edge of the table. The subject views this pin from a position slightly below the edge of the table so that only the point of the pin can be seen. This will prevent any view of the table top.

d) Procedure
The subject is asked to position himself by the edge of the table so that the point of the pin, at 50 cm from the edge, is just obscured by the edge of the table. A chin-rest is adjusted to keep his head at that level. He closes his eyes. The pin is moved closer to one of the three distances. The subject opens one or both eyes and sees the pin. He is asked to hold a slim pointer vertically to one side of the pin at the same distance. When he is satisfied he lowers the pointer to the paper and the position is marked.

The procedure is repeated for the other two distances and for the other condition of vision. The order of the six combinations, of distance and monocular or binocular vision, is randomized.

Results

Find the mean error of judgements under the two conditions of vision. These will be taken as the subject's score using monocular and binocular vision. The difference, with sign, between these two scores is the statistic, d, used in the analysis.

Analysis (variables CD)
A t-test for related samples, a Wilcoxon test, or a sign test can be used to assess the significance of any difference in accuracy between monocular and binocular judgements. You might expect the variance of judgements using one eye to be greater than when using two eyes. Test for a significant difference with the F-test.

Variations

1   Accurate judgements of distance are fairly vital when driving a car; and yet many people are allowed to drive with vision in only one eye. Does the advantage of binocular vision decrease with distance? In driving, distance judgements are usually of over five metres.

   The experiment can be repeated using a suitable target at around ten metres distance. The pointer is moved by the experimenter on the instructions of the subject. Again the subject should be able to see only the top of the target.

2   An interesting variation is suggested by an observation by Gregory in his book, *Eye and Brain*. An after-image is obtained by looking steadily at a bright light. Now look at a screen, say, a blank wall or a plain sheet of paper. The after-image will appear to lie on the screen and hence at the distance of the screen. The apparent size of the after-image will depend on the distance at which it appears to be. It appears small when viewed against a nearby screen and larger when viewed against a distance screen, although the size of the after-image on the retina cannot change. This is a demonstration of the mechanism of size constancy in the visual system [size constancy].

   An after-image is visible with the eyes closed. At what distance does this after-image appear to lie? Two cues to distance are available with the eyes closed: the convergence angle of the eyes and the focus of the lenses [perception: depth perception]. By holding a finger close to the face and trying to focus on it (without, of course, opening the eyes) the convergence and focus of the eyes will give cues of a near object. By imagining looking at a distant object these cues will be of a distant object. Does the apparent size of the after-image change under these different conditions of focus and convergence? Measuring the apparent size of the after-image poses a problem. One possibility is to use naive subjects and ask them simply to judge in which condition the after-image appears larger.

3   The variation of E 13 uses binocular judgements of distance as a skill in which the subject can be encouraged or discouraged.

References

Gregory, R.L. (1966), *Eye and Brain: The Psychology of Seeing*, Weidenfeld and Nicolson

Index guide: depth perception; binocular vision; size constancy; depth cues

E 4   The validity of maze learning as a measure of intelligence

The problem

One of the classic problems in psychology is the nature/nurture debate in intelligence. To what extent is an individual's intelligence limited by genetic, and hence predetermined, factors [intelligence: nature/nurture debate]?

There is the initial quandary of how we are to measure such an elusive quality as intelligence [intelligence: nature of; testing]. This is commonly done by using a suitable IQ test. Whether such a test is a valid measure of intelligence is another problem and happily does not concern us here. Having measured the individual's intelligence we can tackle the nature/nurture question. His intelligence will be determined by two factors:

1 His genetic endowment, fixed at the moment of conception.

2 His upbringing, all the external influences of the environment from the moment of conception.

The debate revolves about the importance of either factor in determining the individual's intelligence. There are two obvious approaches:

1 We can control the genetic endowment and vary the upbringing. If all the subjects have the same or very similar genetic structure then any variation in intelligence is the result of variation in upbringing.

2 We can control the upbringing and vary the genetic endowment. If all the subjects have experienced the same or very similar upbringing then any variation in intelligence is the result of variation of genetic endowment.

This is straightforward in theory. In practice there are problems. It is practically and morally impossible to control or manipulate either of these factors in humans. The nearest we can get to the first approach is to use identical twins; we cannot, however, manipulate their upbringing in the cause of science and must make do with such little variation that occurs naturally. *Measuring* that variation presents vast problems.

An alternative is to use animals. Strains of mice and rats have been developed in which the genetic variation is very little; techniques have been mastered for producing identical twins by dividing the developing embryo. The development of a rat is rapid and its upbringing can be rigorously controlled or manipulated. There is one small problem. How are we to measure the intelligence of a rat? Goodness knows, we have enough troubles with humans. Several studies have used maze learning as an operational definition, and hence measure, of intelligence in rats (Tryon, 1940, and many other studies based on his strains of 'maze-bright' and 'maze-dull' rats, e.g. Cooper and Zubeck, 1958).

Is maze learning a valid measure of intelligence? One test of validity is *correlation* validity. We have a well-established measure of intelligence in humans, using IQ tests. If maze learning is a valid measure of intelligence there should be a high correlation between an individual's performance on a maze-learning task and on an IQ test. This validity is tested in the experiment.

We will try to simulate for humans the conditions of a rat in a maze. The rat cannot see the whole maze, only his immediate surroundings. How can this be simulated short of constructing Hampton Court? The paths of the maze are drawn as single lines with junctions at various points where the subject must decide which path to take. The maze is covered by a large sheet of card with a small hole in the centre. The subject can view the maze only through this hole and so can only see his immediate surroundings:

51.

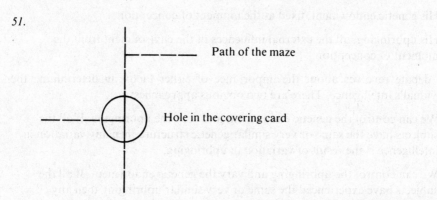

Path of the maze

Hole in the covering card

By sliding the card over the maze the subject can follow any path. Performance on the maze task is measured by the number of wrong decisions the subject makes before the maze is learnt to a criterion of, say, three runs through the maze making no wrong decisions. This measurement determines the structure of the maze. At each junction the subject must be 'right' or 'wrong'; a wrong decision must take him to a dead end.

52.

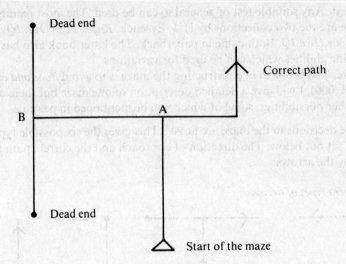

Dead end

Correct path

B — A

Dead end

Start of the maze

In figure 52 the subject can be 'right' or 'wrong' at junction A. The 'wrong' decision takes him to junction B; either decision here will be wrong. Junction B must be replaced by a dead end mark (see 'Apparatus'). The maze-learning task is measured by errors. We will expect a high *negative* correlation between maze performance (errors) and IQ.

The experimental hypothesis is that there is a relationship between performance on the maze-learning task and on an IQ test.

A method

a) Design
Non-causal: We cannot manipulate either variable. One experimental variable is the performance on the maze-learning task measured by the number of errors made before a criterion is reached. The other experimental variable is the performance on an IQ test.

An independent-subjects design is used.

b) Subjects
IQ tests are designed for particular age-ranges. The subjects should all be within this range. It is simplest to use adults initially. Performance on an IQ test can also vary with culture. At the very least, all subjects should have English as their first language. All subjects should be unfamiliar with the particular IQ test chosen.

c) Apparatus

1 The IQ test. Any suitable test of general IQ can be used. The most readily available are the two collections by H.J. Eysenck, *Know Your Own IQ* and *Check your Own IQ*. Both come in paperback. The latter book also has tests for specific abilities which can be used for variations.

2 The maze. The problem in constructing the maze is to avoid *floor and ceiling effects* (p. 000). I will give a detailed description of one maze but there are many other possibilities, some of which will be mentioned in passing.

All the decisions in the maze are at 90°. This gives the six possible types of decision set out below. The direction of approach and the correct path are shown by the arrows.

53. *Six different types of decision*

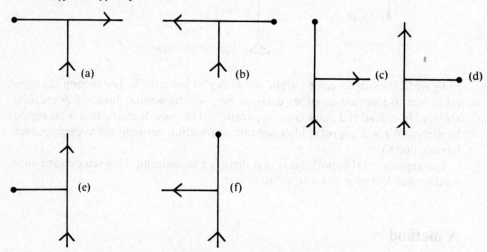

The maze has a total of twelve decisions, two of each type. The order of these decisions is chosen randomly using a die. For example: type d, a, e, c, b, f, d, b, e, c, a, f. The distance from one decision to a dead end or the next decision is 9 cm. and contains one 90° bend after 3 cm or 6 cm, whichever is suitable to fit the rest of the maze.

Dead ends are marked ●. The start is marked △. The finish is marked □.

So, the first four decisions (d, a, e, c) could look like figure 54. The rest of the maze is constructed similarly. The maze is drawn on a sheer of paper and stuck to the centre of a large table.

The covering card which the subject manipulates is square, with each side twice as long as the greatest dimension of the maze sheet. The small observation hole is cut in the centre of this card. The size of the covering card

54. *The start of a maze*

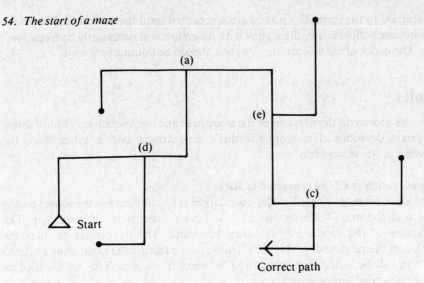

ensures that the subject cannot see any part of the maze as he moves the covering card. The observation hole is 2 cm in diameter so that only one line or decision can be seen at any point on the maze.

d) Procedure

1 The IQ test. Follow the procedure recommended for the test you have chosen. If the test is from a book it may be necessary to get the permission of the author or publisher if you wish to duplicate copies of the test. This should not be difficult if you explain how the test will be used.

It is not necessary to convert the scores on the test to IQ ratings for the purpose of the experiment, although some subjects will want to do so. Others may want you to keep their scores confidential. You must do this.

2 The maze-learning task. Before the subject comes into the room the covering card is placed over the maze with the hole over the start mark. The subject is told that each decision is either 'right' or 'wrong'; there are no decisions on 'wrong' paths. He is instructed to slide the covering card over the maze to follow the path. He is shown examples of a dead end mark and a finish mark. When he reaches a dead end he slides back to the last decision and takes the other path until he reaches the finish. He may, at some point, turn backwards down the maze; the experimenter should spot this and tell the subject, who returns to the last decision. This reversal counts as another dead end and the run continues. The total number of dead ends reached gives the score for each run of the maze.

When he reaches the finish he is asked to turn round while the cover card is returned to the start. The procedure is repeated until the subject reaches the criterion performance, three runs with no errors, not necessarily consecutive. The order of maze learning or IQ test should be counterbalanced.

Results

The errors scored on the first run of the maze are random; the subject cannot know the correct decisions. The score for the maze-learning task is taken from the beginning of the second run.

Analysis (variables CC or converted to RR)
The product-moment or rank-order correlation is found between the scores on the IQ test and the maze-learning task. Try the rank order first – it's quicker. The significance of the correlation can then be found. The hypothesis predicts the direction of the relationship; if maze learning does measure the same thing as the IQ test there will be a negative correlation between the scores. You are justified in using a one-tailed test of significance.

Variations

1   The subjects may unknowingly turn back at some point along the maze. This will happen after reaching a dead end; the subject retraces to the decision and takes the path by which he arrived. Is this more likely to happen at particular types of decision? If so, why? You can test hypotheses by constructing mazes of 'reversing' and 'non-reversing' decisions.

2   The ease of recognizing such reversing may affect the ease of learning the maze. It is possible to construct a maze consisting only of type (a) and type (b) decisions (see figure 53). If the subject reaches a dead end the correct path is always 'straight on at the junction'. A similar maze can be constructed using combinations of the two decisions below:

55.

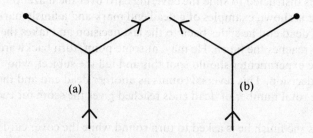

(a)   (b)

When the subject retraces from a dead end he is confronted with another decision: which path to choose. How does performance on the two mazes compare?

3   The maze is an interesting learning task. We have considered whether certain types of decision are easier to learn; it may be more important to look at the position of the decision in the maze. That is, are decisions learnt quickest at the beginning, the middle or the end of the maze? If the experimenter is familiar with the maze he can recognize each decision as it is reached and record the number of errors made at each decision. (Beware! When the experimenter is familiar with the maze there is a great danger of influencing the subject with involuntary sighs or nods as he makes his decision.) The number of errors on each decision for all subjects is then compared with the *expected* number of errors using chi-squared as a test of goodness of fit (p. 32). The hypothesis we are fitting is that there are equal numbers of errors at each decision. A significant difference from these expected frequencies reveals a *serial position effect*.

4   Maze learning might measure a particular sort of intelligence, for example, visual/spatial ability. The experiment can be repeated using an IQ test designed to measure this and other specific abilities. (Some of these can be found in Eysenck's *Check Your Own IQ*.) Does a visual/spatial test show a higher correlation with maze-learning ability?

5   There is some evidence that there is a sex difference in some tasks: males perform better on visual/spatial tasks. Does the same hold with maze learning? If you have found a high correlation between IQ and maze learning then you must consider using a matched-subjects design for such an experiment, using pairs of males and females of similar IQ.

References

Cooper, R.M. and Zubek, J.P. (1958), 'Effects of enriched and early environments on the learning ability of "bright" and "dull" rats', *Canad. J. Psychol.*, vol. 12, 159–64

Eysenck, H.J. (1969), *Check Your Own IQ*, Penguin Books

Eysenck, H.J. (1969), *Know Your Own IQ*, Penguin Books

Tryon, R.C. (1940), 'Genetic differences in maze-learning ability in rats', *39th Yearbook Nat. Soc. Stud. Educ.* (part 1), Public School Publishing Co., Illinois

Index guide: intelligence; maze learning; validity

E 5   Estimating the loudness of an auditory signal with background noise

The problem

My wife and I disagree about the use of a car radio. I like to listen to it; she likes to sleep through it. The optimum loudness of the radio for these two activities is not the same. This leads to much surreptitious adjusting of the volume knob by both parties followed by furious accusations and denials. Curiously, these accusations and readjustments occur most frequently at traffic lights. When the car is stopped at a set of traffic lights the radio *does* sound much louder. We agree to turn the radio down. The lights change and the car speeds up. The radio volume appears to drop to a barely audible whisper – I turn it up and so it goes on. One hypothesis for the behaviour of my radio is that the motion of the car in some way affects the reception of the radio signal. This is easily tested by using the cassette player instead of the radio. It makes no difference; the volume still appears to vary inversely with the speed of the car.

There could be a psychological explanation. As the car's speed increases so does the volume of other noises, of the engine, the tyres on the road, the wind, various rattles, etc. Do I perceive the loudness of the radio relative to these other noises? As the loudness of the other noises increases, the loudness of the radio will appear to decrease. This hypothesis forms the basis of the experiment.

The task of the subject is to judge the loudness of an auditory signal, perhaps a prerecorded radio programme. This is measured by adjusting the volume control to match a standard signal (the target signal). Either of these two signals can be mixed with background noise, representing the odd noises my car makes travelling at speed.

A method

a)   Design
Causal: The independent variable is the level of background noise. Ideally we should like to measure this loudness level. This however requires equipment that

may not be available. We will content ourselves with two conditions of the independent variable. The background noise in my car appears to be a mixture of all the audible frequencies. It sounds rather like a roaring hiss. An approximation to this noise can usually be found on a television by removing the aerial and twiddling with the tuner. This noise is then recorded onto one track of a stereo tape recorder. In one condition of the independent variable the background noise is that normally present in the experimental room from outside, traffic, wind and so on. In the other condition there is the addition of the prerecorded noise at some constant level.

The dependent variable is the subject's adjustment of the loudness of the auditory signal when he judges it to be the same loudness as the target signal. This is measured by the position of the volume control on the tape recorder or amplifier.

A repeated-measures design is used. If the number of subjects is severely limited you could use a single-subject design, but avoid using yourself as the single subject for obvious reasons.

b) Subjects
There are no special restrictions.

c) Apparatus
A stereo tape recorder with separate volume controls for the two channels is ideal. Two mono tape recorders are just as good. Measuring the position of the volume control is easier if they are of the 'slide' type as an accurate scale can be placed alongside the sliding control. Accurate measurement of the position of the volume control is more difficult with a rotating knob.

The target signal can be a passage of prose recorded from the radio. Choose a passage that does not contain great variations in volume. The passage is recorded on one channel of the tape recorder. The noise is recorded on the other channel. The two speakers are placed together at one end of the room. The subject sits at the other end. The experimenter stands next to the tape recorder, behind the subject.

d) Procedure
The subject comes into the room and sits down. The experimenter explains that the subject will hear an extract from a radio programme (the target signal) with or without background noise. After 30 seconds the tape will be switched off. The same tape will be switched on again after 5 seconds but the loudness of the signal will have been altered. The subject's task is to adjust the loudness of the radio programme to its previous level by making hand signals to the experimenter. The subject should move his hand up if he wants the volume increased or down if he wants it decreased. The subject calls out when he thinks the signal matches the target signal in loudness. The subject is instructed to ignore the presence or absence of the background noise.

The experimenter adjusts the volume control to the subject's instructions. It is important that the subject cannot see the volume control; he may match the volumes visually. The experimenter records the position of the volume control. The recorder is switched off, the volume control returned to the target level and the next trial can be run.

The experimenter controls the presence or absence of background noise with either signal by simply pulling out the speaker connection. There are four possible combinations of noise and signal:

Combination	Noise with target signal	Noise with variable signal
1	No	No
2	No	Yes
3	Yes	No
4	Yes	Yes

Each subject is tested on all combinations. The order of the combinations is randomized.

Results

The results of each subject on the four combinations are considered in pairs. For example: for combinations 1 and 2, find the difference between the two positions of the volume control. The hypothesis predicts that the subject will set combination 2 louder.

Analysis (variables CD)

This prediction can be tested with a Wilcoxon test by ranking these differences (with signs) for all the subjects. If the scale on the volume control has few subdivisions there could be several ties in the differences. In this case the less powerful sign test will have to be used.

A similar analysis is used for all pairs of combinations. The hypothesis predicts similar volume settings for combinations 1 and 4, a low setting for combination 3 and a high setting for combination 2. These predictions of direction allow you to use a one-tailed test in the analysis.

Variations

1 In this experiment, and in my car, the subject has to *remember* the loudness of the target signal. The results could be a function of memory rather than of hearing. This can be tested by getting subjects to match signals simultaneously presented. In this variation the target signal, with or without

noise, is presented to one ear, the signal to be adjusted, with or without noise, is presented to the other ear using a pair of stereo earphones. The combinations of conditions are the same as in the original experiment. Two stereo tape recorders will be necessary.

2 In the original experiment the noise and the signal appear to come from the same source; the speakers are placed next to each other at some distance from the subject. The instructions to the poor old subject are to ignore the noise and attend only to the signal. This attention will be easier if the speakers are placed on either side of the subject or if the noise and the signal are presented to different ears using stereo earphones. Will this physical separation of the noise and signal sources affect the subject's ability to judge the loudness of the signal?

3 Does the nature of the signal affect the subject's judgement of loudness? The original experiment uses speech. It could be argued that the subject may infer the loudness of this signal from the intelligibility of the speech. The experiment can be tried with a variety of signals from speech to a single tone.

　By varying the nature of the signal you will also be varying the similarity of the signal and the background noise. This will affect the difficulty of attending to one and ignoring the other, (see the previous variation). This variation can be extended by making the background 'noise' and the signal very similar, say two prose passages. The subject listens to the target passage on its own. He is then asked to adjust the volume of the signal mixed with another prose passage.

4 In the original hypothesis it was suggested that the loudness of the signal is perceived relative to the background noise. This noise was held constant while the signal volume was adjusted. If *both* the noise and the signal are adjusted (on a common volume control) their relative strengths will remain the same. What does the hypothesis predict in this case – and what actually happens?

　The variations are legion.

Index guide: attention; auditory perception; hearing

E 6 Estimation of time and reading speeds

The problem

Many of us would be confident in distinguishing the passing of one minute from one hour. It is not obvious, however, how we do this. There have been many studies of endochronology or 'biological clocks' where regular changes in the body, patterns of eating and sleeping and so on, take place at more or less regular intervals. It is unlikely that the same mechanisms are used in the perception of small passages of time, say a minute or so. In fact we are remarkably bad at estimating such small time spans. McKellar (1962) found that subjects engaged in a boring routine task, after 260 seconds, gave an average estimate of 398 seconds, with estimates ranging from 92 to 720 seconds. On the other hand, I find it remarkable that we can perform even this well.

On what basis do we make these estimates? Normal timekeeping methods rely on counting regular events; a clock 'counts' pendulum swings or the vibrations of a quartz crystal. What can we count – heartbeats? The problem is fascinating but curiously neglected in general textbooks. A good background can be found in *On the Experience of Time* by Ornstein. Loehin (1959) suggests that there are four factors underlying the estimate of time:

1 Interest v boredom. Bored subjects tend to give longer time estimates than interested subjects.

2 Filled time v empty time. Longer estimates tend to occur with filled time rather than empty time.

3 Repetition. If an activity is repeated in two equal periods of time, the second period is perceived as passing more quickly.

4 Passivity v activity. Periods of passivity are estimated as being longer than periods of activity.

All of these suggested factors invite experimentation. They all make some appeal to common sense although, paradoxically, one or two appear to contradict each other.

This experiment looks at the second of these suggestions. The hypothesis is that the estimation of time is influenced by the number of events that occur. Two passages of prose, from the same book, are read at different speeds. Subjects listen to one passage (the *target* passage) for a predetermined time, say 100 seconds. They then listen to the second passage read at a different speed and are asked to stop the tape recorder after the same time as the target passage.

The hypothesis predicts that the subjects perceive time passing more slowly during the passage read at the slower speed.

A method

a) Design
Causal: The independent variable is the relative speeds of the target passage and the second passage. In one condition the target passage is read at the faster speed and the second passage at the slower speed. In the other condition this order is reversed.

The dependent variable is the subject's estimate of time before he stops the tape recorder on the second passage. The hypothesis predicts that this estimate of time is longer in the first condition.

There is some reason to suppose that subjects in *both* conditions will underestimate the time of the second passage (i.e. stop the recorder after the target time). Take a look at Loehin's third suggested factor (see also variation 1).

An independent-subjects design is used. It is likely that there will be considerable variation in the estimates: a pilot study will be useful to give some idea of the number of subjects you are likely to need.

b) Subjects
There are no special restrictions. Subjects are allocated randomly to the two conditions of the independent variable.

c) Apparatus
A tape recorder, ideally one using tape cassettes. This will make the changing of reading speed very simple. Two tapes are prepared before the experiment; both are passages taken from the same book, a novel, to reduce the differences in style and content to a minimum. The passages are read by the same person at two different reading speeds. It is important that these reading speeds remain fairly steady throughout each passage. You can check this by counting the number of words

read in each period of fifteen seconds. Both passages should be at least five minutes long to allow for any wild estimates.

The times of the target and second passages are measured with a stopwatch.

d) Procedure

The experimenter explains to each subject that he will listen to a passage on the tape recorder for a set time. He will then be asked to listen to a second passage for the same amount of time. He is to stop the recorder after the same time as the target passage.

Subjects are very cunning and will, of course, cheat if they can. To prevent the subject counting during the passages explain that you will be asking questions on both passages at the end of the experiment. Check that he cannot see the tape counter on the recorder or the tape spools – it would be very simple to count the revolutions. Check there is no clock in the room. Obviously the subject will be relieved of his watch before the experiment.

The recorder is played and the stopwatch is started from the first word. The recorder is stopped after 100 seconds. The cassette is changed. The second passage is played and the subject stops the recorder when he estimates the time of the two passages is the same.

Give him his watch back and repeat the procedure for the next subject.

Results

The subjects' estimates are sorted into the two experimental conditions. The mean estimate is found for each condition.

Analysis (variables CD)

The difference between the two means can be compared with a t-test for independent samples. Alternatively the estimates can be ranked and the Mann-Whitney test used. The more powerful t-test should be used where possible as there is likely to be considerable variation in the estimates.

The hypothesis predicts the direction of the difference between the means: that is, subjects hearing the slower reading on the second passage will stop the recorder after a longer time. A one-tailed test is justified.

Variations

1   A similar experiment can be used to test the suggestion that the repetition of
    an activity produces shorter time estimates, Loehin's third factor. This is a
    simple order effect.

The experimenter prepares two prerecorded passages from the same book, as before. In this experiment the passages are read at the same speed. The procedure is the same as before; subjects listen to 100 seconds of the target passage and are asked to estimate the same time for the second passage. The independent variable is now the order of the two passages. Remember to counterbalance the two passages to avoid a constant error from any differences in the reading or content of the two passages.

The hypothesis predicts that subjects will underestimate the time of the second passage, i.e. they will stop the recorder after *more* than 100 seconds. This prediction can be tested with a Wilcoxon test. The difference between the subject's estimate and the target passage time (100 seconds) is found. These differences are ranked and the rank sum of the less frequent sign taken and so on.

2   It is possible to test the suggestion that passive periods are perceived as being longer than active periods. The subject compares two passages read from the same book as before. In this variation one of the passages is read by himself. The procedure is similar to the original experiment. The order of the active and passive passages must be counterbalanced. We have suggested that the relative speed of reading will affect the estimate of time; it will be necessary to match the prerecorded reading speed to the subject's reading speed. Before the experiment the subject is timed reading a third, similar passage. The number of words in this is counted beforehand. This will give an estimate of the subject's reading speed. The nearest to this is selected from a stock of prerecorded tapes. It is very simple to record the performances of any previous subjects and use these as prerecorded passages. Label each with its reading speed.

The hypothesis predicts that the subjects will read for longer than they listen. The analysis of the results is the same as for the original experiment.

3   I suggested earlier that estimates of time could be made by counting, unconsciously, some regular bodily event – perhaps heartbeats or breathing. This might be worth testing in a quick variation.

All subjects listen to a target passage. In one condition the subject then performs some vigorous exercise as quickly as possible. This should be short, but exhausting, to raise the heart and breathing rate. The subject now listens to the second passage, read at the same speed as the target passage, and stops the recorder after the same time.

In the other condition the subject rests between the target and second passages. The separation of the two passages is the same in both conditions. If the subject's estimate is influenced by heart or breathing rate the exhausted subject should overestimate the length of the second passage, i.e. stop the recorder sooner.

4   It should be easy enough to find 'interesting' and 'boring' ways of passing the time to test Loehin's first suggested factor.

5   Presumably the old saying, 'A watched kettle never boils' is a formulation of Loehin's third factor. Popular sayings usually contain some grains of truth and can be a rich source of hypotheses to test.

References

Ornstein, R.E., *On the Experience of Time*, Penguin Books
Loehin (1959), 'The influence of different activities on the apparent lengths of time', *Psychol. Monographs*, No. 474.

Index guide: endochronology; perception of time; time; apparent time

E7   Strategies in game playing

The problem

A simple game forms the basis of this experiment. No doubt this game has a name but I do not know it and so a description will have to serve.

Two players face each other. Each can make one of three responses with his right hand:

1   A fist, with the thumb uppermost. This represents a rock (response R).

2   An open hand, held horizontally with the palm facing downwards. This represents paper (response P).

3   The first and second fingers extended in a 'V' pointing away from the body. This represents a pair of scissors (response S).

The players make their responses simultaneously, the winner depending on the combination of responses. If the two responses are the same the players draw. The 'rock' beats the 'scissors' (because it blunts them) but loses to 'paper' (the paper can wrap up the rock). The paper beats the rock but loses to the scissors (the scissors can cut the paper). And so the scissors beat the paper but lose to the rock. Each response draws with one of the opponent's possible responses, beats another and loses to a third.

The object of the game is to guess the next response of your opponent and to produce the appropriate response to win. To make sure that the responses are made simultaneously the players keep to a rhythm. Each holds his right hand in a fist and strikes the table, say, three times together and produces the response on the fourth count. On the fifth count the players strike the table again and the rhythm continues with a response every four counts.

The players will need a little practice at this game until they are immediately aware who has won or lost each encounter of responses. If you feel it to be necessary a small stake can ride on each encounter, the winnings handed over at the end of a session of play.

Consider the behaviour of one player. He makes his response; this can be rewarded if he wins, or punished if he loses. What will his next response be in either case? The theories of operant conditioning might predict that a winning response will be repeated and a losing response changed. Is this prediction supported?

The hypothesis is that there is some relationship between the outcome of a response and the subsequent choice of response.

A method

a)   Design
Non-causal: One experimental variable is the outcome of the player's response, whether a win, a loss or a draw.

The other variable is the subsequent response: is this the same or different from the preceding response?

The experiment uses a single-subject design.

b)   Subjects
There are no special restrictions. The beauty of any experiment based on the playing of a game is the ease of getting subjects who will participate for ages with little or no encouragement.

c)   Apparatus
The experimenter needs a sheet of paper to record the players' responses. A metronome is very useful in providing a regular (and measured) rhythm for the players.

d)   Procedure
The experimenter explains the game to the players, a pair of subjects. They practise until they are thoroughly familiar with the game. Both players should be able to recognize the winner of any pair of responses immediately.

The difficulty with this experiment is the recording of the responses. The experimenter needs some practice in jotting down the responses fast enough to keep up with the rhythm of the players.

At the beginning of a trial the experimenter demonstrates with the help of the metronome the rhythm he wishes the subjects to maintain. This can easily be varied by the number of times the players strike the table between responses (see 'Variations'). The experimenter starts recording after three responses and continues until sufficient responses have been collected or until, as usually happens, the experimenter makes a mistake and gets left behind. It can help to have a second experimenter recording the responses for this reason. After the trial the two lists of responses are checked and any discrepancies discarded.

The subjects are asked whether they were aware of following any tactic or pattern of responses.

Results

The responses of each player are considered separately. At each response the player wins, loses or draws. Considering the winning responses first, the player's next move can be 'the same' or 'different' from the winning response. As a further refinement in analysis, 'different' responses can be categorized as 'up' (the response that would beat the previous response) or 'down' (the response that would lose to the previous response). For example, player A wins with 'rock' (player B produced 'scissors'). If A's next response is another 'rock' the response is scored 'same'. If the next response is 'scissors' the response is 'down'. If the next response is 'paper' the response is scored 'up'. The responses following all A's wins are collected.

When Player A wins the subsequent response is:

Same	Different		
	Up	Down	
Frequency				Total no. of wins

Similar tables of frequencies are found for responses following losing responses and drawing responses.

Analysis (variables DD)
The null hypothesis is that there is no relationship between the outcome of a response and the subsequent choice of response. This is tested using a chi-squared as a test of association.

See, for example, the first and second diagrams on p. 226. Alternatively, chi-squared can be used as a test of goodness of fit. First, does the player show any overall preference for a type of response? See the third diagram on p. 226. The expected frequencies, if there are no overall preferences, will each be one-third of the total number of responses.

A similar analysis can be tried for each of the response outcomes: winning responses, losing responses and drawing responses. Such an analysis will reveal the tactics, if any, that the player is using. The subjects were asked if they were aware

Subsequent response

	Same	Different	(2df)
win			
lose			
draw			

Outcome of response: (label beside win/lose/draw)

Subsequent response

	Same	Different		(4df)
		Up	Down	
win				
lose				
draw				

Outcome of response: (label beside win/lose/draw)

	Same	Up	Down	(2df)
Observed frequency				
Expected frequency				

of using any particular pattern or tactic. Does this conscious tactic agree with his actual play?

Finally, do his tactics support a simple theory of operant conditioning? We should expect that winning responses are repeated and losing responses are changed. Perhaps the tactic reveals that the players will go 'down' after a losing response assuming the opponent will repeat.

Variations

1   One problem in this experiment is that we can expect the tactics of one player to depend on and adapt to those of the other player. It is possible for one player, a confederate of the experimenter, to stick rigidly to one tactic.

    For example: the confederate repeats a losing response, changes 'up' after a win and changes 'down' after a draw. Does the subject spot such a rigid tactic? If so, how long does it take him to learn a winning tactic to a criterion of, say, ten wins in a row? The confederate's tactic can be changed at this point and the number of responses taken by the subject to readjust is measured. The speed of the game will be important in this variation (see the following variation).

2   The game can be played at different speeds. Does this affect the pattern of the players' responses? The speed is simply varied by changing the number of times the players strike the table between responses. One might predict that as the speed increases the outcome of a response becomes less important (as the players have little time to use this information) but overall response preferences increase. The fastest speed will be dictated by the experimenter's ability to record the responses. It is quite simple to make this automatic using a pen recorder. The three possible responses are made by pressing buttons connected to resistances of different value in the circuit used in E 10.

    At the other end of the scale, players can be given as much time as they wish to make a response. They each write down their response and these are then compared before the next response is made.

    A combination of these first two variations could be interesting.

3   This game can be played by very young children. Do they use tactics different to those of adults? I suppose that with some careful designing of apparatus the experiment could be adapted to suit animal subjects in Skinner boxes.

4   There are many other suitable games that can be investigated in a similar way. In the 'match game' there are two players. Each holds a number of matches, from none to three, in his closed hand. They try to guess the total number of matches held in both hands, taking turns to call the first guess. The second

caller cannot repeat the guess of the first. When both have made a guess the hands are revealed and the winner, if any, declared. This is not just a game of chance and players can win consistently by adapting their tactics. What tactics do players use and, more interestingly, are they aware of using them?

Index guide: operant conditioning; thinking; games

E 8   The prisoner's dilemma: a model of industrial behaviour

The problem

Industrial disputes are a familiar feature of many modern societies. In many cases the behaviour of the two parties in these disputes appears nonsensical. Take a typical example that occurred recently in a British shipyard. The shipyard was short of orders and threatened with closure. A contract to build a number of ships was offered to the yard on the condition that there were no disputes. Two unions were in dispute about who should do a particular part of the job, lagging a boiler or some such. If the dispute could be resolved both unions would benefit from the contract; if not the contract would be lost and both unions suffer. The unions could not agree and the contract was lost. The rest of the country was amazed: how could the men be so short-sighted? The pattern is often repeated when a firm goes out of business with employers and employees disagreeing about a relatively trivial matter. What causes such apparently illogical behaviour?

This experiment attempts to simulate this behaviour in a simple game based on the classic problem, the Prisoner's Dilemma (see R. Brown, *Social Psychology*, and Luce and Raiffa, *Games and Decisions*). The dilemma is very simple. Two persons are suspected of a crime. They are taken to separate rooms and interrogated. Each suspect has two alternatives: he can trust the other and keep quiet or inform on the other in an attempt to get a lighter sentence for himself. If both trust each other they get off with no punishment. If both inform on each other they both get five years in prison. If one trusts and the other informs on him, the informer gets a reward while the other shoulders all the blame and gets ten years. The best solution overall is for the prisoners to keep quiet – but can they trust one another?

The experimental game is played between pairs of subjects. Each subject has the choice of 'trusting' or 'informing'. The payoff matrix is given overleaf. The game can be played for pence. If both the subjects choose to trust, each gains 1p from the experimenter. If both inform, each loses 1p to the experimenter. If one trusts and the other informs, the truster loses 3p to the informer.

The subjects' best tactics are clear. If they trust they will all gain; inform and

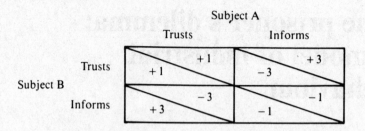

they will all lose. It might appear that the experimenter stands to lose a great deal of money over several trials. If, however, this game is a good model of the situation found in industrial disputes the experimenter might expect to gain. This is the hypothesis.

A method

a) Design
This is hardly an experiment, more a structured observation of behaviour. The variable, the behaviour being observed, is the proportion of informers and trusters.

b) Subjects
There are no special restrictions. If the game is to be played for money the subjects must be fully informed beforehand.

c) Apparatus
A sheet of paper is given to each subject to record his responses. He is also asked to write his name on a small slip of paper. These are collected and placed in a 'hat'.
  It will be helpful if the payoff matrix is displayed for all to see.

d) Procedure
The experimenter explains the game in detail to a group of a dozen or so subjects. He can point out that the most sensible solution is for all subjects to trust each other. A subject cannot, however, make an agreement to trust his partner as this partner is chosen *after* the subject has made his response.
  For the first trial the subjects are asked to make a decision, 'trust' or 'inform', and to record this on the sheet of paper. The subjects' names are now shuffled in the hat and pulled out in random pairs. Each member of the pair reads out his decision and the payoff is made. The subjects record their winnings or losses alongside their decision. A second pair of names is drawn from the hat and so on until all the subjects have been paired and the payoffs made. The names are put back into the hat, the subjects make a second decision and the game continues. The

game carries on for ten decisions or until all the subjects have made the same response for three consecutive trials.

The experimenter can, if he wishes, pay back any profit he has made as he collects the response sheets.

Results and analysis

In the payoff matrix the overall payoff is zero. That is, if the subjects respond randomly we will expect the mean gain of the experimenter to be zero. This prediction can be tested by several groups of subjects using chi-squared as a test of goodness of fit. The hypothesis predicts that the experimenter gains every time. Good for the experimenter – not so good for human nature.

I will leave you to fit the game to the industrial situation. The game has been used as a model of panic behaviour in fires and economic crises (Brown, *Social Psychology*).

Variations

1   You may find that some subjects will trust throughout the experiment. This may be because of the logic of the game – trusting is the long-term sensible solution. It may be that 'trusting' is seen as morally better than 'informing'. Is the same persistence shown if the names for the two responses are interchanged?

2   In the experiment the subjects did not know their partner until their decision was made. If the same partners are kept throughout the ten trials will the subjects begin to trust each other? You might expect the pairs to polarize into two types, trusters and informers. Does this happen?

References

Brown, R. (1965), *Social Psychology*, Collier Macmillan
Luce, R.D. and Raiffa, H. (1957), *Games and Decisions*, Wiley, New York

Index guide: prisoner's dilemma; panic behaviour; games

E9   Personal space in a lavatory

The problem

When two people stand and talk they will stand at a distance at which they feel comfortable. This distance will depend on several factors, e.g. how well they know each other and from which culture they come. Argyle (1967) gives the much-quoted example of an Arab and an Englishman in conversation. The Arab prefers a small interpersonal distance. The Englishman, preferring a greater separation, retreats but the Arab instinctively closes the gap to his preferred distance. They pirouette relentlessly about the floor, the Arab no doubt considering the Englishman unfriendly, the Englishman harbouring graver suspicions about the Arab.

The interpersonal distance, or 'personal space', will depend on the type of interaction. We could ask whether it is maintained even between people who do not appear to be interacting at all. Sommer (1969) found that persons sitting in a public reading room like to have at least one empty seat between themselves and the next reader.

There is a problem measuring this personal space without arousing the suspicions of the subjects. Sommer solved this by using a discrete measurement that could be made at some distance, the seat in which they were sitting. The problem here is that subjects tend to stay for long periods and relatively few observations can be made. They may also have strong personal preferences for particular seats which can obscure the effects of personal space.

The solution suggested here is to use a public lavatory. There is a constant traffic of subjects who stay for a short time. Many observations can be made. The measurement of personal space is discrete – either the urinal or compartment used, depending on the sex of the subject. These advantages do not come without the odd practical problem.

The hypothesis is that subjects will avoid positions adjacent to another person.

A method

a) Design

(For the sake of simplicity I will only outline the investigation in a men's lavatory. The design can easily be adapted.)

Causal: The independent variable is the position of any other people using the lavatory when the subject chooses his urinal. The dependent variable is the choice of urinal, whether or not adjacent to another person.

An independent-subjects design is used.

b) Subjects

Males. They must be unaware of the experiment.

c) Apparatus

One men's lavatory with a row of urinals. One in a college is ideal. You can time your visits for observations to coincide with the end of lectures or lessons. This should give you the maximum number of observations without having to hang around a suspiciously long time.

The observer has a prepared score sheet to record the choice of each subject and the position of any others. For example, if there are four urinals, A, B, C, and D, the score sheet has four columns labelled the same. An entry AB in column C records that a subject chose position C when there were people in positions A and B. An entry of a dash in column D records that the subject chose position D when no one else was using the lavatory.

d) Procedure

The observer must find some legitimate excuse for spending several minutes in the lavatory. I suggest cleaning out fountain pens in the wash basin. This can take ages. If several pens are cleaned you have an excuse for scribbling occasionally to try them out, covering the recording of observations.

A subject enters the lavatory and goes to a urinal. The position of the subject and any others is recorded. It is possible to manipulate the position of the others using several stooges standing at various positions as the subject enters. There is, however, a limit to the time they can stand there. This is unnecessary if there is an adequate traffic of subjects. It may be necessary to make a large number of observations. This experiment is particularly suitable for a group of experimenters to share the observations over a week or so.

Results and analysis

What determines where the subject will stand? The hypothesis suggests that the subject's choice of position will depend on the position of others using the urinal. It may also be that some positions are more popular than others. These preferences must first be established by looking at the subjects' choice when no one else is using the urinals. Significant preferences are found by using chi-squared as a test of goodness of fit. The worked example on page 35 uses data from this experiment.

We can now look at the subject's choice when others are using the urinal. His chosen position can be adjacent or not adjacent to another person.

Take a simple example using a row of three urinals, A, B and C.

Position of others	Chosen position of subject			
	A	B	C	Total
None	15	30	20	65
Someone standing at A	—	3	15	18
Someone standing at B	8	—	12	20 Discard
Someone standing at C	25	11	—	36

The observations made when someone was in B are discarded as the subject has no choice – he has to stand adjacent to B. The observed frequencies of adjacent and not adjacent choices are given below:

	Adjacent	Not adjacent
Observed frequencies	3 + 11	15 + 25

Is this difference significant? Again we will use chi-squared as a test of goodness of fit. The observations in the 'None' condition give the estimate of the relative popularity of A, B and C. These are used to generate the frequencies expected if the position of another person does not affect the subject's choice.

There are 36 observations when someone is in position C and the subject must choose A or B. We know that position B is twice as popular as position A, so we would expect the 36 observations to be divided:

12 in A (not adjacent) and 24 in B (adjacent).

Similarly we would expect the 18 observations when someone was in A to be divided:

$\frac{3}{5} \times 18$ in B (adjacent) and $\frac{2}{5} \times 18$ in C (not adjacent).

The total observed frequencies of adjacent and not adjacent choices are given below:

	Adjacent	Not adjacent
Expected frequencies	24 + 10.8	12 + 7.2

These are compared with the observed frequencies using a chi-squared test with Yates's correction.

Variations

1 The same experiment can be applied to ladies' lavatories with the additional bonus that the variable of occupied compartments can be manipulated by simply closing the appropriate door.

2 Personal space can be investigated in any number of interesting situations. Sommer has used the seating in a reading room. In the same way you could use the choice of seats in a self-service dining room. The problem with these studies is the variation in relationships between subjects. They may be meeting because they are friends. A second problem is the strong preference people can show for particular seats in these places.

3 Argyle points out the cultural differences in personal space. Do these differences apply to spacing in a lavatory? Happily, public loos in colleges are very similar the world over and direct comparisons of behaviour could be made. Do not expect to get a research grant to wander the globe observing behaviour in foreign loos. There are some colleges in Britain for foreign students where such cultural differences could be explored.

4 If the subject is forced to take a position adjacent to someone will this affect his behaviour? We might predict that he would spend as short a time as possible. The effects might be more physiological. I can recall one research finding that the time to start urinating increased the closer the subject stood to the next person. I can foresee some practical difficulties for the intrepid researcher in this field.

References

Argyle, M. (1967), *The Psychology of Interpersonal Behaviour*, Penguin Books
Sommer, R. (1969), *Personal Space*, Prentice Hall, Englewood Cliffs, N.J.

Index guide: personal space; proximity; interpersonal distance

E 10   Eye contact and interpersonal distance

The problem

Relationships between two people can vary enormously in their amount of intimacy. The term 'relationship' here is used in its widest sense to include any response of one person to the other. Two strangers passing in the street may avoid each other's gaze and make only the merest adjustment in direction to avoid bumping into one another. Each has reacted to the other's presence: they have some sort of relationship, however fleeting. It is not very intimate.

A slightly more intimate relationship will be found between a shop assistant and a customer. Questions and answers may be exchanged; they may look directly at one another, smile and so on. If the customer gives his name for some reason, by signing a cheque, the assistant may call him by his name, 'Mr Beer'. The assistant is unlikely to use the customer's christian name – this would be *too* intimate for the relationship and both customer and assistant might feel uncomfortable at such intimacy.

The amount of intimacy in a particular relationship can be expressed in many ways: the proximity of the two people, whether they touch each other – and if so, where; the topic of conversation; the type of language used; the tone of voice; how they address each other; the amount of smiling and eye contact and so on.

The degree of intimacy associated with each of these variables will depend on the culture of the two people. Kissing, for example, is associated with different levels of intimacy in, say, France and Britain. A good and readable background to this subject can be found in Michael Argyle's *The Psychology of Interpersonal Behaviour*. This book includes a splendid example of cultural differences in intimacy.

We have suggested that too much intimacy for a particular relationship will be uncomfortable for the participants – they may be embarrassed. On the other hand, too little intimacy is equally unpleasant – a snub. We strive in a relationship to express the appropriate amount of intimacy for that particular relationship.

We could ask whether there is any interaction between the different expressions of intimacy. That is, if for some reason the degree of intimacy in one form is changed, will this affect the other expressions of intimacy? This is the basis of the experiment.

The variables are two of the expressions of intimacy mentioned earlier: eye contact and proximity. If the distance between the two people is varied will this affect the amount of eye contact? There are three plausible possibilities:

1 No change in eye contact; the two expressions of intimacy are independent.

2 They are directly related; as the physical proximity is increased (the subjects sit closer together) so the eye contact increases. This would suggest that expressions of intimacy must be consistent.

3 They are inversely related; as the physical proximity increases the amount of eye contact decreases. This would suggest that the various expressions of intimacy are balanced to maintain a constant overall level of intimacy.

The experimental situation is an interview between the experimenter and the subject. The hypothesis is that there is a relationship between the amount of eye contact and the distance between the two people.

A method

a) Design
Causal: The independent variable is the distance between the experimenter and the subject. This is varied by the seating arrangements for the interview. In one condition the experimenter and subject are seated at either end of a long table at a distance of 3 metres (long condition).

In the other condition they sit either side of the table at a distance of 1 metre (short condition).

The dependent variable is the amount of eye contact between them. This will depend on the behaviour of the experimenter as well as the subject. There is a serious risk of an experimenter effect. To avoid this the experimenter does not vary his gaze but stares at the subject's eyes throughout each trial.

The measurement of the eye contact presents a problem. It is important that the subject does not realize that eye contact is being measured. On the other hand it is unsatisfactory to have the experimenter measure the subject's eye movements. A little subterfuge is necessary. The subject is asked to take part in an interview designed to measure, say, 'occupational aptitude'. He is told that the interview will be recorded on tape. Before this interview starts, he is told, the experimenter will explain the purpose of the experiment while the technicians set up the recording equipment and adjust the microphones. The two technicians, holding microphones, take up positions close to the experimenter and the subject. They will be recording the eye movements during the experimenter's explanation of the fictitious experiment.

56.

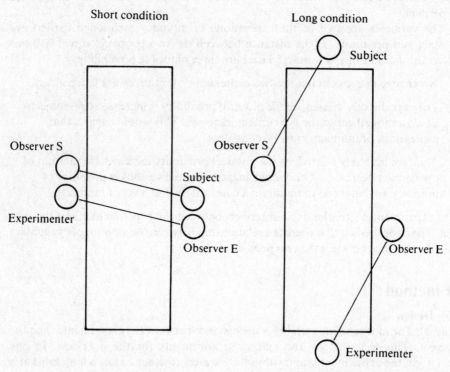

A repeated-measures design is used. Each subject is tested under both conditions of the independent variable. The cover story of adjusting microphones and acoustic levels is used to explain the necessity of changing seats (see 'Procedure').

b) Subjects

The subjects must be unaware of the real purpose of the experiment. Ideally the relationship between the experimenter and the subject should be similar in all cases. This will allow the experimenter to use the same rehearsed 'explanation' for all the subjects. In most cases the subjects will probably know the experimenter by sight and name. If you consider that the sex of the subject will be a significant variable in eye contact it might be as well to restrict the subjects to one sex. This will, of course, restrict the application of your results.

As usual, a pilot study is advisable to estimate the probable importance of these variables.

c) Apparatus

An electric clock is used to measure the amount of eye contact during a set period of the interview. The clock is started by two switches connected in series.

57.

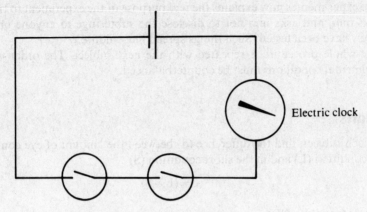

Electric clock

Two push button on-off switches

Each observer holds one switch out of sight. When the person he is watching looks directly at the other person he presses the switch. The clock starts when both switches are being pressed, when there is mutual eye contact between subject and experimenter.

The observers need microphones and a tape recorder to back up the subterfuge.

d) Procedure

The subject comes into the experimental room. The experimenter explains that he will be giving the subject a questionnaire to measure 'occupational aptitude' (or some such fol-de-rol) as part of an experiment. He asks the subject's permission to record the interview. He asks the subject to sit down and suggests that he explains the experiment while the technicians check for 'acoustic level'. The observations are taken during the experimenter's explanation for two reasons:

1　The subject will be more relaxed and off his guard than during what he supposes is the experiment itself.

2　The experimenter must do all the talking during the taking of observations. Speakers commonly break off eye contact as they speak (see *The Psychology of Interpersonal Behaviour*). This variable is avoided if the subject does not speak; the experimenter can also stick to his rehearsed script without interruption.

After one minute of observations the clock is read by one observer and the proportion of mutual eye contact recorded. He then announces to the experimenter that the sound recording level, or whatever, is unsatisfactory and suggests the subject and experimenter use the other seating arrangement. They do so and observations are taken for another minute under the second condition of the IV.

The experimenter now explains the real purpose of the experiment to the subject, thanks him, and asks him not to disclose the subterfuge to anyone until all the subjects have been tested. Such things spread like wildfire.

The whole procedure is repeated with the next subject. The order of the two experimental conditions must be counterbalanced.

Results

For each subject, find the difference (d) between the amount of eye contact in the long condition (L) and in the short condition (S)

$$d = (L - S)$$

Analysis (variables CD)

The statistic (d) is used in the t-test for related samples. Alternatively the differences can be ranked and a Wilcoxon test used. The pilot study will give you some idea of the power needed in any test. You may get away with the sign test.

Variations

1 In the original experiment the subjects are prevented from speaking. It was suspected that a dialogue would affect the amount of eye contact. This suspicion can be tested.

   The experimenter explains that the technicians need samples of speech, to adjust the acoustic level, from the subject and the experimenter. The experimenter asks the subject open-ended questions. Take some care over the content of these questions – this content may be a variable in eye contact. The observers record eye gaze by pressing buttons as before. Four clocks are used to record the proportion of time the subject spends in eye contact when speaking or listening. The electrical arrangement is given in figure 58.

   A third observer, ostensibly operating the tape recorder, operates the pair of two-way switches, A and B. These are thrown to the left when the experimenter is speaking and the subject listens. Clock A1 measures the total time under this condition. Clock B1 measures the amount of eye contact under this condition. Clocks A2 and B2 measure the same events when the subject is speaking. The hypothesis is that the proportion of the time spent in eye contact when the subject listens (A1/B1) is greater than when the subject speaks (A2/B2).

2 It is possible to measure the relationship between eye contact and other expressions of intimacy. Physical contact can be varied by touching the subject's hand or arm. The cover story you concoct to explain this

58.

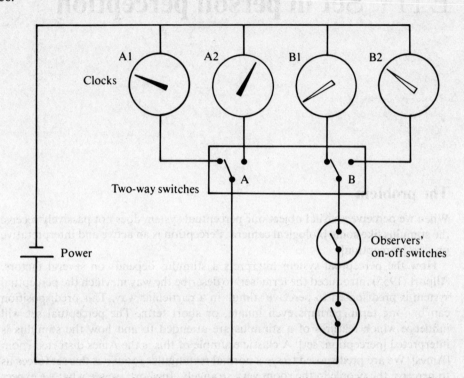

extraordinary behaviour is up to you – I suggest taking the subject's pulse for some reason.

It may be worthwhile considering whether it matters in this variation who is doing the pulse reading. The experimenter carries on a continuous explanation to the subject as before. In one condition the experimenter takes the subject's pulse. In the other condition a confederate of the experimenter does so. Is the effect on eye contact between experimenter and subject the same in both cases? A repeated-measures design is simply explained by the first pulse reader being unable to feel the pulse.

3 There are endless possibilities for studying the relationship between other pairs of expressions of intimacy mentioned earlier.

References

Argyle, M. (1967), *The Psychology of Interpersonal Behaviour*, Penguin Books.

Index guide: personal space; eye contact; intimacy; proximity

E 11   Set in person perception

The problem

When we perceive a visual object our perceptual system does not passively receive the stimulus like some biological camera. Perception is an active and interpretative process [perception].

How the perceptual system interprets a stimulus depends on several factors. Allport (1955) introduced the term 'set' to describe the way in which the perceptual system is predisposed to perceive stimuli in a particular way. This predisposition can be long term, perhaps even innate, or short term. The perceptual set will influence which features of a stimulus are attended to and how the stimulus is interpreted [perception: set]. A classic example of this is the Ames distorted room [Ames]. We are predisposed to see a normal rectangular room but this set forces us to perceive the people in the room very strangely. In short, we see what we expect to see.

A similar process may be involved in perceiving other people. Some information about a person is directly available to our senses: the voice, accent, physical appearance, height, colour of hair, etc. On the basis of these we make judgements of other characteristics: personality, mood, intelligence, health and so on. This perceiving of another person's characteristics is called person perception or [interpersonal perception]. Many studies have examined the way in which we arrive at these assessments. We may associate certain characteristics with visible features. Allport suggests that fat people are seen as being jolly; people whose eyebrows meet are seen as being untrustworthy; and those with high foreheads as being more intelligent.

Some characteristics may be associated with others. Asch (1946) gave subjects a list of characteristics of an imaginary person. They were asked to describe the person. Asch found that the change of one word in the list of characteristics ('warm' or 'cold') could produce very different descriptions. In these studies the subject has only the experimenter's story or list of characteristics to go on. When we meet a person for the first time he is there to be seen and heard. How does our information about him affect our perception? This information could work in two ways. It may affect how we interpret the information we get from visual and auditory perception. It may also affect those perceptions themselves as in the studies of set in visual perception mentioned earlier.

In this experiment a group of subjects interview a man. All the subjects can ask questions and all hear the man's answers. They are all given a brief description of the man before the interview. This description varies in one respect, his occupation. Will this variation affect how they perceive the man? The experimental situation commonly occurs in everyday life. Many important decisions influencing the individual's future are made on the basis of interviews. Typically the interviewers have some information about the individual before the interview. Does this produce a significant set in the judgements? The subjects are asked to assess various characteristics of the man: his personality, intelligence, ambitions, honesty and so on. They are also asked to estimate his height.

The experimental hypothesis is that the subjects' perception of the man will depend on the occupation they believe him to have.

A method

a) Design
Causal: The independent variable is the occupation the subjects believe the man to have. Half the subjects are told that he is a retired professor from the Open University. The other half are told that he is an unemployed labourer. In all other respects their information is identical.

The dependent variable is their perception of the man. The subjects are asked to assess several characteristics of the man using a standard form. Each characteristic is to be measured on a ten-point scale between two extremes (see 'Apparatus').

An independent-subjects design is used.

b) Subjects
The subjects must be unaware of the purpose of the experiment. Other than that there are no restrictions.

c) Apparatus
One man (or woman). Exactly who you choose will depend on the occupations the subjects have been given. He should at least be compatible with your stories. He must not be known to any of the subjects. He must be unaware which subjects have been told which story, or the alternative occupations. It is prudent to give him some idea of the experiment so that he can avoid exposing the deception when answering the subjects' questions.

The subjects are given a duplicated sheet on which to record their perception of the man. Under each characteristic there will be a ten-point scale between two extremes with a space for general comments.

Example:
Intelligence (Please underline the appropriate point on the scale) (Very unintelligent) 1 2 3 4 5 6 7 8 9 10 (Very intelligent) General comments of intelligence:

Which comments you include are up to you. Bear in mind that the subjects must believe they are taking part in the experiment for some reason. I suggest they be told the experiment is to test the reliability of interviewing techniques and their answers will be compared to assess the amount of variation. They are told that the duplicated form is a standard form used in the college for staff or student interviews. The form can be suitably headed. Make sure that the categories are compatible with this story. Some categories are suggested below.

Characteristic	*Extremes*		
Intelligence	Very Intelligent	–	Very Unintelligent
Social ability	Gregarious	–	Solitary
Personality	Introvert	–	Extrovert
Honesty	Very Trustworthy	–	Very Untrustworthy
Imagination	Very Imaginative	–	Very Unimaginative

It is worth having one section for overall impressions. Although these may be impossible to quantify they can be very revealing.

d) Procedure
The subjects are randomly allocated to two groups. The practical problem in this experiment is to give the subjects different stories without their being aware that they are in two experimental groups. Each group is told the (erroneous) purpose of the experiment and told the barest details of the man to be interviewed.

Example:
1 He is married with two children. He lives locally and is a retired professor from the Open University.
2 He is married with two children. He lives locally and is a building labourer but he is unemployed at the present.

The subjects are told that they should not talk to each other until the interview is over as this would affect the results of the experiment. Both groups of subjects are taken into the room where they will interview the man. They are told that, as the experiment is intended to reproduce a general interview, they should avoid specific questions about his background. The purpose of this instruction is to reduce the chance of questions exposing the deception.

The man is brought into the room and introduced to the subjects. They are free to ask him general questions about himself, his opinions, attitudes and so on. If a dangerous question is asked the experimenter should explain that it cannot be asked and pass on to the next one. After half an hour the interview is stopped and the subjects are asked to complete their forms without discussion. When this is done the man stands to leave and the subjects are asked to estimate his height and record these estimates on the form. The forms are collected and the experimenter explains the deception and its purpose.

Results

The forms are sorted into the two experimental groups and the scores on each characteristic are compared.

Analysis (variables CD)
As the characteristics of intelligence, personality, etc., are measured on a ten-point scale there will be many ties on each characteristic. The non-parametric Mann-Whitney test is unsuitable in this case and a t-test for independent samples must be used. The scores of the two groups are compared for each characteristic. Remember that with a significance level of 5% one in twenty characteristics will show a significant difference between groups by chance alone. The comparison of estimates of height does not use a ten-point scale but there are likely to be many ties here also as subjects will tend to give estimates in whole inches. Again, the t-test must be used.

The comments given for each characteristic can be included to highlight significant differences found statistically. Look for any consistent differences in the overall comments. These may be valuable in pointing the way to further research.

Variations

1 This experiment reproduces the conditions found in many interviews. The hypothesis suggests that the interviewer's perception of an individual depends, to some extent, on information (true or false) about the individual. What other variables do we commonly suppose might affect an interviewer?

   Prospective applicants for a job are commonly told that the letter of application is important. The independent variable can be this letter. The subjects are told that they will be shown a letter of application written by the man to simulate the conditions of a real interview. Two letters containing the same information are produced. One is type-written on thick white paper with no errors. The other is hand-written on cheap, lined notepaper with some errors.

A refinement of this variation would be to vary the language used in the two letters. Bernstein (1959) identifies two types of language in Britain: a 'public' language used by relatively uneducated people and a so-called formal language more commonly found in better educated upper- and middle-class people [language: and social class]. Bernstein has suggested that among other effects of these two languages people using the public language are seen as being less intelligent than users of the formal language. It is possible to construct two type-written letters containing the same information but couched in the two different language styles. Details of these language styles can be found in most sociology textbooks.

2   There are many other possibilities of variation in the information given to the subjects. These can be singular points of difference between the stories (as in the original experiment) such as wealth, or rank (if the subjects are all told that the man has recently retired from the army).

Alternatively the backgrounds can differ in many points to give a contrast in social class. This can be built up by giving differences in sports, hobbies, daily newspaper, choice of drinks and so forth.

3   The effect of set in person perception is recognized in our legal system. The jury in a crown court are unaware of any previous convictions of a defendant until they have given their verdict and sentence is being considered by the judge. A variation of the experiment would be to give the information to the subjects after the interview but before they record their assessments. Can the information influence the assessments in this situation?

References

Allport, F.H. (1955), *Theories of Perception and the Concept of Structure*, Wiley

Ames, A. - *see* Ittelson, W.H. (1952), *The Ames Demonstrations in Perception*, Princeton University Press/ OUP

Asch, S.E. (1946), 'Forming Impressions of Personality', *J. Abnorm. Soc. Psychol.*, vol. 41, 258–90

Bernstein, B. (1959), 'A public language: some sociological implications of a linguistic form', *Brit. J. Sociol.*, vol. 10, 311–26

Index guide: person perception; interpersonal perception; set; language

E 12　The risky decisions of groups

The problem

Many decisions that affect our lives are taken by groups after some discussion rather than by individuals. Government committees, the Cabinet, councils, juries, boards of governors and directors discuss a problem and arrive at a group decision. The hope is that this group decision is better than the average of the individual decisions – that is the point of all the chat.

It was a little disquieting when some researchers (e.g. Stoner, 1961; Wallach, Kogan and Bem, 1962) found that group decisions to a range of problems were consistently riskier than the average of the individual decisions. Typically, subjects in these experiments were asked to decide the justifiable risk in some situation, for example, a business deal or marriage. The subjects made their own decision and were then asked to form a group and arrive at a unanimous decision on the same problem. The group decision was usually riskier than the average of the individual decisions.

The decisions made by Stoner's groups did not directly affect the members of the group (neither do the decisions made by juries and others mentioned earlier). Is this fact important in producing this shift to risk? We can design a similar experiment where these decisions have a direct consequence for the subjects.

The subjects are asked to gamble with the experimenter. The experimenter has a bag containing ten red counters. Into this bag he will put some white counters, as many as the subjects wish. One counter is to be picked randomly from the bag. The subjects bet that it will be white. The subject's decision is the number of white counters he wants placed in the bag. Of course he will want an enormous number but there is a catch: the experimenter will only bet with the subjects who decide on the lowest number of counters. So, there is a pressure to take a risk, otherwise the subject will not get a chance at the money. There is also a pressure to be cautious – it's his money. The gamble is repeated with the subjects in groups. The experimenter will bet with the riskiest group. Each member in the group bets the same amount as in the individual condition.

The hypothesis is that the number of white counters to be placed in the bag is smaller in the group decision than in the individual decisions.

A method

a) Design
Causal: The independent variable is whether the subject's decision is made as an individual or as a member of a group after some discussion.

The dependent variable is the decision, the number of white counters the subject wants placed in the bag before he will bet. This is a repeated-measures design. It is not possible to counterbalance the order of the individual and group decisions as the group decision is likely to have an effect on any subsequent individual decision. You can check this by asking subjects to make another individual decision after the group decision – but before the bet is carried out and anyone has lost or won anything. Do the individual decisions show any shift to risk?

b) Subjects
There are some problems here. There may be moral considerations about gambling in some places. This can be avoided to some extent if the experimenter returns any money he wins after the experiment (he may not be able to retrieve any he loses). The subjects should understand the gamble and be asked if they wish to carry on. It is important that they believe all bets are real and have cash to part with.

c) Apparatus
Ten red counters and two or three dozen white counters (any tokens of any colour will do). A bag in which to shake them. Each subject is given a sheet of paper to record his decisions.

d) Procedure
The subjects are gathered together. The experimenter shows them the empty bag and the ten red counters, explains the gamble, and that he will only bet with the lowest five decisions. This number is chosen as the same as the group size in the second condition. The same amount of money will change hands in the two conditions.

The subjects are asked to decide how many white counters must be placed in the bag before they will bet, say, 20p that a white counter will be picked out. They must not discuss this decision with anyone. This decision is recorded on the subject's sheet with his name and any other information the experimenter requires.

The experimenter identifies the five lowest decisions and explains that the bets will be carried out after the group decisions. Subjects are randomly allocated to groups of five. Each group is asked to reach a unanimous decision and told that the experimenter will bet £1 (20p each) with the group making the lowest decision. Under each condition the choice for the subject is the same. His stake and chances of winning have not changed. Each subject records the decision of his group. Finally, subjects are asked to make another individual decision. The subjects' sheets are collected. The experimenter can now go ahead with the various bets. This is not necessary but you might enjoy it. It might also help to persuade your pool of subjects that you occasionally tell the truth. This could be vital in some future experiment.

Results

For each group calculate the average of the individual decisions taken first. You might consider whether the mean or the median is the more appropriate measure of the 'average' decision.

Analysis
The difference between this average and the group decision is the statistic (d) used in a Wilcoxon test or a t-test for related samples.

The hypothesis suggests that the decision of the group will be lower than the average decision of individuals but in this case it would be dangerous to rely on a one-tailed test. Some later research by Nordhøy has found some types of problem which produce a shift to caution in the group.

A second analysis is used to look for any significant difference between the individual decisions before and after the group decision.

Variations

1   In this gamble the odds are in favour of the subject if his decision is above ten white counters. This is obvious to the subjects and may allow little group discussion and hence opportunity for the group to shift to risk. In a simple variation the odds remain the same although this is not so obvious. The independent variable is the certainty of the odds. The variation is in the number of red counters in the experimenter's bag.

The experimenter explains that the red counters will be picked from a box containing 25 red counters and 25 white counters. 20 counters will be picked at random and the red ones placed in the bag. The bag could contain anything from 0 to 20 red counters, the most likely number being 10. The subjects make their decisions before the red counters are picked.

Will this procedure give a different result? You can compare the shift to risk (if any) or the values of the individual and group decisions under the two conditions.

2 Gambling is predominantly a male pastime. Is this reflected in the riskiness of their decisions?

3 Another obvious variable to tinker with is the size of the stakes. If you attempt to vary this the stakes must remain believable. It makes sense to use very low stakes first, carrying out the bets, and then raise the stakes. These large bets need not be carried out after you have collected your information.

4 Gambling is fascinating behaviour. In a straightforward coin-tossing bet we can regard winning as rewarding and losing as punishing. If the subject has control over the size of the stakes we might expect him to reduce the stake after punishment and increase the stakes after reward. Is this so? Is there any pattern of changing the stakes following successful or unsuccessful trials?

References

Nordhøy, F. 1962, *Group Interaction in Decision-making Under Risk*, unpublished master's thesis, School of Industrial Management, MIT (quoted in Brown, R., *Social Psychology*)

Stoner, J.A.F. (1961), *A Comparison of Individual and Group Decisions Including Risk*, unpublished master's thesis, School of Industrial Management, MIT (quoted in Brown, R., *Social Psychology*)

Wallach, M.A., Kogan, N. and Bem, D.J. (1962), 'Group influence on individual risk taking', *J. Abnorm. Soc. Psychol.*, 65, 75–86

Index guide: group decisions; risk; gambling

E 13　Verbal participation and influence in group decisions

The problem

Many of the decisions that affect our lives are made by groups (see E 12). The individuals in these groups will all have their own points of view in any problem. The decision of the group will presumably lie somewhere between these individual points of view. Some people, however, will be more influential in the negotiation than others: that is, the group decision will lie closer to their point of view than to that of their fellows. This may be the result of their wisdom becoming evident to their fellows; it may be the result of other factors. What factors influence success in negotiation? This experiment looks at one possibility – the amount of talking each person does.

On the one hand we could argue that the most influential person in a group decision will be the one who is allowed the greatest part of the discussion. Certainly, many public speakers appear to behave as though this might be a causal relationship. On the other hand the purpose of talking may be to resolve differences of opinion. In this case we could argue that the person who talks the most is the most anxious to resolve the differences and hence the most likely to concede his point of view to achieve that end.

The hypothesis in this experiment is that there is a relationship between a person's verbal contribution and influence in a group decision. For simplicity the groups used in the experiment consist of just two subjects. The problem they have to resolve has no 'correct' answer. The subjects are asked to imagine that they are to hand out a large sum of money to several charities. Their task is to arrange a list of seven charities in the order in which they think the money should be divided: the first charity will be given the most money, the last will be given the least. Each subject makes his own decision first and then they must make a group decision on which they both agree. The experimenter measures the amount of talking each does in reaching this group decision. This is compared to their success in the negotiation.

A method

a) Design

Non-causal: One experimental variable is the subject's success in the negotiation. This is measured by the closeness of the group decision to his original arrangement of the seven charities. The other experimental variable is the amount of talking each subject does. This is measured by the experimenter using two electric clocks, one for each subject. Each clock is started by pressing a switch button connecting the clock to the power supply. The experimenter presses the button whenever the subject is talking.

This is a form of matched-subjects design; a subject's score on both variables is measured relative to the other subject.

b) Subjects

The subjects should be unaware that their amount of talking is being measured. The subjects can be roughly matched for age and any other variable you consider important.

c) Apparatus

The experimenter operates two on/off buttons connected to two electric clocks. All this apparatus should be concealed from the subjects. If necessary the group discussion can be recorded on tape and the measurements of talking taken later.

d) Procedure

The subjects are asked to take part in an experiment on group decision. They are given the list of seven charities and asked to arrange them as described earlier. The seven charities should be as varied as possible. For example: RNLI, Cancer Research, The Salvation Army, Age Concern, RSPCA, Oxfam, NSPCC. The subjects record their individual decisions on a sheet of paper. This is collected by the experimenter.

The subjects are allocated to pairs. Check that the subjects in each pair have made different individual decisions (subsequent discussions would be rather pointless otherwise). Each pair is given the same list and asked to reach a joint decision of the order of 'worthiness'. They should not be allowed to do this by recalling their individual decisions and mathematically dividing the order. The decision should be argued and justified to their mutual satisfaction. The experimenter observes the discussion without being obtrusive and measures the verbal contribution of each subject. He records the joint decision when it is reached.

Results

The subject's original order is compared to the joint decision. The total difference in ranks between these two orders is the subject's score of success in the negotiation.

Analysis (variables CD)

A matched-subjects design is treated like a repeated-measures design in the analysis. The two conditions in this case are 'talking most' and 'talking least'. Take the score of the subject that talks least from the score of the other. The sign of this difference is used in the sign test. If the most frequent sign is positive, this suggests that the most influential person is he who talks the most.

Variations

1 In this experiment there is no 'correct' solution to the task set by the experimenter. No subject can claim a superior skill in the task. Would such a claim influence the decision?

One argument for relying on group decisions is that the specialized knowledge of the individuals is available to the group – but is it used? In this variation the subjects are divided, without their knowledge, into 'winners' and 'losers'. Subjects are asked to take part in a perceptual experiment. The task is to judge the distance of an object. The object is the dim light in a darkened room used in E 14 (p. 254). The subject estimates the distance by positioning a second light. The actual distance of the light is varied between one and four metres. Each subject makes three estimates at different distances. The 'winners' are told, on each trial, that their estimates were within 2 cm of the correct distance – regardless of their actual accuracy. They are congratulated. The 'losers' are told that they were 30–40 cm out on each trial. Each winner is paired with a loser. They are asked to judge another distance and record their estimate silently on a piece of paper. They can then talk and must arrive at an agreed estimate. Does this estimate lie closer to the winner's individual estimate? Can this result be reversed by subsequently reversing their roles in further trials?

In a similar variation, with naive subjects, the winners and losers are each told that their errors in the preliminary trials are the same – around 15 cm. The winners are told that this is remarkably good, the losers that this is rather poor. Will this produce a shift in the agreed estimate?

Index guide: self-perception; group decisions; dominance

E 14 Conformity and the autokinetic effect

The problem

When a dim light, a glowing cigarette end, is viewed in an otherwise dark room the light appears to move. This is the autokinetic effect [autokinetic effect]. It is possible to estimate the distance and direction of this apparent movement. Sherif (1935) used this effect to investigate conformity. Subjects were asked to estimate the distance the light appeared to move. In one condition subjects were unaware of each other's estimates and these varied considerably from subject to subject. In the other conditions subjects reported their estimates aloud. Over several trials the estimates under this condition converged on a group norm [conformity] [Sherif, M.]. This is not very surprising: the subjects had very little information to go on in the darkened room. The *distance* the light appears to move depends on the apparent distance of the observer from the light [size constancy] and this also changes as the observer stares at the light, making the estimate of the distance the light appeared to move rather uncertain. Many subjects also report that the light appears to move without actually going anywhere. This makes the estimation of distance travelled rather difficult.

Estimates of the *direction* of the apparent movement are free from both of these difficulties. This direction is unaffected by the apparent distance of the objects from the observer. It is also possible to state confidently the direction of movement when the light does not appear to get anywhere. Do these estimates of direction show the same conformity as the estimates of distance when subjects report their estimates aloud?

The experimental hypothesis is that there will be closer agreement between the subjects' judgements of the direction of apparent movement of the light when these judgements are made aloud.

A method

a) Design

Causal: The independent variable is whether or not the subjects are aware of each other's judgement of the direction of apparent movement. In one condition the subjects report aloud this direction as the positions on a clock face. When the light is seen as moving vertically upwards the subject reports 'Twelve o'clock'; when it is seen moving horizontally to the left he reports 'Nine o'clock' and so on. In the other condition he keeps quiet.

The dependent variable is the agreement between the two subjects' judgement of direction. Each subject continuously records his judgements under both conditions of the IV by the position of a circular rheostat, a variable electrical resistance. A pen recorder continuously measures the difference between the positions of the two rheostats so measuring the agreement of the two judgements of direction (see 'Apparatus').

A repeated-measures design is used; each pair of subjects judging the direction of apparent movement under both conditions of the IV.

b) Subjects

There are no special restrictions. Pairs of subjects are selected randomly.

c) Apparatus

The experimental room must be light-proof. The subjects sit side by side at a table facing a small dim light source at a distance of, say, three metres. It is important that the light is not bright enough to reveal anything else in the room. The autokinetic effect is destroyed if the observer can see any other object. This is no problem when the lights are first switched out in the room but as the subjects adapt to the darkness they may become aware of other objects by the glow of the light source.

A pen recorder is used in this method of recording the direction of apparent movement.

The details of the electrical set-up will depend on the type of pen recorder. Figure 59 shows a general arrangement. (It may look a little daunting to experimenters with no scientific background. Don't worry; get a physicist to tell you how to put it together.) The power supplies to the two variable resistances, A and B, have the same potential.

The subject records the direction of the apparent movement by the position of the variable resistance. A large pointer is attached to the resistance so that the position can be felt in the dark. When the subjects agree exactly on the direction of movement by setting the resistances to the same position there will be no current through the pen recorder and the pen will record a straight line down the centre of

59.

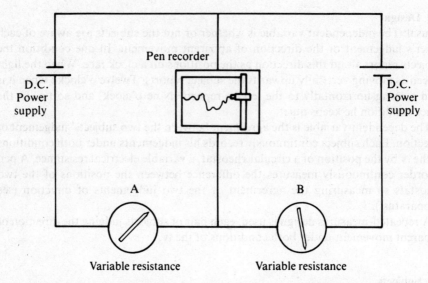

the chart. When they disagree there will be a difference in the two resistances, A and B, resulting in a deflection to the right or left. There is maximum disagreement between the subjects when the pointers are set at 180° to each other.

60. *Maximum disagreement registered on the two resistances*

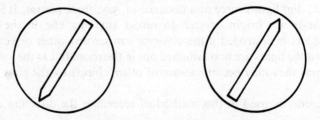

This is not the maximum deflection of the pen. If the higher of the two resistances is increased (or the smaller is decreased) the pen deflection will increase but the agreement of the two subjects will now be closer. We will see how the trace of the pen recorder can be interpreted in the 'Results' section.

Before the experiment begins the pen recorder is adjusted so that the maximum possible deflection is near the edge of the chart.

d) Procedure
The two subjects are brought into the experimental room. The experiment is explained and they are shown how to record the apparent movement of the light by

moving the pointer on the variable resistance to the points around a clock face. They are told that in one condition this direction is also reported aloud. The order of the two conditions is counterbalanced.

The room is darkened and the small dim light is switched on. The pen recorder situated outside the experimental room is started and the subjects observe and record the apparent movement of the light for a predetermined time, say two minutes. A trial under the other condition is run.

The whole procedure is repeated for further pairs of subjects.

Results

The pen recorder will produce a trace something like this:

61.

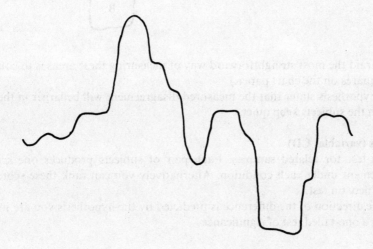

By setting the resistances at suitable levels the experimenter can find the positions on this trace of maximum agreement (that is, the base line, with no deflection of the pen) and maximum disagreement, when the pointers are set at 180° to each other. These lines are drawn on the trace (see figure 62). The amount of disagreement is measured by the area under the curve between the base line and the lines of maximum disagreement (the shaded portion of figure 62). Traces *outside* the lines of maximum disagreement record increasing agreement (areas A and B in figure 62). These areas must be subtracted from the shaded area to give the total measure of disagreement. That is, the measure of disagreement in figure 62 is calculated as:

(Area of shaded portion) − (Area A and Area B)

62.

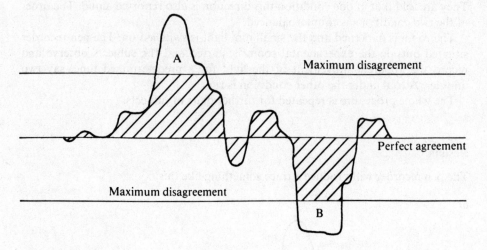

(I am afraid the most straightforward way of measuring these areas is to count the small squares on the chart paper.)

The hypothesis states that the measured disagreement will be larger in the trials in which the subjects keep quiet.

Analysis (variables CD)

Use a t-test for related samples. Each pair of subjects produces one score of disagreement under each condition. Alternatively you can rank these scores and use a Wilcoxon test.

As the direction of the difference is predicted by the hypothesis you are justified in using a one-tailed test of significance.

Variations

These fall into two categories: experiments looking more closely at conformity using the autokinetic effect, and experiments looking at the autokinetic effect itself.

1   Asch (1952) found that conformity increased if the subject believed that the other persons were more competent at the task. A simple variation can test this finding in the autokinetic effect. While the room is still dark, subjects are told that one of them will be given a pair of glasses. These are of plain glass but the subjects are told that they are 'polarizing' or 'low frequency filtering' or some such nonsense and that they will affect the direction of the apparent movement. In fact, *neither* subject is given the glasses; each believes that the

other is wearing them. The subjects report their perceptions aloud. Will the conformity be less in this case where they do not expect to perceive the same movement? (Of course there is no reason why they should agree in the ordinary talking condition.) Their disagreement score can be compared with the scores in both of the first two conditions.

This is an interesting case as there is no suggestion of 'competence' in the original task. However, the suggestion that the two subjects are now visually different could produce the opposite of conformity rather than simply a lessening in conformity.

2   The experimental set-up is ideal for the use of stooges. Several confederates of the experimenter participate with one subject. The confederates have dummy pointers; the pen recorder simply serves to record the judgements of the subject.

On the trial in which the subjects report aloud the stooges all report movement in a predetermined direction. Does the subject conform to this unanimity although there is no suggestion in the autokinetic effect of a 'right' or 'wrong' perception?

3   The autokinetic effect is experienced whether or not the subject is aware that the light does not actually move. You could ask, however, whether the effect is stronger if the subject *expects* a physical movement of the light.

A single subject indicates some movement of the light by pressing a switch activating an electric clock. In one condition the subject is told that the light will be moved by the experimenter during the trial, although no such movement occurs. Under the other condition the subject is told that the light will remain stationary. Such an experiment will use independent subjects.

Do these different expectations affect the amount of autokinetic reported in a trial of some predetermined length?

4   The last variation can be extended by suggesting that the autokinetic effect is correlated with various subject variables. Subjects are told that the autokinetic effect is strongest in persons with, say, high introversion scores on a personality test. The subject is asked to rate himself on an introversion/extroversion scale. This self-assessment is then compared with the amount of autokinetic movement reported. The possibilities here are endless.

5   The autokinetic effect may be correlated with performance on other tasks. A reasonable possibility is a relationship between the amount of autokinetic movement reported and the induced movement on a pendulum (see E 12).

References

Asch, S.E. (1952), *Social Psychology*, Prentice Hall

Sherif, M. (1935), 'A study of some social factors in perception', *Archives of Psychol.*, NY, No. 187

Index guide: autokinetic movement; conformity; size constancy

E 15   Conformity in a Muller–Lyer illusion

The problem

In D 1 subjects are asked to mark the mid-point of a straight line, with or without arrow-heads. A new duplicated figure is used for each subject and subjects are prevented from seeing each other's marked mid-point. This is an elementary precaution to ensure the independence of responses: the subject may be influenced by the response of another subject. We can investigate this influence by allowing the subject to see another (spurious) marked mid-point. Unfortunately subjects in psychology experiments are a suspicious lot. They have a well-founded belief that the experimenter has not been totally candid about the purpose of the experiment. The problem in this experiment is to allow the subject to see the spurious mark without him suspecting that this is the important variable in the experiment. One solution is to make the mark with a sharp pencil and then rub it out. Some trace of the mark will remain to be seen by the subject.

The position of these false marks is varied either side of the mean perceived mid-point. This can be established by carrying out D 1. The hypothesis is that the position of the false mark will influence where the subject places his mark when judging the mid-point of the line.

A method

a)   Design
Causal: The independent variable is the position of the false mark – to the right or left of the mean perceived mid-point. The dependent variable is the position of the subject's marked mid-point.

An independent-subjects design is used. Even the most credulous might become suspicious if he were allowed to see two 'erased' mid-points.

b)   Subjects
The subjects must be naive. Don't use psychology students.

c) Apparatus
The duplicated figures used in D 1 can be used. From this demonstration you will have found the mean perceived mid-point of the arrow-head figure. The distance between this and the actual mid-point can be used as a unit of measurement for placing the false marks. For example, if the line is 20 cm long and the mean perceived mid-point is 9 cm from the left, the false marks are placed at 8 cm and 10 cm from the left of the figure. The false marks are made with a sharp pencil and then rubbed out. Make sure that a discernible mark remains.

d) Procedure
The procedure follows that of D 1. The subject is asked to mark the mid-point of the arrowed figure and the plain straight line. The order of presentation of these two figures is counterbalanced. In this experiment the plain straight line is redundant but it may be as well to use it to deflect the subject's attention from the real purpose of the experiment.

The subjects are randomly allocated to the two conditions of the IV.

Results

The completed figures are sorted into the two conditions of the IV. The position of the subject's perceived mid-point is measured from, say, the sharp end of the figure. The mean of these positions is found for each group.

Analysis (variables CD)
The significance of any difference between these means is found using a t-test for independent samples. The hypothesis does not predict the direction of the difference and so a two-tailed test will be used.

Variations

1   In this experiment the distance of the false marks either side of the mean perceived mid-point is kept constant. You might ponder on the effect of varying this distance. What would we predict might occur as the false is moved further away from the middle of the figure? We might expect that the influence on the subject's response would initially increase, i.e. the subject will put his mark further away from the normally perceived mid-point. On the other hand the false mark must soon reach a position where the subject will judge his (fictitious) predecessor as incompetent in judging mid-points and ignore the mark.

2   We have taken some trouble in this experiment to hide its purpose, of looking at conformity. We can consider the effect of revealing this purpose before the

subject makes his judgement. There are three possible effects on the subject. He could ignore the false mark on the figure. He could conform by placing his mark close to or on the false mark. He could do the opposite, that is, place his mark some distance from the false mark to avoid conforming. A simple variation of the experiment investigates these possibilities.

Subjects are taken in pairs. The experimenter explains that he is trying to measure the effect of seeing another person's judgement of the mid-point of the arrowed figure. Both subjects are given a clean arrowed figure and asked to mark the mid-point with a pencil provided by the experimenter. The experimenter collects the figures, makes some pretence of measuring the mid-points and overmarks with a pen the subjects' marks. They are then asked to make a second judgement on each other's original. In fact they are given back their own figure. The first two possibilities mentioned above, of ignoring the mark or conforming, will predict that the second mark is superimposed on the first. The third possibility, of avoiding conforming, will predict a new mark being made. What actually happens?

Index guide: conformity; visual illusions

E 16   Television in tastes and personal relationships: a balance model

The problem

Studies of conformity look at the tendency of people to change their behaviour to conform with others around them [conformity]. Of course, they may also change their behaviour in order *not* to conform with others around them. Which, if either, of these alternatives is chosen will depend on many factors, not least how the person feels about the people around him. This variable, the subject's feelings towards a second person, is the basis of this experiment.

Many theories have suggested the need for consistency or balance in our attitudes, values and beliefs [attitudes: change in]. For example, Festinger (1957) used the concept of consonance between a person's attitudes, etc., with its opposite, dissonance [cognitive dissonance]. Newcomb (1953) put forward a similar model of cognitive balance. The general principle is straightforward and has applications to a vast range of behaviour. In its essence the theory says that we wish to be similar to people we like and different from people we don't like. There are three variables in this model:

1   Our behaviour (or attitudes, beliefs and so on).

2   The other person's behaviour (or, rather, our *perception* of his behaviour, attitudes and so on).

3   Our feelings towards the other person.

These are represented in a simple diagram (Figure 63). For simplicity we will imagine that each variable can only be positive or negative, denoting approval or disapproval.

Take an example all too familiar to parents of young children. The subject (S), my daughter Emily, likes spaghetti (X). She also likes her friend Juliette (O) - who does *not* like spaghetti (figure 64).

63.

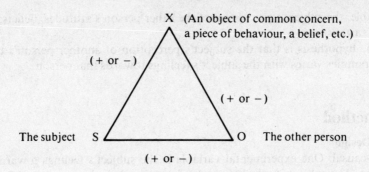

X (An object of common concern, a piece of behaviour, a belief, etc.)

(+ or −)

(+ or −)

The subject   S

(+ or −)

O   The other person

64.

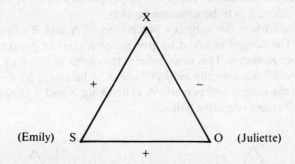

X

+

−

(Emily)   S

+

O   (Juliette)

This is a situation of imbalance. It is uncomfortable to the subject. One of the variables must change. Juliette will not change her attitude to spaghetti so Emily has two choices: she can change her attitude to spaghetti, or she can change her attitude to Juliette. Either of these will produce cognitive balance.

65.

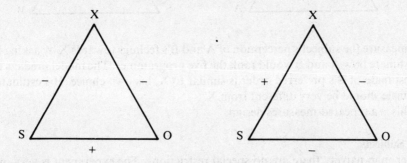

X

−

−

S

+

O

X

+

−

S

−

O

She takes the first choice and conforms, declaring that she never liked spaghetti.

Subjects in Asch's classic experiment on conformity (1952) had the same choice: to reject their own judgement and conform, or to reject the group [conformity].

The following experiment examines the balance model by looking at the third variable, the subject's perception of the other person's attitudes, beliefs, or in this case, tastes.

The hypothesis is that the subject's perception of another person's taste in TV programmes varies with the subject's feelings towards that person.

A method

a) Design
Non-causal: One experimental variable is the subject's feelings towards another person. The subject is asked to think of two people he knows, A and B. A is to be someone he dislikes, B is to be someone he likes.

The other variable is the subject's perception of A and B's taste in television programmes. The subject is asked to give his own taste in programmes by rank ordering five programmes. This rank order is the object of common concern (X) in the balance model. Clearly the subject likes X – he chose it. According to the balance model the subject will perceive A as disliking X and B as liking X if he is to achieve a comfortable cognitive balance.

66.

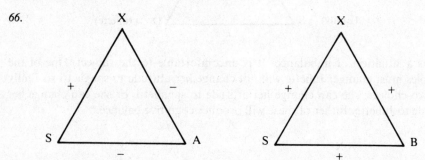

We measure the subject's perception of A and B's feelings towards X by asking him to estimate how A and B would rank the five programmes. The model predicts that his estimate of B's preferred order is similar to X, his own choice. His estimate of A's taste should be very different from X.

This is a repeated-measures design.

b) Subjects
Other than naivety there are no special restrictions. The experiment is very quick and a large number of subjects can be used.

c) Apparatus
The subjects are asked to order five television programmes. This is an ideal response for a questionnaire. The exact form of the questionnaire is up to you. The ques-

tionnaire asks the subject to think of two people, A and B. A is someone he likes, B is someone he dislikes. There is no need for the names of A and B to be written down but the subject must stick to his choice of A and B. The subject is then asked to rank five television programmes in three ways:

1 His own preference.

2 His estimate of A's preference.

3 His estimate of B's preference.

The order in which he is asked for these preferences should be randomized.

The choice of television programmes should cover as broad a range of tastes as possible without any being too specialized. The subjects should at least be familiar with the titles and have a good idea what the programmes are like.

Some of the variations will require more information, e.g. the age or sex of the subject. It is usually a good idea to ask for each subject's name in case you later think of something else you need to know.

d) Procedure

The exact procedure will depend on the questionnaire. To avoid biased sampling (p. 148) it is simplest to find subjects in groups, ask if they will take part in a simple experiment and hand out the questionnaire. It is important that a subject makes his choice of A and B *before* he sees the other question. You could use two sheets of paper or give the first instruction verbally and then hand out the question on TV preferences.

The subjects are asked to write their answers on the sheet without discussing them with anyone.

Collect the answers and thank the subjects.

Results

For each subject find the difference between his own preferred order and his estimate for A. These differences in rank order are measured in the same way as a rank-order correlation.

Example:
The subject's preferred order of the five TV programmes is:

a e d c b

His estimate of A's preferred order is:

d b e a c

a is ranked 1 and 4, difference 3
b is ranked 5 and 2, difference 3

c is ranked 4 and 5, difference 1
d is ranked 3 and 1, difference 2
e is ranked 2 and 3, difference 1
                                    ‾‾

Total difference 10 = Score A

Score B is found in the same way.

Analysis
Each subject will have two scores, score A and score B. These will each be an even number integer between 0 and 12. These results are unsuitable for a t-test as they are hardly continuous. Nor can you use a Wilcoxon test as there will be a large number of ties. The solution is to use a sign test by finding the *sign* of (A − B), see page 86. Although this is not a powerful test you can use a large number of subjects. The balance model predicts that score A will be larger than score B: that is, (A − B) will be positive.

Variations

1   Subjects can be asked to estimate the TV preferences of a third person, C, towards whom they have neutral feelings. The model predicts that the C score will lie between the A and B scores. So (A − C) will be positive and (C − B) will be positive.

2   The experiment looks at cognitive balance using tastes in TV programmes. A similar procedure can be used to test a balance model for beliefs, attitudes or behaviour by asking the subject to estimate the appropriate reactions of persons A and B.
      It is not essential to use a ranking response. If the subject is asked to give some point on a continuum the more powerful Wilcoxon or t-tests can be used. If the subject's response is to be discrete – yes or no to some question – the estimates of A and B's response can be 'the same' or 'different'. A chi-squared test is used.

3   Several studies have found a sex difference in conformity: females tend to be more conforming than males. This could be interpreted in two ways on the balance model:
      a) Females could have a greater need for cognitive balance and hence conform more.
      b) Females tend to choose the alternative of changing *their* response (i.e.

conforming) in order to achieve balance. Males might prefer the tactic of rejecting the group.

In this experiment only one tactic is available to produce a balanced state. A sex difference in this experiment might support the first explanation of sex differences in conformity.

Bearing in mind the behaviour of my daughter you could also look at age differences in this experiment.

References

Asch, S.E. (1952), *Social Psychology*, Prentice Hall

Festinger, L. (1957), *A Theory of Cognitive Dissonance*, Row, Peterson

Newcomb, T.M. (1953), 'An approach to the study of communicative acts', *Psychol. Rev.*, vol. 60, 393–404

Index guide: attitudes; conformity; cognitive dissonance; balance theories

E 17　Visual feedback in the induced movement of a pendulum

The problem

If a pendulum of a bob on a flexible string is held in the hand, the pendulum may begin to swing without any conscious movement of the hand. This apparently 'magical' movement of the pendulum is quite striking. It has been used in many cultures for various mystic purposes. It was believed, for example, that the movement of a pendulum held over a pregnant woman could distinguish the sex of the unborn child by the direction of the oscillation. This is *not* the experiment.

More recently this induced movement of a pendulum has been used to select subjects suitable for hypnosis. The subject holds the pendulum over a simple figure:

67.

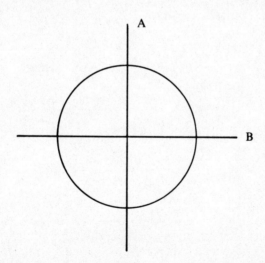

He is asked to ignore the pendulum and concentrate on, say, the line A. After a few seconds the pendulum may begin to swing along the same line. The subject is then asked to concentrate on, say, the circle. The pendulum changes to swing around the circle, and so on. How can we explain this movement? One possible hypothesis is suggested by an experiment of Jacobsen (1932). When a subject was asked to think of hitting a nail with a hammer held in his right hand, Jacobsen recorded periodic bursts of electrical activity in the muscle groups of the right forearm but not in other muscle groups. Similarly, when subjects were asked to imagine counting there was activity in the lips and tongue. Could concentrating on a line give rise to minute muscle activity along the direction of that line, resulting in the swinging of the pendulum? This hypothesis would predict the movement whether or not the pendulum was visible to the subject. We will take this as the null hypothesis. The experimental hypothesis is that induced movement along the line on which the subject concentrates is dependent on the subject seeing the pendulum.

A method

a) Design

Causal: We can manipulate whether or not the subject sees the pendulum.

The independent variable is the visual feedback from the pendulum. Although the subject is asked to ignore the pendulum, in one condition it is visible above the figure, in the other condition it is not. The position of the pendulum should remain unchanged. A possible set-up is given below:

68.

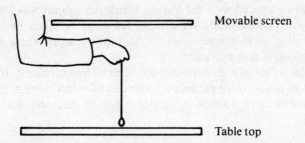

Movable screen

Table top

The target figure is placed on the screen or the table top

There are other suitable arrangements.

The dependent variable is the direction in which the pendulum moves, if it moves at all. The measurement of this gives scope for some ingenuity. One can simply judge the direction of any swing. Is it closer to line A or to line B? A majority decision from a panel of judges can be used.

A better method might be to have two observers, A and B, measuring movement in the directions A and B against measuring grids.

69.

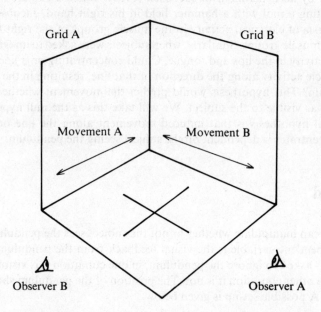

Grid A   Grid B

Movement A   Movement B

Observer B   Observer A

Observer A measures the movement of the pendulum in the direction A by viewing the pendulum against grid A. Observer B does likewise. These observations are eventually compared with the line on which the subject was concentrating. If the subject was concentrating on line A, his score is taken as (A−B). If he was concentrating on B, the score is (B−A). Positive scores show induced movement along the line of concentration.

You can, of course, devise other methods of measurement. If, for example, you have a stop-frame video recorder, things can be much more precise.

The design can be single-subject or repeated-measures with suitable counter-balancing.

b) Subjects

Some subjects may not show any movement of the pendulum. You can't use these in this experiment but hang on to them: *why* they do not swing the pendulum can be investigated in a variation.

c) Apparatus

A pendulum of a bob suspended on, say, 30 cm of cotton. The subject holds the pendulum wearing a thick glove to prevent tactile feedback from the pendulum.

A target figure of a cross is drawn on white card. (If you wish to include the circle (figure 67) then you must devise some way of deciding if the pendulum is tracing a circle.)

Make up a pack of instruction cards of equal numbers of cards marked 'line A' and 'line B'. In practice it is easier to use an ordinary pack of playing cards and colour the lines on the target figure black and red. Suitable instructions must be included if the circle is added to the figure.

The subject stands at a table with a movable screen suspended above it, as in figure 68. A chair with a removable seat is a simple arrangement. The two measuring grids can be fixed to the legs of the chair.

d) Procedure

The experiment is explained to the subject. He is asked to hold the pendulum above the table. One of the two experimental conditions is chosen at random. The target figure is placed on the table directly below the pendulum (in one condition) or on the horizontal screen, directly above the pendulum (for the other condition). The instruction cards are shuffled. One card is taken from the top of the pack, shown to the subject, and placed face down on one side. Neither the experimenter nor the observers see the instruction. The subject concentrates on the line for one minute. The observers take their readings during the last five seconds. The pendulum is stilled by the experimenter, the figure moved if necessary, and the process is repeated by drawing the next instruction card from the pack. After a suitable number of trials the other condition of the IV is tested.

Results

At the end of the testing session the score on each trial is assessed $(A - B)$ or $(B - A)$, as appropriate. A mean score under each condition is taken for each subject. The 'score' of each subject on a condition is this mean.

These results can be analysed using a t-test (for related samples) or a Wilcoxon test, or a sign test, as appropriate.

Variations

1 We have looked at one hypothesis: that the movement is simply the result of minute muscle activity associated with thinking. This may be rejected as a result of the experiment. The movement could be the result of the subject's expectations, a wish to please the experimenter. This could be tested by varying the expectations. All subjects are told to expect movement of the pendulum. Some are told that the normal movement is in the direction of the

line on which they concentrate, others that it is perpendicular to this line. The hypothesis is that the direction of the induced movement depends on the direction expected by the subject.

2   Observation of the first experiment raises a problem. For some subjects the pendulum does not budge. Perhaps these subjects *expect* the pendulum to keep still and so unconsciously make sure it does. The hypothesis is that subjects who show no induced movement are using the visual feedback to keep the pendulum still. This can be tested with suitable equipment – ideally a closed-circuit TV.

The closed-circuit TV is used to *reverse* the visual feedback.

70.

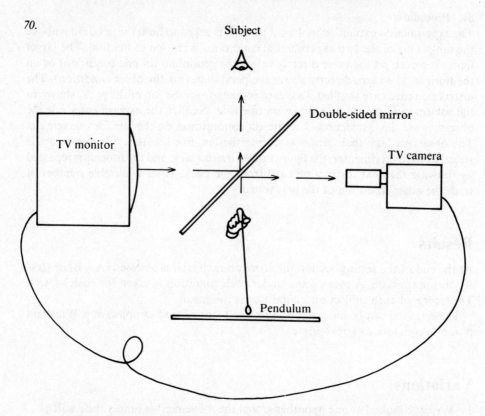

The independent variable is the visual feedback. This is either normal, as in the diagram, or reversed by simply turning the camera or monitor upside down. The dependent variable is the *amount* of movement under the two conditions. The subjects are those who show no induced movement in the first experiment.

The experimental hypothesis predicts large movements of the pendulum under the reversed condition. Minute actions made by the subject to still the pendulum will just increase any movement.

There are many other questions that can be asked. What subject variables are associated with induced movement of a pendulum? Whittaker and Meade (1967) and many others have found sex and age differences in 'persuadability' and conformity. Does the same apply to induced movement? The experiment can be tried as part of a developmental study in schools (I 1).

These experiments raise questions about another induced movement phenomenon – water divining. I leave you to consider this fascinating prospect.

References

Jacobsen, E. (1932), 'Electrophysiology of mental activities', *Amer. J. Psychol.*, vol. 44, 677–94

Whittaker, J.O. and Meade, R.D. (1967), 'Sex and age variables in persuadability', *J. Soc. Psychol.*, vol. 73, 47–52

Index guide: thinking; persuadability; hypnosis

E 18   Sex differences in driving speeds

The problem

There is a popular belief, among men at any rate, that there are differences in the way in which men and women drive cars. One of these supposed differences is the speed of driving, that is, that women drive slower than men. This is the basis of this experiment.

A method

a) Design

Strictly speaking this is a non-causal design. The experimenter does not manipulate either of the experimental variables but simply observes them.

One experimental variable is the sex of the driver, the subject in the experiment. This looks fairly straightforward but you might like to consider what operational definition of this variable you will be using. In practice it is quite easy to spot whether the driver of a car is male or female. Defining *how* this decision is made can be quite tricky.

The other experimental variable is the speed of the car. This is measured by the time taken to cover a particular distance. This standard distance should start when the car is well in view to avoid variation from the experimenter's reaction time. With a little ingenuity these measurements can be made automatically using two pressure detectors, of the type used to ring a bell in a garage forecourt, connected to an electric stopwatch.

An independent-subjects design is used (see page 9).

b) Subjects

The population from which the sample is taken will depend on the time of day and the particular stretch of road you use. You cannot use a random sample but you can try to avoid bias to one group or the other. Common sense should tell you not to take measurements up the road from a home for retired gentlewomen.

c) Apparatus

A road. The choice of road is important in keeping random variation to a minimum. Perhaps the best bet is a country lane. This will reduce variation from pedestrians, parked cars, road junctions, speed limits and so on (but see variation 1).

Some form of stopwatch will be needed.

d) Procedure

The detailed planning of this experiment is considered in Part I. Experimenter effects are avoided if the drivers are unaware that their speed is being measured. Random variation is kept to a minimum by taking observations at the same time of day and with similar conditions of weather, congestion, etc. Observations are discarded when cars are in sight of one another, to ensure independence.

Each car is timed travelling over the standard stretch of road and the sex of the driver is recorded.

Results

There is no need to convert the measurements of the time taken to cover the standard distance into speeds. The individual times are recorded and the means are found for male and female drivers.

Analysis (variables CD)

A t-test for independent samples can be used to find the significance of the difference between the two means. Alternatively, the individual times can be ranked and a Mann–Whitney test used.

The experimental hypothesis suggests the direction of the difference in driving speeds – that women drive slower than men. A one-tailed test can be used.

Variations

1   The experiment is investigating a sexual difference in behaviour that seems to have nothing whatever to do with reproduction. Such differences, real or supposed, are a rich and fascinating source of experimental hypotheses. Several studies have found sex differences in persuadability and conformity (e.g. Whittaker and Meade, 1967; Janis and Field, 1959). These studies agree that females show a greater tendency to conform. This difference could result in the hypothesized sexual difference in driving speeds where there is a speed restriction: females will tend to conform more to this restriction. This could be tested by a similar experiment in an area where drivers are restricted to 30 m.p.h.

If the results of this variation are expressed as speeds above or below 30 m.p.h. they can be compared with the records of convictions for speeding in the same area. Such a comparison might suggest a hypothesis about policemen.

2   The same techniques can be used to look at cultural differences in driving speed between, say, an inner-city area and a rural area. The problem here is to find comparable stretches of road in each place. This variation can be taken a stage further if you are travelling abroad.

In one delightful piece of research an experimenter visited several European cities and deliberately stalled at traffic lights. He measured the time taken before drivers behind him sounded their horns. This varied significantly between countries. More interestingly, it also varied with the nationality of the stalled car, whether native or foreign to the country in question.

3   The intrepid experimenter could investigate another aspect of driving behaviour – the inclination to stop at pedestrian crossings.

References

Janis, I.L. and Field, P., 'Sex differences and personality factors related to persuadability', in C.I. Hovland and I.L. Janis (eds) (1959), *Personality and Persuadability*, Yale University Press
Whittaker, J.O. and Meade, R.D. (1967), 'Sex and Age variables in Persuadability', *J. Soc. Psychol.*, vol. 73, 47–52

Index guide: sex differences; persuadability; conformity

E 19 The effects of sleep deprivation on the performance of simple tasks

The problem

The night before an important examination most candidates tuck themselves up in bed, determined to get a good night's sleep. It is commonly supposed that a night on the tiles with little sleep will impair the candidate's performance in the examination. In fact, there is some reason to argue the opposite. Several theorists in psychology (e.g. Hebb, 1955) have argued that there is an inverted U-shaped relationship between performance and arousal.

71. The hypothetical inverted-U relationship between performance and arousal level

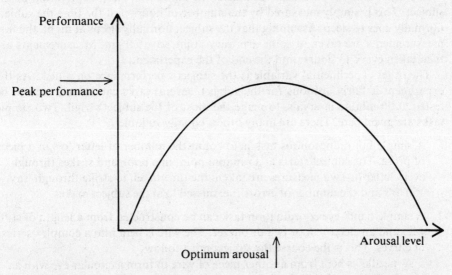

This hypothetical relationship is supported by a considerable amount of evidence. Several experiments by Wilkinson (1960, 1965) have shown that the performance of sleep-deprived subjects (i.e. with low arousal) is improved by an arousing stimulus. The same stimulus given to rested subjects may impair their performance: they have passed the optimum level of arousal. Wilkinson used the arousing stimulus of a loud noise or increased incentives. In these cases the task was fairly monotonous, that is, non-arousing. It is reasonable to suppose that candidates arriving for an important exam are highly aroused – not to say terrified. This may well impair their performance. Sleep deprivation the night before might reduce this high level of arousal to a level nearer to the optimum for performance in the exam.

We cannot test this fascinating hypothesis directly by keeping exam candidates up all night. We can try a related experiment. We predict that there is some relationship between sleep deprivation and performance. The nature of that relationship will depend on the task, whether it is boring or arousing. In a boring task the performance should deteriorate with increasing sleep deprivation. In an arousing task the performance may initially improve with sleep deprivation, to deteriorate as deprivation increases further – an inverted-U relationship.

The hypothesis in this experiment is that there is some relationship between the amount of sleep deprivation of the subject and the performance of some task.

A method

a) Design

Non-causal: One experimental variable is the amount of sleep deprivation of the subject. This is simply measured by the number of hours past the time the subject normally goes to sleep. Assuming that the subject normally sleeps at night, the first measurements are taken at some arbitrary point, say, 9.0 pm. Measurements are then taken every $1\frac{1}{2}$ hours until the end of the experiment.

The other experimental variable is the subject's performance on a task. As the experiment is fairly arduous for the subject, several tasks can be set, each to be tested at 90-minute intervals, to make the most of the subject's vigil. Two simple tasks are given here. There are many others equally suitable.

1   A simple but monotonous task is to count the number of letter 'o's in a piece of prose. The subject starts at a random point in a book and strikes through every letter o. Two measures are taken: the time taken to strike through, say, 150 'o's and the number of errors (i.e. missed 'o's) the subject makes.

2   A simple hand–eye coordination task can be constructed from a length of stiff wire and an electric door bell or buzzer. The wire is bent into a complex series of curves. This is the course the subject must follow.

A 'needle' is bent from another piece of wire to form a circular eye with a handle. This needle is threaded on to the twisting course. The subject's task is to pass the eye of the needle from one end of the course to the other without

72.

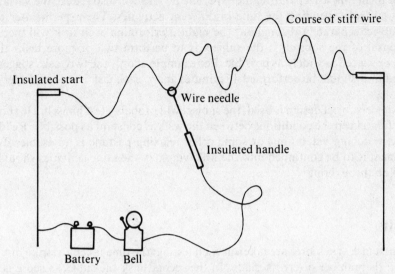

the needle touching the wire of the course. If they do touch, the electrical circuit of the bell is completed; the bell rings and the subject slides the needle to the beginning and starts again. The measurement taken is the *total* distance covered in five attempts.

The size of the needle eye is critical. If it is too large there will be a ceiling effect; the subject will complete the course each time. If the eye is too small there will be a floor effect: he will rarely, if ever, get past the first bend. Ideally the course should become more difficult from start to finish.

The experiment lends itself to a single-subject design, the single subject being the experimenter testing himself throughout the night. The counting of errors in the first task is best left until the experimenter has had a good night's sleep. There is a danger of a large experimenter error in such a design. If you can persuade subjects to undergo sleep deprivation so much the better.

b) Subjects
There are no special restrictions.

c) Apparatus
The apparatus for the hand–eye coordination task has been described. A stopwatch is used to time the first task. The same book is used throughout the experiment to reduce the variation in the proportion of 'o's in the passages.

d) Procedure
The subjects are given a chance to practise the tasks. If several subjects are taking part it will be convenient for them to spend the time together. They can check that

none of them falls asleep during the experiment. This will also reduce the variation in arousal from spending the time in different activities. The experimenter tests each subject separately throughout the night. Performing each task will increase the arousal of the subject; if the subject is to perform two or more tasks these should be spaced as widely as possible. For example, if only the two tasks suggested are used they should be performed 45 minutes apart; each task is repeated every $1\frac{1}{2}$ hours.

If a single-subject design is used, the subject will probably test himself. He should be careful to keep the conditions between the tests as constant as possible. Reading a book, watching video films or some other relaxing pastime is advisable. If the experiment is to be continued into the following day the same activities should be carried on throughout.

Results

In the first task two scores are taken at each testing: the time taken to strike out 150 'o's and the number of errors made. In the second task the subject's score is the total distance travelled along the course in five attempts. The score on each task for each period of sleep deprivation is recorded. This is plotted on a scattergram. We have reason to believe that the relationship, if any, between sleep deprivation and performance may not be monotonic. First, the theory suggests an inverted-U relationship. Second, it is unlikely that arousal decreases monotonically with sleep deprivation; well established circadian rhythms of arousal are likely to produce a low point of arousal in the very early morning. The scattergram will reveal such patterns.

Analysis (variables CC)
For each task, find the rank-order or product-moment correlation between the length of sleep deprivation and the subject's score. Is this significant? Does the correlation differ with the task?

Variations

1 The same hypothesis can be tested with a different design of experiment. The variable of sleep deprivation is measured discretely. One group of subjects, selected at random, is prevented from sleeping all night. A second group sleeps normally. (This is now a causal design as the experimenter manipulates the variable.) Both groups are then tested at the same time in the morning on the tasks used in the original experiment. The advantage of this design is that there will be no effect of practising the tasks. Both groups of subjects have the

same experience of the tasks, both are tested at the same time of day. The disadvantage is that any U-shaped relationship will not be revealed if only two conditions of sleep deprivation are compared. As independent subjects are used there will be more random variation in their performance.

2 It is possible to vary the amount of arousal in the task itself by varying the incentives. This is the difference between a mock examination and the real thing. The task is the same – the rewards and punishments are vastly different. They produce different degrees of arousal (in this case, anxiety). In this variation the incentive on the hand-eye coordination task is varied by using low voltage electric shocks instead of sounding a bell when the needle touches the wire course. Does this increase in the arousal of the task reduce the effect of sleep deprivation?

References

Hebb, D.O. (1955), 'Drives and the C.N.S. (conceptual nervous system)', *Psychol. Rev.*, vol. 62, 243–54

Wilkinson, R.T. (1960), 'Effects of sleep deprivation on performance and muscle tension', in G.E.W. Wolstenholme and M. O'Connor (eds), *The Nature of Sleep*, Little Brown for the CIBA foundation

Wilkinson, R.T. (1965), 'Sleep Deprivation' in O.G. Edholm and A.L. Bacharach (eds), *The Physiology of Human Survival*, Academic Press

Index guide: arousal; sleep deprivation

E 20 **Predicting the weather from the behaviour of cows**

The problem

Animals have often been credited with the ability to predict particular events in the future. This ability is not very surprising – so can we. What is surprising is the claim that some animals can do so more accurately than man or, in some cases, where man, with any amount of sophisticated equipment, cannot do so at all.

In recent years scientists in China have been seriously investigating the claim that major earthquakes can be predicted by the behaviour of several species of wild and domesticated animals. Hopefully this hypothesis cannot be tested in Britain; we have few major earthquakes in Britain – what we have is rain. Our vast experience of rain has resulted in any number of hypotheses connecting its impending arrival with the behaviour of animals. These can be tested.

One of the most commonly held of these beliefs is that of the behaviour of cows in a field. Put simply, the suggestion is that cows lying down is a sign of rain coming. What is not so clear is when this rain will arrive or how many cows should be lying down. We can treat the testing of this belief as an exercise in translating a hypothesis into a practicable experiment with operational definitions of the variables.

The experiment will be carried out in the field – literally. There is little opportunity for the experimenter to control the variables affecting the behaviour of the cows (there is even less opportunity to control the arrival of the rain). One variable that can be controlled is the time of day at which the cows are observed. It seems reasonable to suppose that this will be an important factor in their behaviour. The first task of the experimenter will be to establish the time of day at which the behaviour of the cows is most variable. This will be found by observing a particular herd of cows over several weeks and under different weather conditions at several different times of the day. At each time the number of cows lying down is recorded. The variance of these observations is calculated for each time of day. The experimenter makes the assumption that the time of day has least effect on the cows lying down when the variance is greatest. Observations of behaviour are taken at this time of day for the rest of the experiment.

It seems reasonable to suppose that the number of recumbent cows increases with the likelihood of rain in the near future. How are we to define 'the near future'?

We will consider three periods from the time of observations: the subsequent 6 hours, 12 hours and 24 hours. Each of these periods will be treated as a separate experiment in the analysis of results. For example, taking the six-hour period the hypothesis predicts that more cows will be lying down at the chosen observation time when rain falls in the following six hours than when the following six hours are dry.

A method

a) Design
Non-causal: One of the experimental variables is the behaviour of the cows: that is, how many are lying down at the predetermined observation time. The other experimental variable is the presence or absence of rain in the subsequent period (6, 12 or 24 hours). The amount of rain is not measured. However, some means of detecting rainfall in the field when you are not present will have to be devised. This is best done with some sort of collecting vessel. The operational definition of 'rainfall' will depend on how the rainfall is detected.

A single-subject design is used. The single 'subject' is the herd of cows. The same herd, preferably in the same field, will be used throughout the experiment.

b) Subjects
Cows: I have been told that for some reason these should be dairy cows. It might be as well to find out from the farmer whether the cows will be kept in the field for the duration of the experiment. It may be difficult to estimate this as it will depend on the number of days on which rain falls.

c) Apparatus
Some means of detecting rainfall.

d) Procedure
The cows are observed at several convenient times of the day and the optimum time for observation is decided as described above. The experimenter returns at this time each day and records the number of cows lying down. Check that the total number of cows remains the same. Over the following day he records whether there was any rainfall during the 6 hours, 12 hours and 24 hours after the observations. You may wish to alter these periods depending on the time of observations. Observations are discarded if it is raining at the observation time. This is because you are interested in the cows' reaction to indications of future rain rather than the rain itself; also it saves you from getting soaked.

Results

Taking results for the six hours after observations, find the mean number of reclining cows preceding rain and the mean number of reclining cows preceding a dry period.

Analysis (variables CD)

The t-test for independent samples is used to assess the significance of the difference in means. This is preferable to the slightly less powerful Mann–Whitney test. You will need all the power you can get, as little control of variables is possible and the number of observations is likely to be small.

There may be a large difference in the number of observations in the two groups. If so, check the assumptions of the t-test, particularly the similarity of variance using an F-test (p. 82). The variance will be used in the t-test so the work is not wasted.

The hypothesis predicts the direction of the difference in means: more cows will be found lying down before rain. You are justified in using a one-tailed test of significance. A similar analysis is used with the other two periods following observations.

Variations

1   So far we have only considered that the number of cows lying down increases with the likelihood of rain in the future. There may also be a relationship between the *imminence* or the amount of the rain. Both these hypotheses can be tested during the original experiment if more details of any rainfall are collected. For this variation the experimenter considers only observations after which rain falls in the next twenty-four hours. The experimenter records the time between the observations of behaviour and the beginning of the rain. This time is correlated with the number of cows lying down at the observation time using a rank-order or product-moment correlation. The amount of rainfall is measured in the collection vessel. This amount is correlated with the number of cows lying down.

Correlations measure the monotonicity of a relationship (p. 109). There is some reason to suppose that these relationships (if any) will not be monotonic. For example, if the cows are aware that the rainfall will be very heavy and imminent they may seek shelter. They must get up to do this. Check for any non-monotonic relationship by recording the observations on a scattergram.

2   There are many other more or less silly beliefs about the behaviour of animals. I am assured, for example, that horses can smell fear in humans and react to this fear. This should be easy enough to test. The problem lies in interpreting

the horses' reactions. All horses look frightening to me. Perhaps the solution is to use as an observer someone who makes this claim about horses' reactions to fear. The observer watches the horse as scared or fearless confederates of the experimenter approach the horse one at a time. The observer judges the reactions of the horse in each case. These judgements are later compared with the presence or absence of fear reported by the experimenter's confederates using a chi-squared test of association.

If, incredibly, a relationship is found you might ask whether the horse is 'smelling fear' or reacting to visual signs of nervousness. The fearful confederate approaches the horse upwind or downwind. Alternatively, the horse is blindfolded and approached by fearful and fearless persons.

11　Developmental studies in schools

For ethical and practical reasons it is difficult to use laboratory methods when studying the development of children. Experiments are most conveniently carried out where they occur naturally – in the home and the school. These two situations illustrate the two broad approaches to psychological research: the idiographic and the nomothetic approaches [case studies]. The idiographic approach concentrates on studying the individual and often takes the form of a case study (p. 143). The nomothetic approach uses sampling techniques in order to make *general* statements about human (or animal) behaviour.

Children at home lend themselves naturally to idiographic study. If the experimenter is a parent, brother or sister, or a regular baby-sitter, then any experiments can be part of normal play. Any behaviour is unlikely to be an artificial product of the situation.

Children at school are in sufficiently large numbers, nicely sorted into age groups, for a nomothetic study. An adult in the classroom, perhaps asking them to do seemingly pointless tasks, is part of their normal experience of teachers. After some initial excitement they will settle down and treat you as part of the school scenery.

Approaching the school
Most schools will welcome the occasional researcher – others will not. It is essential to visit the head teacher some time before any proposed work as he or she may suggest some time of the year or term when you would be more welcome to work in the school. You will not be welcomed, for instance, during the first week of the term. Dealing with the head teacher and the class teacher is the most difficult part of the investigation; the rest is child's play.

The head teacher
It is *extremely* important that you have a clear idea of what you wish to do in the classroom – and why. Head teachers are often surprisingly knowledgeable about current child research and can make time-saving criticisms and suggestions. They

will rightly be very dubious of loaning their children to someone who wishes vaguely to 'observe their behaviour'.

Given a clear idea of the investigation a head teacher can suggest the most suitable class (and most amenable teacher) and the time of day when the activity of the children is most suited to the investigation. Be prepared.

The class teacher

Dealing with the class teacher poses different problems. The head teacher can accept you or not; the class teacher has been asked (told) to take you. I will assume she is a woman.

Unlike the head, she will actually have to put up with you during your study, and she may consider herself a good deal busier than the head. She may also feel that, in some sense, you are observing her and her performance in the classroom. A well prepared investigation might set her mind at rest and protect you against a further hazard – the over-helpful teacher. You will be studying her children, of whom she may be proud: their performance reflects her work. Beware of having your subjects selected by the teacher for their 'suitability'. If this is necessary then this biased sampling must be given consideration in the results. It is better to prepare the experiment beforehand and stick to it.

The children

These are rarely any problem except as distractors. It is very easy to get nothing whatsoever done in a morning when surrounded by children. Again, careful preparation will help this. If it seems that your plans are not practicable with the children you have, see the head teacher and discuss the difficulties. If necessary, go away and revise or change the study and start again. Avoid *ad hoc* changes to your experiment in the classroom; they may well ruin the analysis or application of the results or the possibility of collaboration with other researchers.

Schools provide a ready supply of subjects with ages ranging from three and four up to adults of seventeen and eighteen years – the ideal stuff for studying the development of behaviour.

I 1a The development of social behaviour: friendship

The problem

Throughout the time a child is at school he is dealing with a relatively stable population of other children. Some of these children become his friends, others do not. Some of these friendships last, others do not. Does the pattern and stability of these friendships change as the child develops? It seems likely. Anyone with experience of infant children knows that the accolade of 'best friend' can turn on the gift of a sweet or a forgotten party invitation. On the other hand, we adults are not above similar pettiness. The hypothesis is that patterns of friendship depend on the age of the group of children in question; this hypothesis can be tested.

A method

a) Design

Non-causal: One experimental variable is the age of the children. By using the children in a school class we can consider the age as a discrete variable. Two classes are used: the second year of an infant school and the second year of a secondary school. Many schools nowadays do not separate the classes of infants by age group: one class may contain children of ages ranging from four to seven years. If this cannot be avoided it must be taken into account when considering the results. It is worth visiting several schools to find the most suitable grouping of the children.

The other experimental variable is the patterns of friendship within the class. The definition of friendship is tricky. The sociogram, developed by Moreno (1934), has been used by Julienne Ford (1969) to measure friendship in a school class. The construction of such a sociogram gives a good example of the use of an operational definition (p. 16). In this case, the term 'friend' is defined by the instructions given to the subjects. Each child in the class is asked for his name and asked the following:

Pretend there was a small school trip to the zoo. Which three children in the class would you like to go with? No one but I will know your answer. I won't tell any of the children and neither must you. (A suitable variation is given to older children.)

This, of course, does not give a true picture of a child's friendships with all the richness of varying degrees and characteristics. You could ask the child, 'Who are your friends in this class?' but this question will mean different things to different children. The operational definition, if a little artificial, is at least unambiguous; whatever it measures, it measures the same for all the children.

An independent-subjects design is used.

b) Subjects
The two groups of subjects should be chosen carefully. If possible they should have been together for the same length of time and spend the same time together every day. This would be difficult with subjects over thirteen years old where groupings will change for different school lessons. The two groups should have roughly equal numbers and proportion of sexes. If possible they should also have similar home backgrounds.

c) Apparatus
A sheet of paper is provided for each subject to record his name and choice of friends.

d) Procedure
The subjects are asked the question suggested above and their replies are collected. In some of the variations further information will be collected either from the subjects themselves or from the school records. Some children normally in the class may be away. If your time is limited you can restrict their choice of friends to those children in the class on that day. If you will be making other trips to the school you can allow choices from the normal members of the class, collecting replies from the absent subjects as soon as possible.

Results

The results are best displayed in a diagram. Each child in the class is represented by a symbol. An arrow drawn from subject A to subject B represents A choosing B as a friend. Drawing this diagram is not as easy as it sounds; you will probably have to rearrange the symbols several times to produce a clear sociogram of all the patterns of friendship within one class.

For simplicity, in the following two examples a small class of three girls and three boys has been used. Each child has been asked to choose *two* friends. In figure 73, S6 chooses S2, is chosen by S3, and chooses and is chosen by S1. Compare this class to that illustrated in figure 74.

73. *Sociogram of Class I*

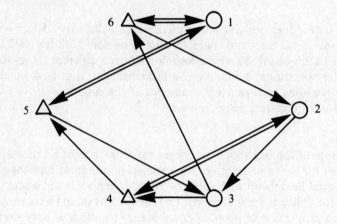

Key:

△   Boy

○   Girl

○ ⟷ △   They choose each other

74. *Sociogram of Class II*

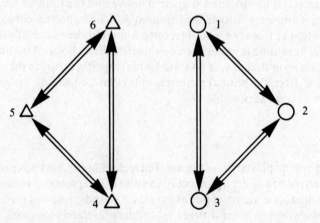

The pattern of friendships in these two classes *looks* different. How can this difference be described statistically?

Analysis

The two sociograms can be compared on several different features.

1 *Sex of chosen friend*
Each choice of a friend can be described as 'same sex' or 'cross sex' – a discrete variable. A relationship between age and sex of chosen friend will use a chi-squared test of association. This will only be accurate if the proportions of the sexes are the same in both classes. For example, for our two fictitious (and remarkably convenient) classes I and II:

	Sex of chosen friend:	
	cross sex	same sex
Class I	10	2
Class II	0	12

Where a single class only is studied, chi-squared can be used as a test of goodness of fit to find whether there is more or less cross-sex choosing of friends than would be expected by random choices. In either of the two classes above, the expected ratio of cross-sex : same-sex choices is 3 : 2. Larger classes with different proportions of boys and girls will have different expectations.

2 *Reciprocated choices*
In a reciprocated choice two subjects choose each other. Differences between the two age groups in the numbers of reciprocated and unreciprocated choices might reflect differences in the stability of these friendships or in the importance given to reciprocation. A chi-squared test is used to assess the significance of any differences. For example:

	Type of choice:	
	reciprocated	unreciprocated
Class I	6	6
Class II	12	0

3 *Hero worship*
The *mean* number of times each child is chosen will always be the same, defined by the instructions to the class. However there may be a difference in the way those choices are distributed; some children being chosen many times, others not at all. This is not the same as differences in reciprocated choices. In the two fictitious groups each child is chosen twice but there are large differences in reciprocation. For each class, find the variance in the number of times each child is chosen. These variances are compared in an F-test to reveal any differences in, perhaps, 'hero worship'.

Variations

1 Julienne Ford has investigated the importance of other variables in friendship: the choice of friends at secondary-school age influenced by the social class of the parents (using the Registrar General's classification of occupations); and the child's racial origins (in schools with a significant immigrant population). It is often said that young children are unaware of such differences as social class and racial origin. This hypothesis can be tested in the infant school, in the same way as sex was considered. If they do not influence the five-year-old's choice of friend, when do they start to become influential?

2 A similar analysis can be tried with other likely variables. Intelligence, the previous school of secondary children and personality spring to mind, but there may be others equally or more important. In each case it is worth considering whether all choices or just reciprocated choices are the most revealing experimental variable.

3 For unreciprocated choices only, is there a tendency for a younger child to choose an older child? The same question may be asked with all the variables suggested in the other variations. That is, the second variation asked whether children of similar intelligence chose to be friends. This variation asks whether there is a tendency to choose a person of higher intelligence, or lower intelligence.

References

Ford, J. (1969), *Social Class and the Comprehensive School*, Routledge and Kegan Paul, London

Moreno, J.L. (1934), *Who Shall Survive?* Nervous and Mental Disease Pub. Co., Washington

Index guide: friendship; development; socialization; sociogram

I 1b   The development of cognitive behaviour

The problem

Jean Piaget and several others have described the cognitive development of the young child in terms of stages of development [Piaget; cognitive development]. One of the stages identified by Piaget – the pre-operational stage – occurs between the child's second and seventh years. It is classically illustrated by the absence of the concept of the conservation of matter. A pre-operational child is shown two quantities of 'stuff' (Plasticine, water, beads) and is shown that the two quantities are equal. The shape of one of these quantities of stuff is changed (by moulding, pouring into a different container, or placing the beads in a different pattern). The pre-operational child does not see that the amount of stuff remains the same despite any change in shape. He will now claim that one quantity is *more* or *less* than the other, although no stuff has been removed from either.

A typical experimental set-up might be two identical glass beakers. Some water is poured into one and the child is then asked (or helped) to pour the same amount into the other beaker. The child agrees that the two beakers hold the same amount of water. The water in one beaker is now poured into a taller, thinner beaker. 'Is there the same amount in each beaker now?' you ask. The child replies that the taller beaker has more 'because the water is higher'. Occasionally he will say it holds less 'because it is thinner'.

Carrying out this demonstration raises some questions. How do you show the child that the two beakers held the same amount of water to begin with? By pointing to the height. If the child poured the water himself, poorly, you show him there are not the same amounts because the *height* is not the same in the two beakers. It is quite possible that the child thinks, in some way, that 'amount' is the same thing as 'height'. That is, his confusion is with terminology rather than the concept of matter.

This hypothesis can be tested. One way is to leave out any discussion with the child about the equality of two amounts of water.

A method

a) Design

Non-causal: One experimental variable is the age of the child. This can be measured discretely by using two age groups in a school. One group consists of pre-operational children aged around five or six. The second group is aged around eight or nine. Alternatively a continuous range of children can be used; this will require a different analysis of the results.

The other experimental variable is the child's grasp of the concept of the conservation of matter. This is measured without any comparison of two beakers of water.

One beaker contains some water. The child is asked to mark the height of the water on a strip of paper attached to the side of the beaker. The water is poured into another container of a different shape and the child sees that no water is spilt. He is then asked, 'If I pour the water back into the beaker, where will it come up to?' He marks the position on the same strip of paper attached to the beaker. The difference, if any, between the two marks is the child's score. The hypothesis is that this score is greater in the younger group.

An independent-subjects design is used.

b) Subjects

Two age groups of children. As these will come from different classes of the school beware of selection by their teachers. A difference in their selection criterion, however well meant or unconscious, could produce a constant error in the results.

c) Apparatus

A glass beaker – a measuring cylinder is ideal. A thin strip of paper runs from the top to the bottom of the beaker. After each child has made his two marks his name and age (or class) are recorded on the strip.

d) Procedure

Each child is tested individually away from other children. The beaker is half filled with water and the child marks the height. The water is poured into a different container, taller and thinner or shorter and fatter, next to the first beaker. He is asked to mark the position the water will reach when poured back into the first beaker. He does so; the strip is removed and replaced by another ready for the next subject.

Results and analysis

The treatment of results depends on the performance of the children. We might expect a child who understands the conservation of matter to make both marks at the same point; the pre-operational child could make the second mark above or below the first. If this happens we cannot use a t-test to compare the mean score of the two groups. The variance of scores will be wildly different; the older children predominantly scoring zero. We cannot use an F-test; the distribution is hardly Normal. Unfortunately, the non-parametric alternative is also out as there will be a very large proportion of ties amongst the older, concrete operational children. A possible solution is to score the child's performance discretely. The second mark either is or is not at the same place as his first mark. It is now possible to use a chi-squared test of association between the age group and the child's performance.

Where only one or two children score zero you can use the Mann–Whitney test.

There is a second interesting analysis of the results. Piaget's developmental theories involve stages. But what does this predict for the scores of children who do not have the concept of the conservation of matter? Do they perform equally badly on this test until such time as it dawns on them, to perform perfectly thereafter? Or does the score on this test gradually decrease with age?

The experimenter discards all the zero scores. There is now no problem in using the Mann–Whitney test to find any difference between the age groups. What does such a difference mean to a theory of developmental stages?

Variations

1 One explanation of the pre-operational child's tendency to claim that a tall, thin beaker contains more water is that of **perceptual dominance.** Perhaps the child understands perfectly the concept of the conservation of matter, but right there in front of his eyes are two lots of water, one twice as high as the other. There may be a conflict between what he knows to be so and what appears to be so. In the pre-operational child the perceptual information dominates. (Goodness knows, it does with us sophisticated adults in visual illusions.) This can be tested.

The subjects are children who did not place both marks in the same place in the original experiment. In one condition the child is shown the water in the second beaker (as above). In the other condition the water is poured into the second beaker out of sight of the child; all he sees is the empty beaker with a mark to show the original height of the water. Where will he place his mark now? If the mark is placed elsewhere is there any pattern to its position?

The hypothesis of perceptual dominance will predict a difference between the scores under the two conditions in the pre-operational child. A repeated-measures design can be used with suitable counterbalancing. A Wilcoxon test is used to reveal any significant differences.

2 A similar procedure can be devised to investigate conservation of number [cognitive development]. A comparison between a child's performance on such

a test and on the conservation of matter test described above will establish how closely such cognitive abilities are associated. This is important if we wish to maintain the idea of an overall stage of cognitive development.

3   There are several other characteristics described by Piaget which distinguish the pre-operational stage in cognitive development. A large-scale investigation could compare the performances of children on these different characteristics. In effect, such an investigation examines the validity of these performances as measures of cognitive development.

Piaget and Inhelder (1948) describe egocentrism in the pre-operational child. A three-dimensional scene is constructed of objects laid out on a table top. Several pictures are drawn of the scene from different points around the table. The task of the child is to pick out the picture that would be seen by a doll that is moved around the table. A simple experiment is to present the child with two pictures: the doll's view and the child's view (see figure 75 on the following page). A pre-operational child will pick out the view as he sees it; the concrete operational child will pick out the doll's view. Each child can be given several trials to get a score of egocentrism.

The role of perceptual dominance can be assessed by a modification of this experiment. Does the child's selection improve if *neither* of the two pictures he is shown is of his point of view?

References

Piaget, J. (1954), *The Construction of Reality in the Child*, Basic Books
Piaget, J. and Inhelder, B. (1948), *The Child's Conception of Space*, Humanities Press, New York

Index guide: Piaget; cognitive development; pre-operational stage

75.   Plan view of table top scene.

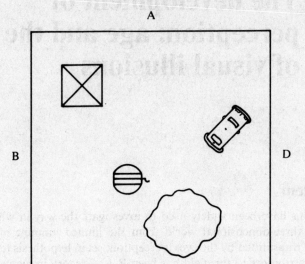

Picture of the scene from position C.

I 1c   The development of perception: age and the size of visual illusions

The problem

Visual illusions have been widely used to investigate the way in which the brain constructs a three-dimensional world from the limited amount of information collected and transmitted by the eyes [perception: set in hypothesis testing]. One of the major contributors to this field has been R.L. Gregory in his two books, *Eye and Brain* and *The Intelligent Eye*. Gregory and others have tried to account for visual illusions in a variety of ways. It is clear that no one mechanism can account for all illusions and there has been much argument as to which illusions are the result of one mechanism and which another.

A neglected facet of this argument is the difference in the way illusions are affected by the development of the individual. That is, the size of some illusions increases with age; others decrease. It is arguable that illusions that are differentially

76. The Ponzo Illusion

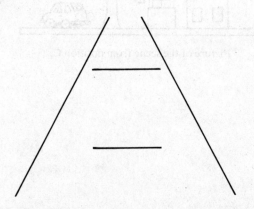

The lower bar is the same physical size as the upper bar

affected by age involve different mechanisms. Parrish, Lundy and Leibowitz (1969) show such a difference between the Ponzo (or railway line) illusion and the Poggendorf illusion.

77. The Poggendorf Illusion

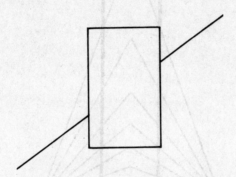

The two oblique strokes are on the same line

A valuable investigation could be made of these and other illusions, with subjects of four to seventeen years, to establish which illusions increase with age and which decrease. The size of the investigation can be varied by the number of illusions tested; several experimenters could combine their work to produce a comprehensive study.

A method

The design of the experiment is much the same whichever illusion is being tested. One experimental variable is the age of the child. This can be measured discretely, by class or age group, or continuously. The other experimental variable is the child's performance on the visual illusion task: that is, the size of the visual illusion. Measuring the size of the illusions is more of a problem. The best technique will depend on your resources and the illusion in question. We will consider a few illusions.

In the Hering figure overleaf, the normal illusion is that the line appears bent. But how bent?

There are two basic methods of measuring illusions. One method is to match the illusion with a line that actually is bent. The subject is given a choice of bent lines and is asked to select the one which most nearly matches the line in the illusion. Each comparison line has a known radius of curvature, its measure of 'bentness'. An alternative is to devise some method of bending a comparison line. The subject

78. *The Hering Fan Illusion*

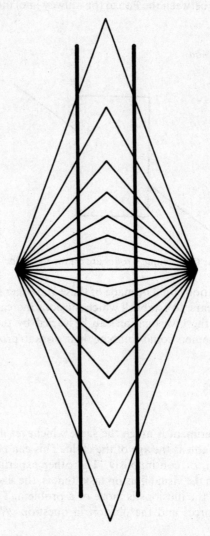

twiddles the apparatus until the illusion is matched and the experimenter measures the amount of bend in the comparison line.

There are difficulties with these matching techniques. The subject has to switch attention between the illusion and the comparison figure. This can affect the size of the illusion. Judgements such as the 'bentness' of a line may be difficult for a young child to make conscientiously.

The second technique is to 'null' the illusion. The distorted element of the illusion figure is changed until the illusion disappears. The amount of change necessary to null the illusion is a measure of the size of the illusion. The Poggendorf illusion is particularly suited to this method. The apparatus below is made from two rectangles of board and a large piece of white card. The subject's score sheet has the oblique stroke (A) and is fixed to the left-hand board.

79.

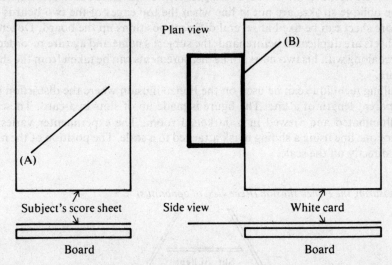

When the two boards are slid together the black-edged rectangle overrides the score sheet.

80.

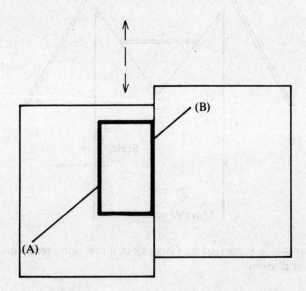

The subject slides the left-hand board along the edge of the other board until the two oblique strokes (A) and (B) appear to be in line. A pencil line is drawn along the lower edge of the overriding rectangle to record the position of the subject's score sheet. The process is repeated using a ruler to ensure the oblique strokes are in line. The position of the score sheet is recorded. The magnitude of the illusion is the difference between the two recorded positions of the score sheet. It is important that the oblique strokes are not in line when the top edges of the two boards are. The score sheet can be fixed at several different positions up the board. Dozens of score sheets are duplicated beforehand; the subject's name and age are recorded on the sheet along with his two marks. The measurements can be taken from the sheets at leisure.

A nulling technique can be used on the Ponzo illusion where the distortion is of the apparent length of a line. The figure is made up of slots in a card. These are back-illuminated and viewed in a darkened room. The experimenter varies the length of one line using a sliding mask attached to a scale. The position of the mask is read directly off the scale.

81. Measuring the Ponzo Illusion (Rear view of apparatus)

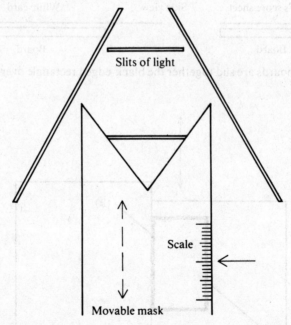

A similar apparatus is suggested by Gregory in a matching technique to measure the Muller–Lyer illusion.

82. *Measuring the Muller-Lyer Illusion (after Gregory 1966)*

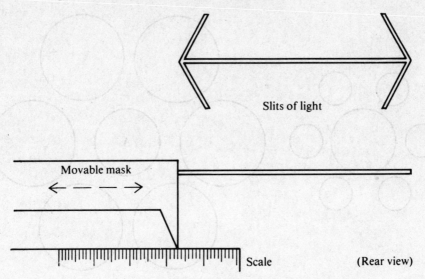

Slits of light

Movable mask

← — — →

Scale   (Rear view)

This could be improved by using the double-ended mask used for the Ponzo measurement so that the varying slot always remains centrally below the Muller-Lyer figure.

A very quick nulling technique for measuring a Muller-Lyer type illusion is given in D 1 (p. 162).

One simple nulling technique can be used for all these illusions – particularly where resources are limited. To measure any illusion the experimenter produces a series of figures which are identical with the exception of the element that is normally distorted in the illusion. This element is varied in each of the figures and the subject selects the figure in which the illusion has disappeared (or is least apparent), for example, using a 'frame of reference' illusion (see figure 83). In this figure the two inner circles have the same diameter. The diameter of circle A is varied slightly in each of a dozen or so figures. The subject selects the figure in which the two inner circles appear the same size. The experimenter records the subject's choice and hence the magnitude of the illusion. The figures can be displayed sequentially or all together in a large display. In either case the order to position must be randomized between subjects to avoid constant errors.

Results and analysis

In most cases the subjects' scores will be measured continuously. The mean magnitude of the illusion can be taken for any age group and age groups compared in

83. Frame-of-reference illusion

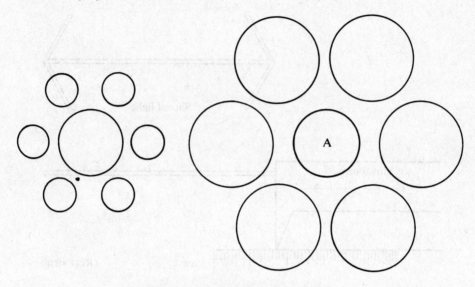

pairs using a t-test or Mann–Whitney test. If the subjects' ages are measured continuously then the magnitude of the illusion can be correlated with age. In most cases it will be advantageous to test each subject several times on the illusion and take the mean score as the subject's performance.

Variations

1 There is a tendency to think that developmental studies stop when the subject becomes an adult. An elaboration of this experiment could look at the way old age affects illusions – visual, that is.

References

Gregory, R.L. (1966), *Eye and Brain: the Psychology of Seeing*, Weidenfeld and Nicolson

Gregory, R.L. (1971), *The Intelligent Eye*, Weidenfeld and Nicolson

Parrish, M., Lundy, R.M. and Leibowitz (1969), 'Effect of hypnotic age regression on the magnitude of the Ponzo and Poggendorf illusions', *J. Abnorm. Psychol.*, vol. 74, 693–8

Index guide: visual illusions; development; perception

12   Animal behaviour in zoos

Observations of natural behaviour

Most of the experiments in this book study human behaviour. This reflects a bias in psychology as a whole. No doubt if aardvarks studied psychology they would concentrate on aardvark behaviour. We concentrate on humans. One advantage of this bias is the avoidance or minimizing of experimenter effects, that is when the act of observing a piece of behaviour changes the behaviour itself. Psychologists look pretty much like any other humans and part of the 'natural' behaviour of humans is interacting with others. This is not so with animals. If we wish to observe the natural behaviour of animals we must be reasonably confident that this behaviour is not affected by our observations. There are several approaches to this problem.

We may choose the simpler animals whose behaviour we can suppose is unaffected by our presence. Many insects, and perhaps some fish and crustacea, can be studied in this way. We must always bear in mind the possibility of affecting their behaviour (some relatively sane people believe that plants can detect and react to the presence of humans). Many experiments of this sort are suggested in *Experimental Animal Behaviour* by Hansell and Aitken.

Studying the natural behaviour of higher animals presents a problem. Most animals wisely avoid humans. Studying the behaviour of these animals must always be a compromise. On the one hand we can remain so concealed as to make observing the animal very difficult and selective. This tactic can be used successfully if the animals are relatively static, e.g. birds sitting on a nest. Here the observer can crouch in a hide to watch the nest but he cannot follow the birds anywhere else. On the other hand we can observe the animal more freely and hope that the behaviour we see is not affected by the observations. The exact form of the compromise will depend on the species and its tolerance of man. The movements of badgers, for example, have only recently been studied by radio tracking. The animal is trapped and drugged. A small radio transmitter is fitted to a light collar around the badger's neck and he is released. The movement of this shy animal can be monitored over several weeks by taking cross bearings with two direction-finding radio receivers.

In this case the observers remain perfectly concealed, often several miles away from the animal. However, the observations of behaviour are severely limited with this technique alone; we only know where the badger is, not what he is doing. There is always the possibility that lugging around a radio transmitter will affect the badger's behaviour.

More detailed observations can be made if the observer can get closer to the animal, with a consequently greater risk of affecting its behaviour. This risk can be reduced if the animals are allowed to get used to the experimenter and tolerate his presence. Perhaps the best known of such studies is Jane Van Lawick-Goodall's classic study of chimpanzee behaviour, *In the Shadow of Man*. When starting her observations Jane Goodall spent several months observing chimps from a distance and gradually moving closer until they would all but ignore her. Even then it is unlikely that their behaviour was totally unaffected by her presence.

These studies are difficult and time consuming. They are impossible as short-term experiments. Observing animals in zoos is a practicable compromise.

Observations in zoos

This compromise between observation and the experimenter effect is a key problem in all zoos. The public come to the zoo to see the animals; in particular they come to see the behaviour of the animals. If they wished only to look at the shape and colour of the animals they would be better off in a museum; museums are warmer, cheaper, you don't have to walk so far and you can get closer to the animals – but they don't move.

To encourage the animals to behave as naturally as possible they could be enclosed in reproductions of their normal habitat. Unfortunately, the natural behaviour of most animals is to hide from the humans who have paid good money to see them. The zoo must compromise in its design of enclosures. On the one hand the enclosure can be small and bare, and the behaviour of the all-too-visible inmate will be to sit disconsolately in the farthest corner. Many older zoos still have this type of cage. The behaviour of the animal bears no resemblance to its natural behaviour. On the other hand, the enclosure can be spacious and naturalistic, allowing the animals to behave naturally – that is, to run away as far as possible and stay out of sight. Some of the larger enclosures in Whipsnade, a zoo designed to encourage animals to breed, suffer from this problem. I have seen a fair sized crowd of people stand for hours in front of a large empty enclosure in Whipsnade, convinced that there was something there if only it would come out.

Many zoos have reached ingenious compromises. In London Zoo's 'nocturnal world' the pattern of night and day is reversed so that visitors can watch, in dim lighting, the activities of noctural animals. There is a fair chance of observing a pick-pocket at work as well.

As zoos improve their animal enclosures they try to strike the best balance between ease of observation and natural behaviour. This is also the best balance for a short-term study of animal behaviour by the psychology student. We cannot assume that the behaviour observed is natural. The animals are in an artificial, restricted enclosure and are exposed to many human observers. On the other hand, just as in Van Lawick-Goodall's study of chimps, we may suppose that the animals have become accustomed to humans and, to a large extent, ignore them. Some of the animals' behaviour will be a product of the restricted space. Territorial behaviour, for example, may become obsessive or distorted in some way. Other natural behaviour may be impossible; it would be impractical and messy to allow the big cats to hunt and kill live prey. Such blocking of instinctive drives can result in displacement or redirected activities [displacement activities]. The enormous advantage of zoos is that the animals are accessible. Much research time in natural conditions is spent finding the creatures. Where time is limited to one or two visits the zoo can guarantee that the animals will be there. Any number of species is available. Some will be more suitable than others at different times of the year or day. The zoo staff will be able to advise you about this.

Approaching the zoo
Always contact the zoo before any proposed visit. Most zoos welcome researchers and are prepared to give help and advice. Many have educational departments. In some cases these are unimaginative affairs, devoted to handing out leaflets. In most cases they can be a considerable help. The initial contact with a zoo is best left to an experienced psychologist, usually your tutor. He can make clear to the zoo staff the requirements and resources of the experimenters; most research carried on in zoos is zoological rather than psychological. He should establish the *level* of the proposed studies. Much of the work of the zoo's education department will be with young school children and the description and explanation of animal behaviour may be a little simplistic.

In this initial approach the zoo might suggest the most suitable species for study. The zoo may specialize in a particular range of species. It is worth finding out these specialities. As pointed out in the previous section, zoos are constantly improving their facilities for observation; naturally these improvements tend to be concentrated on the species in which the zoo specializes. Twycross Zoo near Leicester, for example, specializes in primates. These details of specialities and other information about the British zoos can be found in a recent publication, *Animals on View* by Anthony Smith. A phone call to your nearest zoo will give you some idea of the species available and the types of behaviour that can be observed.

The preliminary visit
The next step ideally is to arrange a preliminary visit to the zoo. Again, this is best left to your tutor; it will be much cheaper. Most zoos give vastly preferential rates

to educational visits. The zoo may also offer to put on a lecture to accompany the visit. This will be extremely helpful when it comes to looking at the beasts themselves. All observation is selective (p. 16); it is easy enough for us humans to select the important feature of any piece of human behaviour. If we are interested in a person's reaction to something we may look at his face: does he smile, frown, avert his eyes and so on? In an animal the facial expression may not change but a reaction will be revealed in some other way. It is helpful to know where to look. A short lecture or discussion can also point the way to the questions to be asked about the animal's behaviour.

During the preliminary visit you can take a look at several species and pick the most suitable for your study. Of course you may be interested only in a particular species but practical considerations may suggest a change. Usually this study will just be one of the experiments required for some psychology examination. In this case it is best to be flexible about the species and the aspect of its behaviour to be studied. Be guided by the zoo staff to some extent. They will probably be able to suggest some well established and easily studied piece of behaviour. If covering familiar ground is unsatisfying, you are free to choose your own.

When you have settled on a species and a particular aspect of its behaviour the zoo staff will probably be able to suggest some background reading. Make a sketch of the enclosure and take a few notes on the animals. One of the problems in watching any group of animals is the identification of the individuals. Jot down any identifying characteristics. The zoo staff will also be able to help with this. You could also ask them for details of age and sex of the animals and the family relationships between them. This will all save time during the actual experiment, a vital consideration if the zoo is any distance from home.

Try recording some of your observations, that is, run a pilot experiment. You may find that a tape recorder is necessary to record details without looking away from the action. Will the observations be qualitative or quantitative? This will depend on what is being observed. You may find it an advantage to lose some of the richness of the behaviour and count specific events. This will allow a statistical analysis of the results and simplify the recording of behaviour. In most cases a description of the behaviour will be more appropriate.

Consider the possibility of two or three observers studying different aspects of behaviour in the same group of animals. The results can be pooled to give a larger-scale and richer investigation.

Check with the zoo on the most suitable time for the study. You will need to consider feeding times, arrangements for cleaning the enclosure, days and times with the least interference from the public and so on. As with any experiment detailed planning pays dividends.

The study

It is pointless here to give details of a study of a particular group of animals: the details will depend on the species, how they are kept and how many there are. We can take a look at the possibilities in a typical example, the social behaviour in a group of monkeys. The monkeys and apes make good subjects for these experiments. They are fairly active and unafraid of humans. They often have elaborate social behaviour. The individuals are usually quite easy to recognize after a little observation.

Many monkey groups have a hierarchical social structure. Typically, the old males have the highest status, with the older females, young males and young females having descending ranks. This structure is by no means rigid and is best regarded as a loose framework on which to fit the observations.

A social hierarchy can be revealed in several different aspects of behaviour:

1 *Grooming*

This is a common behaviour in monkeys and apes. Many seemingly delightful hours are whiled away as one individual calmly picks through the fur of another, an action that appears pleasurable to both parties. The grooming can be mutual or one-sided. If one-sided, do the groomer and the groomed depend on relative social status? It is quite simple to record who grooms whom throughout the period of observations.

2 *Feeding*

A variety of food is placed inside the enclosure by the keeper at feeding time. Some items of food will be more popular than others. Is the distribution of these favourite goodies dependent on social status? There are several possibilities. The highest-ranking individual may prevent all the others from picking the food until he or she is satisfied and leaves the food to the next highest. There may be a free-for-all scramble, the highest-ranking individual being more successful in the scramble. There may be some other pattern or no discernible pattern at all. Do these feeding patterns result in different diets for different status positions?

3 *Responses to novel stimuli*

In some cases the zoo staff may be prepared to introduce novel stimuli into the enclosures. Does social status determine who approaches the object first? This may depend on the nature of the object, whether potentially dangerous. There is a widespread fear of certain objects in humans regardless of any previous experience. Many people are frightened of snakes and spiders without having been harmed by either. Is such a response to snakes innate in the species of monkey under study? The zoo staff may be prepared to place a rubber snake in the enclosure. Is the reaction different from that to any other novel stimulus?

4 *Sexual responses*

In many species of monkey and ape it is easy to identify females who have come into season and are ready for mating. Does the social status of the male or the female determine who mates with whom? Do high-ranking females mate with high-ranking males and so on down the hierarchy or do high-ranking males mate with all females? At the same time you might ask which partner chooses the other. That is, does the female select the high-ranking male and present herself to him, or does the high-ranking male win the right to the female in competition with the other males – on whom is the onus of selection, if any?

If you wish to study these patterns of mating it is advisable to arrange with the zoo that they will give you a call when a suitable female is coming into season. If observations have to be made over several days the work can be shared between several experimenters, each of whom studies some other aspect of behaviour at the same time.

I have been talking of 'high-ranking' individuals and social status as if the animals had little labels tied around their necks. How is this status recognized? You can start by observing encounters between the various individuals. Who gets out of whose way? There are usually recognizable gestures of threat, submission and dominance in these social species. A chat to the zoo staff during the preliminary visit and some background reading will help you to identify these.

These then are examples of the sort of questions that can be asked of social behaviour in a group of monkeys. Several experimenters could combine their findings to compare social behaviour patterns in two or more species of monkey. Of course, there are many other species and questions.

The results

It is quite likely that your observations will be descriptive rather than quantitative. This is a perfectly legitimate type of psychological study. You may find, however, that the normal format for writing up the work is unsuitable for a series of descriptive observations. It is not clear, for example, when a dominant male pig-tailed monkey threatens a youngster, what exactly is the 'hypothesis' or the 'procedure'. The normal format must be abandoned or altered. As with any experimental write-up the object is to provide a clear, simple description of the events.

In many cases the description of, say, a submissive gesture is best made with a drawing rather than words. If you think that your drawing will bear little resemblance to the real thing you can take photographs. Non-professional photographs are often a little disappointing. The gesture you want may be in the shade or rather far away; a professional will take dozens of shots to get the one he wants. The best solution is often to trace the illustration you need from the photograph, enlarging the drawing if necessary.

Finally
Always give a copy of the report to the zoo. They will be interested in your findings for guiding future visitors and researchers. Some zoos are prepared to display these findings and observations beside the animals' enclosure for the benefit of the public. The zoo will normally want to edit the findings and provide professional illustrations but it is extremely satisfying to see your work up there for all to see.

References

Hansell, M.H. and Aitken, J.J. (1977), *Experimental Animal Behaviour: A Selection of Laboratory Exercises*, Blackie

Smith, A. (1977), *Animals on View*, Weidenfeld and Nicolson

Van Lawick-Goodall, J. (1971), *In the Shadow of Man*, Collins (also in paperback by Fontana Books)

Index guide: animal behaviour; social behaviour; ethology

Table A   Critical values of chi-squared

The results are significant at a particular level if the observed value of chi-squared is greater than the table value

Degrees of freedom	Significance level, p .05	.02	.01	.001
1	3.84	5.41	6.63	10.83
2	5.99	7.82	9.21	13.81
3	7.81	9.84	11.34	16.27
4	9.49	11.67	13.28	18.47
5	11.07	13.39	15.09	20.51
6	12.59	15.03	16.81	22.46
7	14.07	16.62	18.47	24.32
8	15.51	18.17	20.09	26.12
9	16.92	19.68	21.67	27.88
10	18.31	21.16	23.21	29.59
11	19.67	22.62	24.72	31.26
12	21.03	24.05	26.22	32.91
13	22.36	25.47	27.69	34.53
14	23.68	26.87	29.14	36.12
15	24.99	28.26	30.58	37.67
16	26.23	29.63	32.00	39.25
17	27.59	30.99	33.41	40.79
18	28.87	32.35	34.80	42.31
19	30.14	33.69	36.19	43.82
20	31.41	35.02	37.57	45.31

Degrees of freedom	Significance level, p .05	.02	.01	.001
21	32.67	36.34	38.93	46.78
22	33.92	37.66	40.29	48.27
23	35.17	38.97	41.64	49.73
24	36.41	40.27	42.98	51.18
25	37.65	41.57	44.31	52.62
26	38.88	42.86	45.64	54.05
27	40.11	44.14	46.96	55.48
28	41.34	45.42	48.28	56.89
29	42.56	46.69	49.59	58.30
30	43.77	47.96	50.89	59.70
32	46.19	50.49	53.49	62.49
34	48.60	52.99	56.06	65.25
36	50.99	55.49	58.62	67.98
38	53.38	57.97	61.16	70.70
40	55.76	60.44	63.69	73.40
42	58.12	62.89	66.21	76.08
44	60.48	65.34	68.71	78.75
46	62.83	67.77	71.20	81.40
48	65.17	70.12	73.68	84.04
50	67.50	72.61	76.15	86.66

Table B Area under the standard Normal curve

The table value gives the proportion of the whole distribution between the mean and a standard score (z). See figure 19 (p. 64)

Second decimal place

z	0	1	2	3	4	5	6	7	8	9
0.0	.0000	.0040	.0080	.0120	.0160	.0199	.0239	.0279	.0319	.0359
0.1	.0398	.0438	.0478	.0517	.0557	.0596	.0636	.0675	.0714	.0754
0.2	.0793	.0832	.0871	.0910	.0948	.0987	.1026	.1064	.1103	.1141
0.3	.1179	.1217	.1255	.1293	.1331	.1368	.1406	.1443	.1480	.1517
0.4	.1554	.1591	.1628	.1664	.1700	.1736	.1772	.1808	.1844	.1879
0.5	.1915	.1950	.1985	.2019	.2054	.2088	.2123	.2157	.2190	.2224
0.6	.2258	.2291	.2324	.2357	.2389	.2422	.2454	.2486	.2518	.2549
0.7	.2580	.2612	.2642	.2673	.2704	.2734	.2764	.2794	.2823	.2852
0.8	.2881	.2910	.2939	.2967	.2996	.3023	.3051	.3078	.3106	.3133
0.9	.3159	.3186	.3212	.3238	.3264	.3289	.3315	.3340	.3365	.3389
1.0	.3413	.3438	.3461	.3485	.3508	.3531	.3554	.3577	.3599	.3621
1.1	.3643	.3665	.3686	.3708	.3729	.3749	.3770	.3790	.3810	.3830
1.2	.3849	.3869	.3888	.3907	.3925	.3944	.3962	.3980	.3997	.4015
1.3	.4032	.4049	.4066	.4082	.4099	.4115	.4131	.4147	.4162	.4177
1.4	.4192	.4207	.4222	.4236	.4251	.4265	.4279	.4292	.4306	.4319
1.5	.4332	.4345	.4357	.4370	.4382	.4394	.4406	.4418	.4429	.4441
1.6	.4452	.4463	.4474	.4484	.4495	.4505	.4515	.4525	.4535	.4545
1.7	.4554	.4564	.4573	.4582	.4591	.4599	.4608	.4616	.4625	.4633
1.8	.4641	.4649	.4656	.4664	.4671	.4678	.4686	.4693	.4699	.4706
1.9	.4713	.4719	.4726	.4732	.4738	.4744	.4750	.4756	.4761	.4767
2.0	.4772	.4778	.4783	.4788	.4793	.4798	.4803	.4808	.4812	.4817
2.1	.4821	.4826	.4830	.4834	.4838	.4842	.4846	.4850	.4854	.4857
2.2	.4861	.4864	.4868	.4871	.4875	.4878	.4881	.4884	.4887	.4890
2.3	.4893	.4896	.4898	.4901	.4904	.4906	.4909	.4911	.4913	.4916
2.4	.4918	.4920	.4922	.4925	.4927	.4929	.4931	.4932	.4934	.4936
2.5	.4938	.4940	.4941	.4943	.4945	.4946	.4948	.4949	.4951	.4952
2.6	.4953	.4955	.4956	.4957	.4959	.4960	.4961	.4962	.4963	.4964
2.7	.4965	.4966	.4967	.4968	.4969	.4970	.4971	.4972	.4973	.4974
2.8	.4974	.4975	.4976	.4977	.4977	.4978	.4979	.4979	.4980	.4981
2.9	.4981	.4982	.4982	.4983	.4984	.4984	.4985	.4985	.4986	.4986
3.0	.4987	.4987	.4987	.4988	.4988	.4989	.4989	.4989	.4990	.4990
3.1	.4990	.4991	.4991	.4991	.4992	.4992	.4992	.4992	.4993	.4993
3.2	.4993	.4993	.4994	.4994	.4994	.4994	.4994	.4995	.4995	.4995
3.3	.4995	.4995	.4995	.4996	.4996	.4996	.4996	.4996	.4996	.4997
3.4	.4997	.4997	.4997	.4997	.4997	.4997	.4997	.4997	.4997	.4998
3.5	.4998	.4998	.4998	.4998	.4998	.4998	.4998	.4998	.4998	.4998
3.6	.4998	.4998	.4999	.4999	.4999	.4999	.4999	.4999	.4999	.4999
3.7	.4999	.4999	.4999	.4999	.4999	.4999	.4999	.4999	.4999	.4999
3.8	.4999	.4999	.4999	.4999	.4999	.4999	.4999	.4999	.4999	.4999
3.9	.5000	.5000	.5000	.5000	.5000	.5000	.5000	.5000	.5000	.5000

Table C   **Critical values of t**

The results are significant at a particular level if the observed value of t is greater than the table value

This table gives values for a *two-tailed* test. For a *one-tailed* test the significance levels are halved.

Degrees of freedom	Significance level, p .1	.05	.02	.01	.001	Degrees of freedom	Significance level, p .1	.05	.02	.01	.001
1	6.31	12.71	31.82	63.657	636.62	21	1.72	2.08	2.52	2.83	3.82
2	2.92	4.30	6.96	9.92	31.60	22	1.72	2.07	2.51	2.819	3.79
3	2.35	3.18	4.54	5.84	12.92	23	1.71	2.07	2.50	2.807	3.77
4	2.13	2.78	3.75	4.60	8.61	24	1.71	2.06	2.49	2.797	3.74
5	2.01	2.57	3.36	4.03	6.87	25	1.71	2.06	2.48	2.787	3.72
6	1.94	2.45	3.14	3.707	5.96	26	1.71	2.06	2.48	2.779	3.71
7	1.89	2.36	2.99	3.499	5.41	27	1.70	2.05	2.47	2.77	3.69
8	1.86	2.31	2.90	3.35	5.04	28	1.70	2.05	2.47	2.76	3.67
9	1.83	2.26	2.82	3.25	4.78	29	1.70	2.04	2.46	2.756	3.66
10	1.81	2.23	2.76	3.169	4.59	30	1.70	2.04	2.46	2.75	3.65
11	1.80	2.20	2.72	3.106	4.44	40	1.68	2.02	2.42	2.70	3.55
12	1.78	2.18	2.68	3.05	4.32	60	1.67	2.00	2.39	2.66	3.46
13	1.77	2.16	2.65	3.01	4.22	120	1.66	1.98	2.36	2.617	3.37
14	1.76	2.14	2.62	2.977	4.14	∞	1.64	1.96	2.33	2.576	3.29
15	1.75	2.13	2.60	2.947	4.07						
16	1.75	2.12	2.58	2.92	4.01						
17	1.74	2.11	2.57	2.898	3.96						
18	1.73	2.10	2.55	2.878	3.92						
19	1.73	2.09	2.54	2.86	3.88						
20	1.72	2.09	2.53	2.84	3.85						

Table D Critical values of F

The results are significant at the 5% level (for a two-tailed test) if the observed value of F is greater than the table value

df_S \ df_L	1	2	3	4	5	6	7
1	648	800	864	900	922	937	948
2	38.50	39.00	39.17	39.24	39.30	39.33	39.35
3	17.44	16.04	15.44	15.10	14.89	14.74	14.62
4	12.22	10.65	9.98	9.60	9.36	9.20	9.07
5	10.01	8.43	7.76	7.39	7.15	6.98	6.85
6	8.81	7.26	6.60	6.23	5.99	5.82	5.70
7	8.07	6.54	5.89	5.52	5.29	5.12	4.99
8	7.57	6.06	5.42	5.05	4.82	4.66	4.53
9	7.21	5.71	5.08	4.72	4.48	4.32	4.20
10	6.94	5.46	4.83	4.47	4.24	4.07	3.95
11	6.72	5.26	4.63	4.28	4.04	3.88	3.76
12	6.55	5.10	4.47	4.12	3.89	3.73	3.61
13	6.41	4.97	4.35	4.00	3.77	3.60	3.48
14	6.30	4.86	4.24	3.89	3.66	3.50	3.38
15	6.20	4.76	4.15	3.80	3.58	3.41	3.29
16	6.12	4.69	4.08	3.73	3.50	3.34	3.22
17	6.04	4.62	4.01	3.66	3.44	3.28	3.16
18	5.98	4.56	3.95	3.61	3.38	3.22	3.10
19	5.92	4.51	3.90	3.56	3.33	3.17	3.05
20	5.87	4.46	3.86	3.51	3.29	3.13	3.01
21	5.83	4.42	3.82	3.48	3.25	3.09	2.97
22	5.79	4.38	3.78	3.44	3.22	3.05	2.93
23	5.75	4.35	3.75	3.40	3.18	3.02	2.90
24	5.72	4.32	3.72	3.38	3.15	2.99	2.87

		df_1						
		8	9	10	12	15	20	24
	1	957	963	969	977	985	993	997
	2	39.37	39.39	39.40	39.42	39.43	39.45	39.4
	3	14.54	14.47	14.42	14.34	14.25	14.17	14.1
	4	8.98	8.90	8.84	8.75	8.66	8.56	8.51
	5	6.76	6.68	6.62	6.52	6.43	6.33	6.28
	6	5.60	5.52	5.46	5.37	5.27	5.17	5.12
	7	4.90	4.82	4.76	4.67	4.57	4.47	4.42
	8	4.43	4.36	4.30	4.20	4.10	4.99	3.95
	9	4.10	4.03	3.96	3.87	3.77	3.67	3.61
	10	3.85	3.78	3.72	3.62	3.52	3.42	3.37
	11	3.66	3.59	3.52	3.43	3.33	3.23	3.17
df_S	12	3.51	3.44	3.37	3.28	3.18	3.07	3.02
	13	3.39	3.31	3.25	3.15	3.05	2.95	2.89
	14	3.29	3.21	3.15	3.05	2.95	2.84	2.79
	15	3.20	3.12	3.06	2.96	2.86	2.76	2.70
	16	3.12	3.05	2.99	2.89	2.79	2.68	2.63
	17	3.06	2.99	2.92	2.82	2.72	2.62	2.56
	18	3.01	2.93	2.87	2.77	2.67	2.58	2.50
	19	2.96	2.81	2.82	2.72	2.62	2.53	2.45
	20	2.91	2.84	2.77	2.68	2.57	2.46	2.41
	21	2.87	2.80	2.73	2.64	2.53	2.42	2.37
	22	2.84	2.76	2.70	2.61	2.50	2.39	2.33
	23	2.81	2.73	2.67	2.57	2.47	2.36	2.30
	24	2.78	2.70	2.64	2.54	2.44	2.33	2.27

Table E   Critical values of L for the sign test

Results are significant if the observed value of L is equal to or less than the table value

This table gives values for a *two-tailed* test. For a *one-tailed* test the significance levels are halved.

T	Significance level, p			
	0.1	0.05	0.02	0.01
5	0			
6	0	0		
7	0	0	0	
8	1	0	0	0
9	1	1	0	0
10	1	1	0	0
11	2	1	1	0
12	2	2	1	1
13	3	2	1	1
14	3	2	2	1
15	3	3	2	2
16	4	3	2	2
17	4	4	3	2
18	5	4	3	3
19	5	4	4	3
20	5	5	4	3
21	6	5	4	4
22	6	5	5	4
23	7	6	5	4
24	7	6	5	5
25	7	7	6	5
26	8	7	6	6
27	8	7	7	6
28	9	8	7	6
29	9	8	7	7

T	Significance level, p			
	0.1	0.05	0.02	0.01
30	10	9	8	7
31	10	9	8	7
32	10	9	8	8
33	11	10	9	8
34	11	10	9	9
35	12	11	10	9
36	12	11	10	9
37	13	12	10	10
38	13	12	11	10
39	13	12	11	11
40	14	13	12	11
41	14	13	12	11
42	15	14	13	12
43	15	14	13	12
44	16	15	13	13
45	16	15	14	13
46	16	15	14	13
47	17	16	15	14
48	17	16	15	14
49	18	17	15	15

Table F Critical values of U for the Mann–Whitney test

The results are significant at the 5% level if the observed value of either U or U′ is smaller than the table value

N_a is the size of group A; N_b is the size of group B.

N_a	N_b=20	19	18	17	16	15	14	13	12	11	10	9	8	7	6	5	4
2	2	2	2	2	1	1	1	1	1	0	0	0	0	–	–	–	–
3	8	7	7	6	6	5	5	4	4	3	3	2	2	1	1	0	–
4	13	13	12	11	11	10	9	8	7	6	5	4	4	3	2	1	0
5	20	19	18	17	15	14	13	12	11	9	8	7	6	5	3	2	
6	27	25	24	22	21	19	17	16	14	13	11	10	8	6	5		
7	34	32	30	28	26	24	22	20	18	16	14	12	10	8			
8	41	38	36	34	31	29	26	24	22	19	17	15	13				
9	48	45	42	39	37	34	31	28	26	23	20	17					
10	55	52	48	45	42	39	36	33	29	26	23						
11	62	58	55	51	47	44	40	37	33	30							
12	69	65	61	57	53	49	45	41	37								
13	76	72	67	63	59	54	50	45									
14	83	78	74	67	64	59	55										
15	90	85	80	75	70	64											
16	98	92	86	81	75												
17	105	99	93	87													
18	112	106	99														
19	119	113															
20	127																

Table G Critical values of T for the Wilcoxon test

The results are significant at a particular level if the observed value of T is smaller than the table value

This table gives values for a *two-tailed* test. For a *one-tailed* test the significance levels are halved.

		Significance level, p			
		0.100	0.050	0.020	0.010
	5	0			
	6	2	0		
	7	3	2	0	
	8	5	3	1	0
	9	8	5	3	1
	10	10	8	5	3
	11	13	10	7	5
	12	17	13	9	7
	13	21	17	12	9
	14	25	21	15	12
N	15	30	25	19	15
	16	35	29	23	19
	17	41	34	27	23
	18	47	40	32	27
	19	53	46	37	32
	20	60	52	43	37
	21	67	58	49	42
	22	75	65	55	48
	23	83	73	62	54
	24	91	81	69	61
	25	100	89	76	68
	26	110	98	84	75
	27	119	107	92	83
	28	130	116	101	91
	29	140	126	110	100
	30	151	137	120	109

Table H **Random numbers**

44 91 13 32 97	75 31 62 66 54	84 80 32 75 77	56 08 25 70 29
37 30 28 59 85	53 56 68 53 40	01 74 39 59 73	30 19 99 85 48
75 20 80 27 77	78 91 69 16 00	08 43 18 73 68	67 69 61 34 25
65 95 79 42 94	93 62 40 89 96	43 56 47 71 66	46 76 29 67 02
05 02 03 24 17	47 97 81 56 51	92 34 86 01 82	55 51 33 12 91
94 21 78 55 09	72 76 45 16 94	29 95 81 83 83	79 88 01 97 30
34 41 92 45 71	09 23 70 70 07	12 38 92 79 43	14 85 11 47 23
53 14 36 59 25	54 47 33 70 15	59 24 48 40 35	50 03 42 99 36
88 59 53 11 52	66 25 69 07 04	48 68 64 71 06	61 65 70 22 12
65 28 04 67 53	95 79 88 37 31	50 41 06 94 76	81 83 17 16 33
73 43 07 34 48	44 26 87 93 29	77 09 61 67 84	06 69 44 77 75
48 62 11 90 60	68 12 93 64 28	46 24 79 16 76	14 60 25 51 01
28 97 85 58 99	67 22 52 76 23	24 70 36 54 54	59 28 61 71 96
02 63 45 52 38	67 63 47 54 75	83 24 78 43 20	92 63 13 47 48
76 96 59 38 72	86 57 45 71 46	44 67 76 14 55	44 88 01 62 12
77 45 85 50 51	74 13 39 35 22	30 53 36 02 95	49 34 88 73 61
29 18 94 51 23	76 51 94 84 86	79 93 96 38 63	08 58 25 58 94
72 65 71 08 86	79 57 95 13 91	97 48 72 66 48	09 71 17 24 89
89 37 20 70 01	77 31 61 95 46	26 97 05 73 51	53 33 18 72 87
81 30 15 39 14	48 38 75 93 29	06 87 37 78 48	45 56 00 84 47
83 71 46 30 49	89 17 95 88 29	02 39 56 03 46	97 74 06 56 17
70 52 85 01 50	01 84 02 78 43	10 62 98 19 41	18 83 99 47 99
25 27 99 41 28	07 41 08 34 66	19 42 74 39 91	41 96 53 78 72
63 61 62 42 29	39 68 95 10 96	09 24 23 00 62	56 12 80 73 16
68 96 83 23 56	32 84 60 15 31	44 73 67 34 77	91 15 79 74 58
87 83 07 55 07	76 58 30 83 64	87 29 25 58 84	86 50 60 00 25
49 52 83 51 14	47 56 91 29 34	05 87 31 06 95	12 45 57 09 09
80 62 80 03 42	10 80 21 38 84	90 56 35 03 09	43 12 74 49 14
86 97 37 44 22	00 95 01 31 76	17 16 29 56 63	38 78 94 49 81
85 39 52 85 13	07 28 37 07 61	11 16 36 27 03	78 86 72 04 95
97 05 31 03 61	20 26 36 31 62	68 69 86 95 44	84 95 48 46 45
75 89 11 47 11	31 56 34 19 09	79 57 92 36 59	14 93 87 81 40
09 18 94 06 19	98 40 07 17 81	22 45 44 84 11	24 62 20 42 31
84 08 31 55 58	24 33 45 77 58	80 45 67 93 82	75 70 16 08 24
79 26 88 86 30	01 31 60 10 39	53 58 47 70 93	85 81 56 39 38

01 61 16 96 94	50 78 13 69 36	37 68 53 37 31	71 26 35 03 71
46 68 05 14 82	90 78 50 05 62	77 79 13 57 44	59 60 10 39 66
00 57 25 60 59	46 72 60 18 77	55 66 12 62 11	08 99 55 64 57
24 98 65 63 21	47 21 61 88 32	27 80 30 21 60	10 92 35 36 12
28 10 99 00 27	12 73 37 99 12	49 99 57 94 82	96 88 57 17 91
07 10 63 76 35	87 03 04 79 88	08 13 13 85 51	55 34 57 72 69
92 38 70 96 92	52 06 79 79 45	82 63 18 27 44	69 66 92 19 09
99 53 93 61 28	52 70 05 48 34	56 65 05 61 86	90 92 10 70 80
93 86 52 77 65	15 33 59 05 28	22 87 26 07 47	86 96 98 29 06
18 46 23 34 27	85 13 99 24 44	49 18 09 79 49	74 16 32 23 02
24 53 63 94 09	41 10 76 47 91	44 04 95 49 66	39 60 04 59 81
22 06 34 72 52	82 21 15 65 20	33 29 94 71 11	15 91 29 12 03
07 16 39 33 66	98 56 10 56 79	77 21 30 27 12	90 49 22 23 62
29 70 83 63 51	99 74 20 52 36	87 09 41 15 09	98 60 16 03 03
57 90 12 02 07	23 47 37 17 31	54 08 01 88 63	39 41 88 92 10
33 35 72 67 47	77 34 55 45 70	08 18 27 38 90	16 95 86 70 75
49 41 31 06 70	42 38 06 45 18	64 84 73 31 65	52 53 37 97 15
65 19 69 02 83	60 75 86 90 68	24 64 19 35 51	56 61 87 39 12
92 09 84 38 76	22 00 27 69 85	29 81 94 78 70	21 94 47 90 12
98 77 87 68 07	91 51 67 62 44	40 98 05 93 78	23 32 65 41 18
00 41 86 79 79	68 47 22 00 20	35 55 31 51 51	00 83 63 22 55
57 99 99 90 37	36 63 32 08 58	37 40 13 68 97	87 64 81 07 83
12 59 52 57 02	22 07 90 47 03	28 14 11 30 79	20 69 22 40 98
31 51 10 96 46	92 06 88 07 77	56 11 50 81 69	40 23 72 51 39
96 11 83 44 80	34 68 35 48 77	33 42 40 90 60	73 96 53 97 86
85 47 04 66 08	34 72 57 59 13	82 43 80 46 15	38 26 61 70 04
72 82 32 99 90	63 95 73 76 63	89 73 44 99 05	48 67 26 43 18
91 36 74 43 53	30 82 13 54 00	78 45 63 98 35	55 03 36 67 68
77 53 84 46 47	31 91 18 95 58	24 16 74 11 53	44 10 13 85 57
37 27 47 39 19	84 83 70 07 48	53 21 40 06 71	95 06 79 88 54
34 18 04 52 35	56 27 09 24 86	61 85 53 83 45	19 90 70 99 00
11 20 99 45 18	48 13 93 55 34	18 37 79 49 90	65 97 38 20 46
27 37 83 28 71	00 06 41 41 74	45 89 09 39 84	51 67 11 52 49
10 65 81 92 59	58 76 17 14 97	04 76 62 16 17	17 95 70 45 80
59 71 74 17 32	27 55 10 24 19	23 71 82 13 74	63 52 52 01 41
33 73 99 19 87	26 72 39 27 67	53 77 57 68 93	60 61 97 22 61
87 14 77 43 96	43 00 65 98 50	45 60 33 01 07	98 99 46 50 47
72 87 08 62 40	16 06 10 89 20	23 21 34 74 97	76 38 03 29 63
73 96 07 94 52	09 65 90 77 47	25 76 16 19 33	53 05 70 53 30
79 96 23 53 10	65 39 07 16 29	45 33 02 43 70	02 87 40 41 45
20 21 14 68 86	87 63 93 95 17	11 29 01 95 80	35 14 97 35 33
85 43 01 72 73	08 61 74 51 69	89 74 39 82 15	94 51 33 41 67
59 97 50 99 52	08 52 85 08 40	87 80 61 65 31	91 51 80 32 44
72 68 49 29 31	89 85 84 46 06	59 73 19 85 23	65 09 29 75 63
88 02 84 27 83	42 29 72 23 19	66 56 45 65 79	20 71 53 20 25

Index